T0287059

CAROLINE MILLS

CAMPING ROAD TRIPS UK

30 ADVENTURES WITH YOUR CAMPERVAN, MOTORHOME OR TENT

Bradt GUIDES

Bradt Guides Ltd, UK
Globe Pequot Press Inc, USA

First published February 2023
Bradt Guides Ltd
31a High Street, Chesham, Buckinghamshire, HP5 1BW, England
www.bradtguides.com
Print edition published in the USA by The Globe Pequot Press Inc,
PO Box 480, Guilford, Connecticut 06437-0480

Text copyright © 2023 Caroline Mills
Map copyright © 2023 Bradt Guides Ltd; includes map data © OpenStreetMap contributors
Photographs copyright © 2023 Individual photographers (see below)
Project Manager: Daniel Austin
Cover research: Pepi Bluck, Perfect Picture

ISBN: 9781804690604

British Library Cataloguing in Publication Data
A catalogue record for this book is available from the British Library

Photographs
Photographers & picture libraries all credited alongside individual photos. Images from
the author are credited (CM).

Front cover Kylesku Bridge in northwest Scotland (Alan Copson/AWL); campervan amid
bluebells in the Forest of Dean (David Chapman/Alamy)
Back cover Motorhomes parked up at Dartmoor National Park (Maciej Olszewski/
Shutterstock)
Title page Campervan in Cornwall (Ian Cumming/Axiom - Design Pics/SuperStock)

Map David McCutcheon FBCart.S

Typeset by Ian Spick, Bradt Guides
Production managed by Jellyfish Print Solutions, printed in the UK
Digital conversion by www.dataworks.co.in

AUTHOR

Caroline Mills (⊘ carolinemills.net) is an experienced travel writer who has spent a lifetime camping, caravanning and motorcaravanning. Her travels in campervans and motorhomes have taken her extensively throughout the UK and mainland Europe. While appreciating the value in seeing Britain's popular landmarks (many included in this guide), Caroline's passion is for discovering lesser-known destinations, seeking out and embracing what's special about places regarded as ordinary. Utilising road trips as the basis for deeper exploration of an area, this may be for the joy of finding rare wildflowers in Teesdale, the excitement of meeting a jewelled lizard in Jersey, exploring aesthetic riverside mills in Lancashire, or discovering aviation heritage in Lincolnshire. Mills writes extensively about camping, caravanning, campervans and motorhomes for magazines, newspapers and websites, and has authored or contributed to eight travel guides, including three for Bradt. Caroline is a member of the British Guild of Travel Writers and tweets from 🐦 @CarolineMills99.

ACKNOWLEDGEMENTS

A hearty thank you to all the wonderful team at Bradt Guides for bringing this book to fruition: to Hugh and Laura for marketing and publicity, to Emma Gibbs for proofreading, Ian for creating the fabulous design, David McCutcheon for the map design and, most of all, to Daniel Austin and Anna Moores for editing, and providing much thoughtful advice and perceptiveness.

DEDICATION

To my lovely mother, Ann (1937–2022), who left this world during the final stages of writing this book. Her zest for life and poetry lives on, her encyclopaedic knowledge of wildflowers a legacy never forgotten.

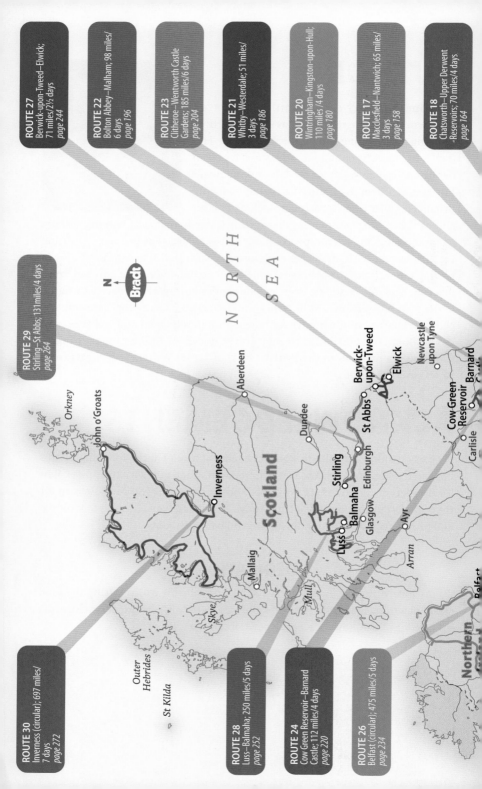

N

Bradt

N O R T H

S E A

Orkney

John o'Groats

Aberdeen

Dundee

Inverness

Scotland

Berwick-
upon-Tweed

St Abbs

Elwick

Newcastle
upon Tyne

Stirling

Edinburgh

Mallaig

Balmaha

Glasgow

Barnard
Castle

Luss

Cow Green
Reservoir

Skye

Ayr

Carlisle

Mull

Arran

Outer
Hebrides

St Kilda

Northern

Belfast

ROUTE 19
Cranwell–Lincoln; 112 miles/4 days
page 172

ROUTE 9
Wicken Fen–Hickling Broad;
319 miles/8 days
page 90

ROUTE 10
Clipsham–Lyddington; 67 miles/
3 days
page 106

ROUTE 13
Ludlow–Kington; 72 miles/3 days
page 128

ROUTE 7
Dover–Sandwich; 42 miles/4 days
page 68

ROUTE 8
Leith Hill–Rathfinny Estate;
204 miles/5 days
page 76

ROUTE 12
Tewkesbury–Worcester; 80 miles/
4 days
page 120

ROUTE 6
Southbourne–Adgestone;
155 miles/6 days
page 58

ROUTE 11
Stinchcombe Hill/Kelmscott;
61 miles/3 days
page 112

ROUTE 1
St Helier (circular); 50 miles/4 days
page 2

ROUTE 25
Kilkeel–Rostrevor; 127 miles/4 days
page 228

ROUTE 16
Britannia Bridge–Aberffraw;
129 miles/3 days
page 154

ROUTE 15
Pontcysyllte Aqueduct–
Betws-y-Coed; 168 miles/5 days
page 146

ROUTE 14
The Mumbles–Abergavenny;
240 miles/5 days
page 134

ROUTE 5
Malmesbury–Dyrham; 120 miles/3 days
page 50

ROUTE 4
Bideford–Castle Cary; 131 miles/7 days
page 38

ROUTE 2
Duchy of Cornwall Nursery–Trewethett
Farm; 225 miles/5 days
page 10

ROUTE 3
Tavistock–Ashburton; 193 miles/5 days
page 26

ENGLISH CHANNEL

IRISH SEA

Isle of Man

England

Wales

Isle of Wight

Kilkeel

Aberffraw

Britannia Bridge

Anglesey

Betws-y-Coed

Aberystwyth

The Mumbles

Cardiff

Kington

Abergavenny

Bideford

Minehead

Trewethett Farm

Duchy of Cornwall Nursery

Penzance

Tavistock

Ashburton

Castle Cary

Dyrham

Stinchcombe Hill

Malmesbury

Kelmscott

Worcester

Tewkesbury

Ludlow

Pontcysyllte Aqueduct

Nantwich

Macclesfield

Chatsworth

Sheffield

Upper Derwent Reservoirs

Clitheroe

Leeds

Bolton Abbey

Wentworth

Castle Gardens

Lincoln

Kingston-upon-Hull

Wintringham

Cranwell

Clipsham

Lyddington

Derby

Birmingham

Wicken Fen

Cambridge

Ipswich

Hickling Broad

Luton

London

Reading

Salisbury

Poole

Southbourne

Adgestone

Brighton

Leith Hill

Rathfinny Estate

Sandwich

Dover

St Helier

Jersey

CONTENTS

← Enjoying the views over Loch Kishorn – route 30 (SeraphP/Shutterstock)

FEEDBACK REQUEST

At Bradt Guides we're aware that guidebooks start to go out of date on the day they're published – and that you, our readers, are out there in the field doing research of your own. You'll find out before us when a fine new family-run site opens or a local attraction changes hands and goes downhill. So why not tell us about your experiences? Contact us on ✆ 01753 893444 or ✉ info@bradtguides.com. We will forward emails to the author who may post updates on the Bradt website at ⊘ bradtguides.com/updates. Alternatively, you can add a review of the book to Amazon, or share your adventures with us on social media: ⓕ BradtGuides 🐦 @BradtGuides & @CarolineMills99 ⓞ BradtGuides

INTRODUCTION

'To me there's nowhere like it and never will be. This is my life – my world.'

Hannah Hauxwell

Along a quiet country lane that ends as a farm track sweeping into the hills, and five miles from any village, sits a small stone barn. It is surrounded by low stone walls and fine meadows. On the opposite side of the Blackton Reservoir, over which the stone barn looks, are more meadows that creep up the hillside towards the rocky outcrop of Goldsborough Carr. The only way to, ultimately, reach the barn is on foot, along the Pennine Way. It is a remote place.

In June, the hay meadows that surround the barn smell of summer, crammed with red clover, buttercups, ragged robin, yellow rattle and delicate pignut flowers among the sward. The remote stone barn is empty now, except for a board with the words quoted above. It once housed a cow that belonged to Hannah Hauxwell, a lady who rose to prominence on television in the 1980s for living here alone without electricity or running water.

The fields that were once her life – and a harsh existence at that – is now a nature reserve, Hannah's Meadow. They are collectively a Coronation Meadow, deemed some of the best hay meadows in Britain. Hannah's little world – these meadows – are the best of Britain. There is, indeed, 'nowhere like it and never will be'.

↑ Shore Caravan Site, Achmelvich – route 30 (CM)

Hannah's Meadow is one of the very special places to visit and be able to see the best of the UK within this collection of road trips. The UK has some of the most iconic and varied scenery in the world. Its cities are vibrant and rich with culture, its provincial market towns a delight to mooch around and its countryside, well... it is unique.

Whether the wild, remote Highlands of Scotland, the upland hay meadows of the North Pennines, pretty hedgerows in Rutland or the multi-fingered river creeks in Cornwall and Devon, the UK has so much variation to explore.

There are, of course, many destinations within the UK that remain extraordinarily popular with tourists and several, such as Snowdonia or the Yorkshire Dales, are included within this guide. But I'm always keen to seek somewhere different, somewhere new (to me, at least), to champion the ordinary and find interest in less likely locations. I'm eager to encourage readers to visit that 'elsewhere', too; for crowds to disperse, so that traditional tourist locations that are often stretched beyond capacity remain economically viable but ecologically sustainable destinations.

Consequently, there are some notable – but deliberate – omissions in this book. You won't find, for example, a road trip in the Lake District. Much is written about

↑ Exploring the Pennine Way – routes 18 & 24 (Duncan Andison/Shutterstock)

this area that doesn't require repetition here; the roads can become clogged in high season, and it would be inappropriate for me to encourage more road traffic to already busy narrow lanes.

Instead, I offer an alternative close by; in this instance the Forest of Bowland Area of Outstanding Natural Beauty, which sees fewer people converging on the hills but, in my view, is no less pleasing on the eye. In place of the city of York, allow me to introduce the city of Halifax. Discover a hidden and oft-forgotten corner of Kent, a quiet valley of Herefordshire and Cheshire's claim on the Peak District.

Why *camping* road trips? For me, camping immerses one in a locale more than any other form of accommodation. The sound of a tent or awning zip echoing into the night, or gently falling rain on the roof of a campervan as you drift off to sleep; the smell of slightly singed marshmallows, oozing with stickiness inside; snuggled in blankets beside the warmth of an autumn campfire with its scent of oak smoke, and mesmerised by the flickers of the flame; contemplating a three-quarter moon and the stars while listening to the babble of a nearby stream in the dark; waking up in a field to morning dew and a blackbird's song. There is, no doubt, that camping gives beguiling access to nature, to velvet nights and the harmony of sunrise. It is my life – my world; there's nowhere like it and there never will be.

These 30 micro-adventures in *Camping Road Trips: UK* offer a selection suitable for anyone who likes to camp, whether in a small campervan, a motorhome or tent and car/bicycle/motorbike (and, if you don't like to camp, I've provided the websites to find alternative accommodation). These road trips are not a commute from A to B at speed. Each is as much about slowing down, getting to know places and spending time on foot, by bike or boat as it is about spending time on the road. These are not journeys to be rushed, but to get out of the vehicle (or leave it at a campsite) and explore; an opportunity to highlight a locale, its character and personality.

I recommend that you have a look at the *How to use this guide* (page xii) section before you find yourself loading up your vehicle for a first road trip. And, if you wish to venture further afield, there's always *Camping Road Trips: France and Germany*, with another 30 adventures to enjoy, from touring through the Alps or the Pyrenees, to sampling cider in Normandy (not while driving!) and gorgeous Baltic beaches in Germany.

Happy travels!
Caroline Mills
carolinemills.net
@CarolineMills99

HOW TO USE THIS GUIDE

This section is not intended to be a 'how to go camping' guide or 'how to buy a motorhome'. For this type of general information, I recommend reading the excellent advice and articles in the numerous camping and motorhome magazines and websites or, if I may, suggest one of my other books, *The Camping Pocket Bible*.

There are 30 road trips within this guide. For each trip, introductory information indicates the counties through which you'll travel, the start and finish locations and the distance and time. At the end of each trip is an **Essentials** box with information on **getting there & around**, **parking**, **accommodation** and a list of recommended websites where you can **find out more** about a region or specific location or attraction.

Look out, too, for **Top tips**, which provide extra information on detours, recommended tour extensions or the use of public transport, and **Souvenir** boxes, offering suggestions to keep memories of your travels alive.

TIME The time given is the minimum number of days you should allocate to each trip; I really want you to be able to enjoy being on the road and take time to savour moments, and you may well wish to spend more time in certain locations than I (in some cases with family) did.

DISTANCE These are not exact to the last mile, so please use them as a rough guide only, not to set your fuel gauge. I start and stop the mileometer for each trip and, by the time I've taken a couple of wrong turns, or pulled into an appealing farm shop, the distance of any trip won't be exact.

GETTING THERE & AROUND Allow me to let you into a secret: I hate sat nav. I've used it a couple of times and I find my brain switches off; it stops me from being alert, from tuning in to my immediate location and noticing landmarks, because I know that someone else is doing the navigating for me. In many instances, there are woeful stories of the speaking robot sending drivers to the wrong place.

Please use sat nav if you need to (and it *is* helpful on occasion). But to get the most out of these road trips, I encourage you to switch it off and get out a good road atlas or map. I'm not the only one concerned that we're losing our map-reading and natural navigation skills or sense of direction. Besides, much of the fun of a road trip is plotting a route, joining the dots, and locating where you are in relation to other places. Nor does sat nav tell you whether you like the look of the terrain you might be driving through.

Road signage is not always first-class in Britain, especially in rural areas, but if you take a wrong turn and you can't spin round for a couple of miles, don't worry about it; that's when you spot the riverside parking area you like the look of sitting by for afternoon tea, or the ruined castle on the hilltop tucked among the trees.

Neither does it matter if you don't follow these routes exactly. You may be more interested in horseriding than I am and prefer to take the road that's signposted to a livery yard. You may not feel the need to take a detour to a family attraction if you're touring alone or as a couple. You may also find a road closure that forces a diversion – or you may well find a prettier route. Please use these road trips as inspiration to create your own itinerary, based upon your own interests and your own timescale. Hence, I've included a general set of directions but, often, these tours include back roads and lanes without a name or number. That's when *you* get the road atlas out and plot the route!

My preference for a good road atlas of Britain is the AA's *Big Easy Read Britain*, which covers 2.5 miles to the inch. When touring Northern Ireland, I use The AA's *Road Atlas Ireland*. Do make sure your road atlas is up to date.

If you're not familiar with driving in the UK, I recommend taking a look at the AA's advice (⊘ theaa.com/driving-advice/driving-in-great-britain). There is

↑ Make the most of sunrises and sunsets when camping (Robert Coppinger/Shutterstock)

useful general information about driving in the UK, speed limits and the travel documents required.

More and more cities have or are introducing environmental anti-pollution schemes such as low emission zones. A good website to visit to check the status of any location is: ⌀ urbanaccessregulations.eu.

Notes on parking are devoted to coachbuilt motorhomes and campervans that need to avoid height barriers.

ACCOMMODATION The accommodation recommended for these road trips varies tremendously in size, location and style – from holiday parks to small campsites, club sites (open to members and non-members), licensed sites exclusively for members of camping clubs to overnight stops in car parks and consenting 'wild' camping spots. Some are very basic and utilise a dedicated motorhome/campervan area of a general parking area, others are campsites with multiple facilities.

There are specific road trips within the guide that allow opportunities for experiencing camping off-grid in car parks or permitted camping zones. These include road trips 4 (Devon), 27 (Northumberland) and 28 (Loch Lomond and the Trossachs National Park). Note that all those used are legally designated overnight parking areas, be that by a local district council, a national park authority or a private landowner. Road trips 4 and 27 allow campervans/motorhomes only; 28 allows tents, too. In these instances, I have also provided alternative campsite suggestions.

There are also many opportunities on these road trips to stay on small sites that allow no more than five campervans, motorhomes, or caravans/trailer tents, sometimes with the addition of tents. These campsites are granted licenses by virtue of being under the umbrella of a membership organisation and, thus, can only be used by paid-up members (although, you can join on the spot) of the relevant camping club such as The Camping & Caravanning Club (CCC), and the Caravan and Motorhome Club (CAMC). These are known as Certificated Sites (CS) and Certificated Locations (CL) respectively.

While it would require users of this guide to purchase membership to stay on these small five-van sites, I thoroughly recommend such a purchase. Not only will you have access to those referred to in this guide, but you can also access more than 2,000 Certificated Sites/Locations (along with other membership benefits). Many are in extraordinarily beautiful settings, often remote, and often peacefully quiet. They can also be significantly less expensive than a campsite with a multitude of facilities. However, most of these sites request advance booking – even if that is a few hours in advance, providing space is available. Therefore, some forward-planning may be required.

WALK ON THE WILD SIDE

DISCOVER MORE TO THIS CHANNEL ISLAND THAN THE TRADITIONAL BEACH HOLIDAY BY EXPLORING THE ISLAND'S FOOTPATHS

WHERE	Channel Islands: Jersey
DISTANCE/TIME	50 miles/4 days
START/FINISH	St Helier (ferry port)

As I stand clifftop-high on Jersey's most southwestern tip, it's a beacon of light that lures me seaward. The mottled rocks are rough, their jaggedness bewildering. Though a smooth cream ribbon path, extending out into the Atlantic Ocean, is enough to entice me to the little mountain on which Corbière Lighthouse stands firm.

A hesitant sun shoots a single beam of light across the steely blue sea as if to beckon me further. But I'm too mesmerised by the goldfinches that dart around me – and the oystercatchers, whose long orange beaks appear as needle-like as the rocks – to keep focus on the little lighthouse and the sunbeam beyond.

Minutes later I turn seaward again, ready to begin my walk along the causeway. To no avail. The ribbon path has vanished ghostlike beneath the might of the Atlantic and will not reappear for several hours. I'm grateful for my timing; I wouldn't relish a hazardous swim to shore, caught out by the incoming tide that now pounds those sabre-toothed rocks. But the tide's hindrance of my seafaring wander gives me an opportunity to sit a little longer on the blustery clifftop and appreciate Jersey's wild side.

↑ Sunset at Noirmont Point (PatrickBieniek Germany/Shutterstock)

Jersey, the largest (at 45 square miles) and most southerly of the inhabited Channel Islands, is known for its impressive sandy beaches. It's also known for its annual crop of Jersey Royal potatoes, for its financial services industry – centred on the quaint capital, **St Helier** – and for Jersey Zoo, founded by the conservationist Gerald Durrell, whose pre-Jersey childhood was played out in the autobiographical television series *The Durrells*.

What is, perhaps, less well known is Jersey's remarkable, diverse scenery; that the island has its own national park teeming with wildlife; or that it's a fabulous place to go walking. Though measuring just nine miles by five, Jersey has miles of footpaths and walking trails, including the 48.5-mile coastal path that circumnavigates the island. There is also a network of Green Lanes – peaceful, narrow lanes (not suited to motorhomes!) where walkers, cyclists and horseriders have priority over motorists.

The National Trust for Jersey cares for more than 1,500 vergées (a measurement equivalent to 0.44 acres) of land across 170 sites on the island and the organisation has created a range of self-guided walks on much of its own land (available to download from its website), including a 3.5-mile circular walk around **Noirmont Point** and Portelet Common on the south coast.

It's here that I choose to begin my series of 'wild Jersey walks'. Except that I don't quite follow the guided route, for it's when I step off-course, following steep paths down to the distinctive black-and-white-banded Noirmont Tower, that my walk truly comes alive.

A pallet of colours bursts forth: first vibrant yellow gorse, then pink sea thrift, bluebells, navelwort, heather, oxeye daisies and Jersey's very own spotted rock-rose. But these pale by comparison to the tropical vibrancy of succulents with hot and fiery pinks and purples. These hottentot-figs, or ice plants as they're also known, may look visually appealing or even 'at home' on Jersey's Riviera-like south coast, but, originating from South Africa, they're not native to the island and their invasive nature is harming its ecological balance.

Wildflowers are not the only showstoppers on my walk from Noirmont Point to **Le Fret Point**, at the tip of Portelet Common. My every footstep is accompanied by a flash of goldfinches enjoying every seedhead and a rainbow of butterflies – from reddish orange to violet – warming themselves on the radiator rocks.

These footsteps must be slow and methodical, for a rustle beneath the heather bells alerts the sound of tiny feet, and a head emerges from the undergrowth. It's a privileged encounter with the most jewel-like lizard that can be found on British soil – the European green lizard. His emerald body with azure blue head is dazzling. He isn't the only one I see that day – I meet his cousin a few hundred yards further on as I make my way to Portelet Bay.

Any walk is enhanced by a decent place to take a break and wanderers on this south-coast walk are spoilt with the popular Portelet Inn, perched above Portelet Bay, and the wonderful beachside Portelet Bay Café. Both serve excellent, home-cooked food using island produce.

Replenished, I continue west by road to **Corbière Point** – and its lighthouse with causeway – before turning north for the sweeping views over **St Ouen's Bay**. The largest of Jersey's beaches, taking up most of the west coast, St Ouen's Bay is a favourite among surfers – and the sunsets are vintage. With the noisy whoosh of breaking waves in the background, I head for the adjacent Jersey Wetland Centre.

While Jersey may be a small island, it would be churlish to think the landscape is the same island wide. Far from it. The south coast has a warm microclimate with wildlife to match; the north coast is far more rugged while the southeast coast extends considerably twice daily with one of the largest tidal variations in the world.

But, on the west coast, there are sand dunes aplenty and a combination of marsh and wetland habitats. The Wetland Centre is free to enter and there's information on the landscape in this part of the island. Binoculars are available for visitors to look over the nature reserve, which includes St Ouen's Pond. I'm fortunate enough to see a rare marsh harrier during my visit. You don't need to be a regular birdwatcher or informed ecologist to appreciate the importance of what you see here – like the causeway leading to Corbière Lighthouse, the landscape and the wildlife entices you to thirst for more.

→ La Corbière was Britain's first concrete lighthouse in 1874 (Neil Balderson/Shutterstock)

SOUVENIR

The most southerly vineyard in the British Isles is Jersey's La Mare Wine Estate. Guided tours are possible and there's a fine café/restaurant.

In addition to excellent quality wines and spirits, the estate also makes cider, a nod to Jersey's traditions in the 1600–1700s when 20% of the island was covered in cider orchards (long before the Jersey Royal potato became the island's most famous crop). For something unique to Jersey, why not pick up a jar of Black Butter, also made at La Mare Wine Estate? This 'butter' is a combination of cider, apples, lemon, sugar, liquorice and spices that are boiled for days until it turns into a black, jammy conserve. It is fabulous with cheese.

The vineyard is situated near the village of St Mary, in the north of the island.

In late spring and early summer, the meadows north of St Ouen's Pond and the Wetland Centre erupt into a showy display of more than 40,000 orchids. The most colourful of these meadows is **Noir Pré**, with five orchid species carpeting the ground, including the Jersey orchid, which only grows wild in Jersey and neighbouring Guernsey. The fields and wildflowers en masse are a magnificent sight from the designated footpaths and the meadows glow as the sun slips into the Atlantic Ocean during my visit.

The coastal path around Jersey is remarkable but it is perhaps at its most stunning along the north coast, where the path rises and falls with the rugged hills that ascend from the sea and the tiny valleys that intercept. In place of the giant sweeping bays and beaches seen on the south and west coasts, there are secluded bays and tiny harbours in the north. These bays, each with its own beachside café, make ideal stopping points to take a breather from the clifftop panoramas.

Following an overnight stop at Rozel Camping Park, a delightful site within a five-minute walk of the sea and with pitches overlooking the French coast, I begin an early morning stroll at **Vicard Point**, three miles northwest. I find it a glorious introduction to the north, with a blue sea as backdrop to foxgloves and orchids, and a meeting with a red squirrel.

Further west, **Bonne Nuit Bay**, with its line of little red fishing huts, provides a scenic sea-level stop before a walk around the **Mourier Valley** and **Devil's Hole**. On either side of the valley is grazed heathland, where the National Trust for Jersey has introduced rare-breed Manx Ioaghtan sheep to nibble away at the invasive bracken.

The conservation practice has worked for it has allowed the recolonisation of the very rare chough, a bird that had become extinct in Jersey. There are now a dozen or so breeding pairs, all of which tend to reside around the rocky ledges of the north coast. They're not the only rare birds on the island; there are also a dozen puffins, which can be seen around the cliffs at Plémont.

But my walk does not finish at Devil's Hole. While the coastal paths along much of the north coast are deserted, visitors arrive en masse to Devil's Hole, one of the island's most well-known beauty spots. A ten-minute descent on foot from The Priory Inn at **St Mary's** introduces you to the dizzying height of this collapsed cave and the vast crater that now exists, where the waves crash dramatically around the rocks. You can peer into the hole from an observation platform, which also offers fine views towards Rouge Nez and, arguably, the prettiest stretch of coast on the island.

My favourite section of Jersey's coastline, around **Grosnez Point**, was yet to come. It's late evening by the time I reach the headland, the island's most northwesterly point, and a moderate storm can be seen brewing at sea. A streaky sky makes the expanse of charcoal grey sea appear all the greater, though on land the light appears mystical as it filters through the ruined arch of the atmospheric 14th-century Grosnez Castle and across the heather-strewn plateau.

With much of the coastline explored, I venture inland the following day. The morning is soggy, but it matters not, for the gentle rain makes the inland valleys appear all the more luscious and green.

↑ The keep at Grosnez Castle in springtime (Gary Le Feuvre/Shutterstock)

Hamptonne Woods is my starting point on foot, where red squirrels are resident. There's also a collection of willow sculptures along the footpath that represent the life cycle of the crapaud toad, a species native to Jersey and unique in the British Isles. The woods open out into the most idyllic valley – the Waterworks Valley – which winds its way south to St Helier. I don't venture that far, instead returning beside an impressive river of cow parsley to visit Hamptonne Country Life Museum.

The museum, housed in a magnificent collection of traditional farm buildings, offers a glimpse into the rural life of yesteryear. There's plenty to see, including traditional livestock, such as placid Jersey cows, in the surrounding paddocks.

The museum is perfect when the weather is too inclement to be out on the clifftop paths, as is a visit to Le Moulin de Quétival, Jersey's last surviving watermill. The working mill is mid-way along another of Jersey's scenic valleys, **St Peter's Valley**, which has a dedicated foot- and cycle path to enable exploration from top to bottom.

I have one more walk that I'm particularly keen to do, which requires an exhilarating 15-minute boat ride in a RIB. **Les Écréhous**, six miles east of Jersey, can be seen from Rozel Camping Park. The notable collection of rocks and sandbanks are part of Jersey's archipelago and its national park, with all but three islets submerged at high tide. The wildlife is remarkable: the archipelago is designated and protected as a Ramsar site because of its international ecological importance.

On my 'seafari', I have the opportunity to watch gannets plunge into the sea at death-defying speed and view Atlantic grey seals basking on the rocks. Common terns shriek overhead, the only sound as I step off the boat on to a tiny middle-of-nowhere sandbank with a turquoise sea all around.

↑ Hamptonne Country Life Museum (CM)

The isolation – and the silence (or at least silence from human habitation) – is enthralling and, were it not for the incoming tide once again, I could quite happily stay a week!

But it's time to leave, not just Les Écréhous but Jersey, too. As I take one last walk – this time merely around the viewing deck on the high-speed *Liberation* as it skirts the south coast of the island – a pod of playful dolphins appears. Like a little flotilla behind the ferry, they seem to offer a final farewell from Jersey.

ESSENTIALS

GETTING THERE & AROUND
Condor Ferries operates a year-round service, with crossings from 3½ hours, connecting the UK through Poole & Portsmouth to the Channel Islands (Guernsey & Jersey); also from St Malo in France.

There are two high-speed ferries, the *Condor Liberation* & *Condor Voyager*, while the *Commodore Clipper* provides a longer, conventional service for all-weather, year-round crossings. All ferries accommodate campervans & motorhomes.

A permit is required for campervans/motorhomes to enter Jersey. This is obtained when booking your campsite (the campsite will apply for the permit on your behalf). Motorhomes may travel around the island with a permit although, due to the narrow roads, unless you're travelling with the smallest of campervans, I'd recommend you leave the motorhome at a campsite and use the extensive bus network. Buses travel to the remotest of places on the island. Your visit to the island will be far less stressful and it will avoid the irritation of locals going about their daily business.

If you are travelling by road: from St Helier, A1/A12 to Beaumont (for Hideaway Stopover); A1/B57 to Noirmont Point, then circumnavigate the island clockwise via Corbière, B35 to l'Étacq, B55 & B33 to St John & Trinity; B31 to Rozel (for campsite). Distances between locations are small, thus they are easy to pinpoint on a road map.

ACCOMMODATION
I stayed at: Rozel Camping Park, St Martin (open May–Nov); Hideaway Motorhome & Caravan Stopover, Beaumont Hill (this adults-only, *aire*-style stopover is the only site on the island open all year). Other campsites on Jersey include: Beuvelande Campsite; The Palms Campsite.

For an extraordinary glamping experience, hire a pod at Durrell Wildlife Camp, in the grounds of Jersey Zoo, and listen to the animals that the camp overlooks.

FIND OUT MORE
Condor Ferries ⌕ condorferries.co.uk   **Jersey Seafaris** ⌕ jerseyseafaris.com
Jersey Tourist Board ⌕ jersey.com   **Liberty Bus** ⌕ libertybus.je
National Trust for Jersey
⌕ nationaltrust.je

2 TREMENDOUS CORNWALL, COFFEE & COURGETTES

TEST YOUR TASTEBUDS ON A FOOD & DRINK TOUR

WHERE	Cornwall
DISTANCE/TIME	225 miles/5 days
START/FINISH	Duchy of Cornwall Nursery/Trewethett Farm

Searching for Tregony in my road atlas is like looking for the proverbial needle. Everywhere in Cornwall, it feels – village, house, street or campsite – begins with the prefix 'Tre'.

In Kernowek, the Cornish language, *Tre* means homestead or settlement, and there are thousands of examples across the county. I'm grateful to pass through the hamlets of Truthwall and Trink simply for a change of vowel.

It's not for place names that I've come to Cornwall, though. Rather, for its delectable food. And there seems no better way to set up a foodie tour of the county than to start with a cooked breakfast at the **Duchy of Cornwall Nursery** near Lostwithiel.

The nursery overlooks the rolling green hills and woods of the River Fowey valley, and the 13th-century remains of Restormel Castle – the home of the first Duchy of Cornwall, The Black Prince. As part of the Duchy estate, the half-century-old nursery has sustainability credentials, growing and selling a huge selection of plants.

↑ St Agnes Heritage Coast (Ian Woolcock/Shutterstock)

In its pine-framed barn, built using timber from the estate, the café serves breakfasts, lunches and teas in front of a massive stone fireplace, and with oak-framed gothic-arched windows through which are exceptional views of the valley.

I opt for the 'Duchy' breakfast, a full English of local sausage, bacon and eggs. 'But, I'll forgo the Hog's Pudding,' I tell the waiter. 'Do you know what Hog's Pudding is?' he asks. Blushing with my ignorance, I anticipate it to be a black pudding. Indeed no, it's a slice of spicy sausage, a Cornish delicacy that dips very well into my golden-yolked poached egg.

A mile south, in Lostwithiel, I'm tasting cider at **Fowey Valley Cidery and Distillery** beside the wooded river. The valley was once renowned for a Cornish cider-making tradition that's long vanished: Victorian tourists would take boat trips upstream from Fowey to look at the spring apple blossom.

Local historian Barrie Gibson rescued one of the overgrown riverside orchards to make delicious sparkling cider from its apples. The cidery, a modern barn on a small industrial estate, is not especially romantic. But inside Barrie is preparing for the season's harvest. Some apples have already arrived. Says Barrie, 'We cannot make sufficient cider to supply the demand from our own crop, so local residents with apple trees bring nets of apples. In return, they receive a bottle of cider.'

Barrie makes a champagne-style sparkling vintage cider by the traditional method used to produce champagne that's hand-turned on riddling racks every day to remove the sediment. He runs cider-making classes, and tours explaining the cider-making process too. As he explains on the tour, 'To be called an English cider it only needs 35% apple juice (from anywhere in the world); the rest is often made up using inexpensive imported corn syrup and forced carbonation. Here, the cider is made entirely from local apples and is naturally carbonated from the fermentation process.'

I move southwest to **St Austell Brewery** for a guided tour. Here I learn of the 170-year history of the brewery, set up by local farmer Walter Hicks in 1851. My tour includes a tasting of seven beers and a token to receive a pint at the brewery's on-site bar. As I'm driving, I redeem my token in the shop for a bottle of St Austell's lager, Korev (the Cornish word for beer).

Thus far, I've not seen much of Cornwall's magical coastline, but that changes on a visit to the **Lost Gardens of Heligan**, which look over Mevagissey Bay. It's not Heligan's Jungle valley or the Pleasure Gardens for which I visit on this occasion but for its Productive Gardens and Home Farm.

Celebrated for being rediscovered and restored by Tim Smit (of Eden Project fame), Heligan's gardens were part of a 200-acre estate. Its walled Kitchen Garden supplied Heligan House and the wider estate workforce with fruit and vegetables for centuries. Now the Productive Gardens, which purposefully grow heritage varieties not suitable for large-scale commercial production, and Home Farm,

↑ The Productive Gardens at Lost Gardens of Heligan (chrisdorney/Shutterstock)

with its rare and heritage breeds of farm animals (the only farm in the southwest with Rare Breeds Survival Trust status), supplies the on-site Heligan Kitchen.

I'm in time for a late lunch but there is also the opportunity to book a Lost Supper, a seven-course tasting dinner without a menu. That is, the menu, using the produce from the garden, is planned on the day, after the gardeners have listed what's available and what's in season. The food 'miles' are reduced to 157yds, from plot to plate.

Adjacent to the entrance of Heligan is **Lobb's Farm Shop**. It's the retail window of the three Lobb brothers, who own a farm apiece around Heligan. Between them, they rear cattle and sheep to produce grass-fed beef and lamb and grow an array of vegetables – all of which can be bought at the award-winning farm shop and butchery, along with a wide selection of other Cornish-made products. I come away with a veritable feast for my first campsite dinner, at Higher Kestle Farm, one of the Lobb-owned farms within walking distance of Heligan.

SOUVENIR

Every food and drink location I visited here has something worthwhile to take away. There are many others! From fudge shops to gin distilleries, farm shops to seafood sellers – and not forgetting Camel Valley Vineyard, which also produces outstanding sparkling wines. Many – including Ann's Pasties – will deliver by mail order to your door.

↑ Camel Valley Vineyard (SubstanceTproductions/Shutterstock)

Inclement weather greets my morning drive to the **Tregothnan Estate** at St Michael Penkevil, crossing the River Fal at Tregony. It's not a relaxing route for large vehicles, but the high-hedged drive highlights the beauty of south Cornwall's creeks and steep, wooded valleys. A lost jungle of oaks and pines, the scenery is below canopy, quiet and remote.

The Tregothnan Estate was reputedly the first place in Britain that grew tea bushes and made homegrown English tea. It's possible to pre-book tours of the tea plantation, situated on the west bank of the Fal River at Coombe. I choose to visit the Woodyard Shop, a tiny cabin on the estate that sells multiple kinds of tea and suitably plain accompanying biscuits. It also sells cups of tea – not particularly elegantly, in a paper cup. But with a tiny tea garden surrounded by enclosing trees, it's a restful place to sit a while.

My journey takes me to the coastal edge of the **Roseland Peninsula** and Portscatho, where a short walk north along the South West Coast Path leads to The Hidden Hut. This al-fresco wooden servery, overlooking **Porthcurnick Beach**, has become a destination diner in recent years. It doesn't simply serve whipped-cream-topped hot chocolates to passing walkers, its street-food menu of fresh, seasonal fare and its one-dish feast nights are legendary. People make a point of coming here, as I have, despite the £15 per portion menu. Lunch, as the clouds disperse to leave soggy sand pitted by raindrops, tastes divine for having a sea-salty breeze accompaniment.

It's a long route from the Roseland Peninsula to drive around the extensive Fal Estuary via Truro to reach southwest Cornwall. I choose the more scenic option, by taking the King Harry Ferry, which crosses the Fal between Philleigh and Trelissick. The five-minute crossing provides a wonderful if all-too-brief glimpse of this fjord-like ria, where giant ships can be seen anchored mid-stream when mothballed.

I continue west to Lynher Dairies at Ponsanooth. The name is not that familiar but its product, Cornish Yarg, is one of Cornwall's best exports. The creamy-textured hard cheese is made from the milk of farms within a 20-mile radius of the dairy, including its own pedigree herd of Ayrshire cows. After a couple of taste tests, I pick up a wedge of nettle-wrapped Yarg and a piece of Cornish Kern, a World Cheese Awards winner.

Skirting Helston, I drive the length of the **Lizard Peninsula** for a circular walk from the mainland's southernmost village. My walk to Lizard Point, and the return through the Lizard National Nature Reserve towards Kynance Cove, is a sublime excuse to go armed with an ice cream from Roskilly's, whose farm is on the peninsula. And its little parlour in the village is next to Ann's Pasties, another institution of The Lizard.

Ann has won countless awards for her pasties, which were initially made for family and friends. So good are they, however, that there are now three shops on

↑ Lizard Point (CM)   → Roskilly's ice cream, based on the Lizard Peninsula (CM)

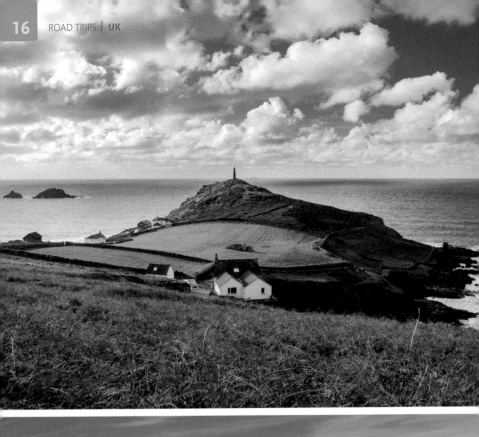

the peninsula – in Helston, Lizard and Porthleven, the last a foodie town of cafés, pasty shops, harbourside pubs and upmarket seafood restaurants. Following an overnight stay at Teneriffe Farm Campsite (which sells homemade sausages and burgers from the farm), and an early-morning walk across the headland to Mullion Cove, it's to Porthleven that I descend to pick up one of Ann's Pasties for lunch.

I arrive soon after opening time and, entering the shop, the aroma knocks the senses. The shop assistant warns the pasty is piping hot, having just come out of the oven. I announce I'm hungry, having not eaten breakfast. 'That'll be torture then, waiting for it to cool down,' she says. It is. Moments later, on my way to Penzance and Trengwainton Garden, I have to pull over and break off a piece of golden crust. Then another…

The National Trust's **Trengwainton Garden** is, like Heligan, filled with exotic plants and woodland walks. It's also renowned for its walled kitchen garden and orchards, the produce from which is sold to visitors. The garden is unique in the UK in having a series of sloping beds, built shortly after 1816, to increase food production for the estate. Then, the Year Without a Summer, much of the world saw global food shortages following an eruption of Mount Tambora in Indonesia that created a volcanic winter, the coldest summer temperatures for 250 years and complete crop failure.

Half a mile from Trengwainton is the small town of **Newlyn**. Its narrow streets and fishermen's cottages perch on the hillside overlooking the harbour and Mount's Bay. This is one of the best places from which to buy fresh seafood from the numerous stalls beside the wholesale fish market. But Newlyn has another celebrated resident – Jelbert's.

The tiny building has all the unpretentiousness of a 1960s shopfront; little has changed in more than 100 years, including the family that make the ice cream. There's one flavour – vanilla – served from one tub, and there are two choices – with or without a flake and with or without clotted cream on top. Frankly, the latter is a must. For all its modesty, Jelbert's is regarded as the best ice cream in Cornwall; adults that came on their holidays as children now bring their own children and grandchildren to savour the delight of eating a Jelbert's ice cream – with clotted cream on top – looking out towards St Michael's Mount.

My drive continues around the edge of Cornwall's big toe, where the scenery of rolling hills and higher moors inland is as inviting as the occasional views out to sea. I bypass Land's End in favour of **Cape Cornwall**, at the northern end of Whitesand Bay, and a part of the Cornish Mining UNESCO World Heritage Site.

Despite the warmth and stillness of the day, the wind whips up white horses against the rocks surrounding the cape, which splits the Atlantic currents. The headland is so captivating, it's a place I return to later in the evening to watch the sunset, with my fish and chips from Jeremy's in St Just.

↑ Cape Cornwall, the site of a former tin mine (Ian Woolcock/Shutterstock) ← The harbour at Newlyn fishing village (Andy333/Shutterstock)

The road from St Just to St Ives is one of the prettiest in Britain. Its landscape of tiny fields, bordered by low walls and unsymmetrical hedges, stretching to the north coast, with rocky, bracken-lined moorland to the south, is mesmerising; I find myself stopping every few yards to admire its beauty. Along the route are reminders of heavy industry – mine shafts and chimneys from long-closed tin mines that form part of the heritage coast.

At the idyllic village of **Zennor**, where the Tinners Arms offers another reminder, I stop to walk the coast path to Zennor Head with views of the craggy cliffs and emerald seas washing over impossible-to-reach beaches. Zennor is also home to Moomaid of Zennor, another from-the-farm artisan manufacturer of ice cream. Moomaid's most popular ice cream, Shipwreck (with honeycomb, sea salt and dulce de leche caramel) is sold in its busy parlour in St Ives, but so, too, in Zennor where the little café garden is a charming retreat.

I skip St Ives on this occasion, though there are plenty of excuses why I should stop (The Allotment Deli on Fore Street being one of them), to continue my foodie

↑ Views from Zennor Head (CM)

journey. My first stop beyond St Ives is Trink Dairy, a short spur off the A3074. Here, the Knowles family keep a herd of Friesian and Jersey cows. As I arrive, it's milking time. The cows can be seen in the milking parlour through viewing windows while I buy milk from the vending machine (milkshakes also available); I'm so engrossed, the cows are returning to the fields by the time I leave.

Fifteen minutes northeast, I'm at Trevaskis Farm, near Connor Downs, which specialises in pick-your-own fruit from the 28 acres of orchards and tunnels of soft fruits. I'm too late for strawberries and currants, but there are still plenty of late-summer raspberries to pick, along with varieties of apple not found in supermarkets. There's also a very popular restaurant but I've earmarked a pasty from St Agnes Bakery for lunch; if Ann's Pasties win best pasty from the south coast, the tiny village bakery is certainly granted top spot from the north. Munched on St Agnes Head, they taste even better.

I'm full! But I have three more places I'm eager to visit. The Beach Hut, overlooking the tremendous **Watergate Bay**, beloved by surfers, is a trendy

↑ St Agnes (Tim Woolcock Photography/Shutterstock)

wave-riding hang-out. It's as modern as St Agnes Bakery is traditional; menus, ordering and payment are made by mobile app. Ingredients are local and, mostly, vegetarian. It's essential to book for dinner in the summer months, where the huge panoramic windows frame, but don't stop, the rolling surf in front of you.

I opt for the quieter breakfast session, when only the most hardened surfers are taking to the waves, and a small band of yoga enthusiasts are squidging sand between their toes. I say quieter, for listening to the roar of the ocean on a post-breakfast walk along the bay invigorates the senses.

My drive along the coast road to **Padstow** is close to matching the road between St Just and St Ives for beauty. A stop to walk along the cliffs overlooking Bedruthan Steps is essential, along with admiring the string of pretty villages with stone and white-washed cottages. The Cornish Arms, at St Merryn, appeals as a place to stop, were it lunchtime. It's owned by the Steins, as are many of the restaurants and cafés in Padstow. So, too, Rick Stein's Cookery School, where visitors can take part in a demonstration or cooking course to learn new skills – often in relation to his cookery books and television series.

It's the home of one of Rick Stein's former chefs that I next visit. At Trerethern Farm, on the southern outskirts of Padstow, Ross Geach works the land (it has been in his family for more than 130 years), where he runs Padstow Kitchen Garden. Growing a vast variety of vegetables, Ross sells much of his produce to

↑ Padstow Lifeboat Station (Ian Woolcock/Shutterstock)

top-class restaurants (including Stein's Seafood Restaurant in Padstow), but he also sells direct from the farm.

There's nothing high-class about the farm shop – it's an old shipping container. But inside are gems from the soil, fresh-picked and immediate. On sale are spring onions, beetroot, salad leaves and courgettes – plus their edible flowers. I come away with a bag of leaves so full of flavour that they don't need dressing.

Three miles south, I reach my final foodie destination, Trevibban Mill Vineyard. The sun, with its late summer warmth, sweetens the pinot noir grapes that embellish the rows of vines. A diminutive tractor hums in the distance as it mows the grass between each row. I sit on the terrace to lunch on local artisan bread and Cornish cheese with superlative views over the vines and St Breoch Downs. I could take a guided walking tour and tasting. But I'm driving. So, I purchase a bottle of award-winning sparkling pinot noir rosé to take away.

This evening, I sit at Trewethett Farm, my campervan pitched overlooking Trewethett Gut, Lye Rock, Willapark and the Two Sisters, with the Atlantic swirling around them. I pop the cork on my chilled bottle of Trevibban Mill fizz. As the tiny bubbles rise, I watch the sun descend beyond the horizon, turning clouds flame orange and the sea white. Merlin at neighbouring Tintagel Head, it seems, has performed wizardry. It's a magic combination.

↑ Trewethett Farm CAMC (CM)

ESSENTIALS
GETTING THERE & AROUND
NB This road trip is best suited to those touring with a small campervan no more than 18ft (5.5m) long, 6ft 6in (2m) wide and 8ft (2.5m) high, or with a car/bicycle. Larger, coachbuilt motorhomes may struggle on some of the narrow, rural Cornish lanes with high-sided Cornish walls/hedges; please attempt only if particularly adept at reversing long distances uphill and around tight bends.

The Duchy of Cornwall Nursery is situated on a rural lane one mile north of Lostwithiel. A390 to Lostwithiel for Fowey Valley Cider. A390 to St Austell. Follow brown tourist signposts for St Austell Brewery. B3273 south to Pentewan then rural lane west to Heligan/Lobb's/High Kestle Farm. Rural lanes to St Michael Penkevil, via Tregony, to Tregothnan Estate, then to A3078 via Lamorran & Ruan Lanihorne. A3078 south & rural lane to Portscatho. Return to A3078 towards St Mawes/B3289 north then use the King Harry Ferry across the Fal River to Trelissick to reach the A39 south. A393 to Lynher Dairies. Return to A39 then southwest on A39 then A394 to Helston. A3083 south to Lizard. A3083 north to Penhale, B3296 west to Mullion, rural lane south towards Predannack for Teneriffe Farm Campsite. Return to Mullion, then rural lane to Poldhu Point & Cury, A3083 north to Helston, then A394/B3304 for Porthleven. A394/A30 west to Penzance. Rural lane northwest to Trengwainton Garden then south on local roads to Newlyn. B3315/A30/B3306 to St Just. B3306 northeast to St Ives. A3074 south (rural lane spur to Trink Dairy) & A30 northeast to Connor Downs for Trevaskis Farm. A30 northeast/B3277 to St Agnes (and rural lanes to St Agnes Head). B3285 to Perranporth & Goonhavern/A3075 north/A392 east (briefly)/A3058 northwest/ B3276 to Watergate Bay. B3276 to Padstow/A389 south (for Padstow Kitchen Garden)/B3274 & rural lane to Trevibban Mill Vineyard. Return to A389/A39 northeast to Camelford then B3266 north/B3263 to Tintagel & Trewethett Farm.

Parking without height barriers: unless otherwise mentioned here, all food/drink attractions have parking space for motorhomes. For Hidden Hut at Porthcurnick Beach, park at Portscatho car park and walk the 500yds north along the coast path (do not attempt to reach Porthcurnick Beach direct via Rosevine). For the Lizard, use the large car park in The Square. At Porthleven, there are Kittos Field or Withy Field car parks. For Newlyn, try Tolcarne Inn car

↑ Mullion Cove (Lukasz Pajor/Shutterstock)

park or roadside along Strand. St Just has a large, free car park off Lafrowda Close. There's an NT-owned car park at Cape Cornwall, but note that the road is narrow and steep for short sections. Zennor's village car park charges just £1 for all-day parking. At St Ives: leisure centre car park/use park & ride here, or at St Erth & take the 10-min train. St Agnes has a village car park, but for more space park at St Agnes Head & walk. Watergate Bay Car Park is off Tregurrian Hill (the car park nearest to The Beach Hut has a height barrier), if not taking the 10-min downhill walk from the campsite. At Padstow, use Harbourside car park or leisure centre park & ride.

ACCOMMODATION I stayed at: Higher Kestle Farm, St Ewe; Teneriffe Farm Campsite, Predannack; Kelynack Caravan & Camping, Kelynack (St Just); The View at Watergate Bay, Tregurrian; Trewethett Farm CAMC, Tintagel.

Cornwall gets unsustainably busy during summer school holidays and I would encourage anyone that doesn't have to visit during July and August to avoid these months. All these campsites are open from March/April to October, some for longer, and ever more campsites in Cornwall open year-round. You'll find it far more relaxing to be able to drive along quieter roads out of season, and many businesses will be very grateful to receive your custom!

FIND OUT MORE

Visit Cornwall visitcornwall.com

All the food and drink locations featured also have their own websites so do check opening days and times before visiting.

TOP TIP: BREAKFAST AND A WALK TO ST IVES

Park in Zennor village car park, fill up with breakfast at Moomaid of Zennor café (opens 09.30), then walk the South West Coast Path for six miles to St Ives in time for lunch. Take the bus back to Zennor. For a shorter walk, begin with mid-morning coffee at Moomaid of Zennor, take the circular walk using the Field Path to the coast, returning to Zennor along the coast path for lunch at the Tinners Arms. The pub serves plenty of locally caught fish and seafood alongside pub classics.

3 THE CREAM OF DEVON TEA

**DISCOVERING DARTMOOR, BRITAIN'S OCEAN CITY
& A BRITISH TEA PLANTATION (& A TINY, HIDDEN
CORNER OF CORNWALL BY BOAT)**

WHERE	Dartmoor & Plymouth, Devon
DISTANCE/TIME	193 miles/5 days
START/FINISH	Tavistock/Ashburton

The Galápagos Islands, some 6,000 miles away in the Pacific Ocean, seem very far away from where I'm sat on Devil's Point overlooking Plymouth Sound. Yet, I feel a connection while I watch ships anchored beside the Breakwater on a heat-hazy morning, and puce pink valerian flutters in the coastal breeze around the point. Charles Darwin left here on HMS *Beagle* in 1831. His five-year voyage as a young naturalist, which included documenting The Galápagos Islands, would eventually lead him to write *On the Origin of Species* and a changed perception of the natural world.

Fast-forward a little short of 200 years, and **Plymouth** has become renowned for its research of marine biology, conservation and ocean pollution, and is at the forefront of changing human behaviour impacting marine life, creating Britain's first National Marine Park in Plymouth Sound. Little wonder, then, that Britain's Ocean City is also at the forefront of sustainable tourism.

I begin my visit of the city with a walk along Plymouth's Waterfront Walkway. The complete route, with details available via the Plymouth Trails app from the Visit Plymouth website, is 9 miles. I cover a third of this, walking from Sutton Harbour and the Barbican, past the Royal Citadel, The Hoe, Millbay and around Devil's Point to Royal William Yard.

Views are powerful, whether of Mount Batten across the mouth of the River Plym (the Cattewater); of Smeaton's Tower, the red-and-white symbol of the city that stands on the Hoe; of Drake's Island, sitting in the middle of the sound; or of Cornwall and the Tamar Valley when rounding the corner of Devil's Point.

Royal William Yard was once the victualling yard for the Royal Navy, where bread was baked and beer brewed to supply naval ships. The impressive complex of listed buildings has been restored and taken by a supply of waterside restaurants and boutiques. They surround a small marina from where it's possible to catch one of Plymouth's Waterlinks, the ferries that operate between various stops around the city and its surrounds. As the focus of my visit to Plymouth is the ocean, it seems like the appropriate (and environmental) way to travel for my return to the Barbican; some of the boats are solar-powered.

Overlooking Sutton Harbour is the National Marine Aquarium, where I visit next. The award-winning and very popular family attraction showcases marine life that can be found in Plymouth Sound, and then links it to the life of oceans across the globe.

The aquarium was born out of the scientific research on marine biology taking place in Plymouth. This is the public space to present ideas in an entertaining

← Plymouth Hoe (David Jeffrey Morgan/Shutterstock)

TOP TIP: SIX GREAT PLACES TO EAT IN PLYMOUTH

Rockfish & Sardine Bar Choose the restaurant for relaxed and leisurely table service and a theatre-kitchen experience, or the Sardine Bar for a zingy and quick take-away.

The Waterfront On the Grand Parade, an attractive contemporary dining experience (including brunch) in a listed Art Deco building right on the water's edge, as the name suggests.

Plymouth Gin Brasserie Serving dishes using local produce within the historic Plymouth Gin distillery, in the Barbican.

Ocean View Bar & Dining at the Dome Newly opened venue overlooking the sea on The Hoe, with an Art Deco interior. Popular for early evening drinks but also a great place for a Devon Cream Tea.

Piermaster's House Open from 7am for breakfast plus brunch, lunch and dinner. Attractive outdoor deck overhangs the water by the Barbican Landing Stage.

The Orangery or **The Farriers** Both in Mount Edgcumbe Country Park; choose The Farriers for lunch and The Orangery for morning coffee and cake or afternoon tea.

way. It's run by the charity Ocean Conservation Trust, which also manages the Plymouth Sound National Marine Park. This project aims to connect people to marine environments, to demonstrate how everyone is connected to the ocean wherever they live, and how oceans are affected by human behaviour.

That includes experiencing the marine park first-hand. The trust offers boat-trip experiences, free snorkel safaris (with all the equipment provided) and, in the summer months, Beach Explorer sessions. The public can get involved in the trust's citizen-science projects and sign up to, for example, weekly beach-clean litter picks. All the rubbish is returned to the labs at the aquarium, where it's weighed and the data analysed to understand where it's coming from and how it could be prevented from reaching the oceans.

There's also a chance for visitors to get involved in the trust's Seagrass Project, aiming to plant and restore seagrass meadows in the sound. Says Olly Reed, Communications Manager at the Aquarium, 'Seagrass can store and "bury" carbon up to 35 times faster than rainforests, so it's a really important part of the ocean and the ecosystem.'

The seagrass lab, and information about the project, is on view at the aquarium, where visitors can also find out about eating fish from sustainable sources, talk to Ocean Discovery Rangers – all trained marine biologists – about the aquarium's conservation-breeding programmes, watch diving demos, and discover the importance of the oceans on mental health. Concludes Olly, 'it's all about falling in love with the ocean. People will want to look after it then.'

Suitably inspired, I can't wait to get on the ocean so, the following morning, I catch the ferry from Plymouth's Barbican Landing Stage to **Cawsand**. This tiny, colourful village lies on the other side of the River Tamar, in Cornwall. The ferry wedges itself against the petite beach while travellers walk a gangplank to reach not so *terra firma*. It's an exciting way of arriving in the county.

There are walks aplenty from Cawsand – the ferry captain recommends one to nearby Rame Head – but I spend a morning exploring Mount Edgcumbe Country Park. The intention is to walk the South West Coast Path around the headland to the tiny village of **Cremyll**, where another ferry connects to Plymouth. But I'm lured by a steep path through wild vegetation up to Maker Heights, from where I gain superlative views of the south coast and, as I traverse the Deer Park, views north of the Tamar Valley and Plymouth.

Mount Edgcumbe Country Park is a must-see on any green tourism itinerary. There's a day's walking to be done, whether around the coastline or through the hay meadows and woodlands; there's also an off-road cycle trail. Guided tours of the impressive stately home are available for a small charge, otherwise the entire country park is open to the public free of charge. Also here, among the formal gardens descending to the sound, is a reserve devoted to protecting the endangered black bee, the UK's original native honeybee, the population of which is dwindling. Visitors can view the work of the reserve from special platforms.

The short ferry crossing from Cremyll across Plymouth Sound to Royal William Yard is the perfect end to a beautiful visit and gives an introductory view of the

↑ Cawsand and Kingsand (Gordon Bell/Shutterstock)

Tamar Valley. Plymouth Boat Trips, who operate the Waterlinks, also offer various cruises, including a one-hour tour of the harbour and a half-day trip up the tidal River Tamar to **Calstock**.

Much of the Tamar Valley is designated as an Area of Outstanding Natural Beauty and my all-too-brief visit to the once-busy inland port of Calstock demonstrates why. There are steep wooded slopes beyond open buttercup meadows and the historic signs of former mining activity – this is also part of the Cornwall and West Devon Mining Landscape, designated a UNESCO World Heritage Site in recognition of when the area was a hive of industrial activity extracting copper and tin.

By morning, I'm back at the Barbican Landing Stage to pick up another ferry, this time for a visit and guided tour of **Drake's Island**. Easily viewed from the mainland, this tiny, rocky islet guards the entrance to Plymouth's marinas. The island became a small garrison during the Tudor and Napoleonic wars. Until very recently, it was off limits to the public.

Now nature has reclaimed much of the island and it's possible for visitors to venture here. Bob, the Island Warden, meets the tour group at the jetty, where he explains the history and ecology of the 60yd-wide island as we set off on a walking tour around the ramparts and through a series of tunnels and magazine chambers. Unlikely bedfellows, an assemblage of self-seeded wildflowers cling to decaying ammunition stores and, as Bob tells comical anecdotes of social island history, resident parent geese lead their goslings up old artillery ramps.

Returning to the mainland, I feel I can't leave Plymouth without supper from the ocean. Rockfish, situated beside Plymouth's fish market, and one of the

↑ Drake's Island with Mount Edgcumbe Country Park beyond (Mykola Romanovskyy/Shutterstock)

restaurants pledged to the city's green tourism project, seems a fine place to go. Run by renowned seafood ambassador Mitch Tonks, the day's menu is determined solely by what has been caught sustainably and locally, using Marine Stewardship Council-certified seafood.

I could dine in the restaurant with table service, but I happen to be in town on the third Friday of the month. That's when Rockfish's Sardine Bar runs Fish Friday, where fish and chips are sold for £3 per portion. The queues are long; it's understandably very popular but it's an opportunity to discover how to enjoy fish from sustainable sources.

As I end my trip to Plymouth, tucking into deliciously light and crispy batter and tasting a fish I'd never ordinarily think to order, small fishing boats in vivid colours are returning to the harbour. I've walked, and walked some more, used ferries to get around and got to know the National Marine Park that little bit better.

But it's time to venture inland where rivers and tiny streams still connect me to the ocean. My first stop inland – just – is Saltram, a National Trust park whose meadow gardens, parkland and steep wooded cliffs drop down to the River Plym at its mouth. There are views of Plymouth Harbour to ease one into inland scenery gently, but my eyes are already averted to the gardens, where blackbirds scurry amid the sunny glades of springtime meadow flowers, azalea bushes blousily bloom and a beekeeper suited up like a Martian tentatively studies beehive frames for honeycomb.

Exiting through unremarkable Plympton, I drive north towards Lee Moor, curious at giant slabs of white something I can see in the distance. Those white

somethings are vast china clay pits and slag, a modern-day nod to Dartmoor's mining past. From the village of Wotter, built to house the clay-pit workers, are fine views, offering one last glimpse of the sea before I turn into Dartmoor National Park on the road to Meavy and **Yelverton**.

The moors here show not only the fresh scars of industry, but that of former heavy labour as a walk from Cadover Bridge, which crosses a narrower River Plym, highlights. Across the moorland are the disused workings of tin mines and ancient settlements. These are soon left behind, though, and in their place come extraordinary views of Sheeps Tor and the green and verdant foothills of Dartmoor.

The early evening light is magnificently soft, casting a rich glow across the fields and tors. I don't want to waste a drop of that sunlight. Beyond Yelverton, crossing Whitchurch Common to the east of Tavistock, I spy an anomalous tor in a relatively flat, distant landscape. It's distinctive and alluring; I cannot resist venturing to take a closer look, so I head north out of Tavistock, turning west at Mary Tavy.

The deserted road through the park opens extensive views that force me to stop for a while to take them in. But I can see that what sits upon the now not-so-distant tor is a church, perched like a wedding-cake topper. It's detached from its parish at Brentor by several fields and sits prominently alone.

The climb to **St Michael de Rupe** takes my breath away. Not because of its steepness – though it *is* steep (coffin bearers must have winced in days of old) – but for the views. This is some resting place, for the living as well as the departed. There's little flat space at the summit of the tor upon which to sit the diminutive church. But the space that surrounds the church appears immeasurable and ethereal. My brief walk back to the campervan is one filled with a sense that I have just seen the whole of southwest England.

In the morning, I mosey into **Tavistock**, a town of pleasurable size to explore on foot. At its heart, yet with views of Dartmoor at every turn, is the town's former abbey buildings and Pannier Market, which has taken place for more than 900 years. The lovely market building, which offers themed markets five days a week, is enveloped by a partly covered pedestrian walkway with cafés and shops.

A heritage trail from the abbey includes a wander along the River Tavy and the historic canal wharf, a once-important route to export copper and tin to the inland quays at Morwellham and Calstock. Tavistock, which is the only town in Devon to be part of a UNESCO World Heritage Site, is known as a stannary town. These towns, found only in Devon and Cornwall, were the collectors of tin coinage, a local tax on refined tin.

In thick fog, I leave Tavistock and climb to the viewpoint on top of Pork Hill, on the western edge of Dartmoor. Views, at this moment in time, are not to be had –

↑ Combestone Tor on Dartmoor (Sebastien Coell/Shutterstock) ← Tavistock Abbey (CM)

though on an evening earlier in my trip, I had ventured up to find a panorama that's almost a match for those at Brentor church. But this early morning, my only company is a group of Dartmoor ponies, standing in the parking area like a set of delinquent boy racers – was it they, manes flying, that had created the circular doughnuts on the tarmac?

The ponies move on. In their place comes the sound of skylarks, and then a rare glimpse of them on the ground as they feed on titbits in the coarse grass.

At **Merrivale**, it is merry indeed, lying below the layer of dense cloud as the sun attempts to peep. The tiny River Walkham flows through the green vale, above which are hardened moors, with stone and rock scattered like a war zone. The fog rises and falls like the swell of the sea. A hardy hiker, with hefty rucksack and all the gear, drifts in and out of sight as the fog comes down hard again. Sheep graze roadside, seated for warmth.

By the time I reach the centre of the moor, I realise how unrelenting the bleak openness is by comparison to the cosseted fields of the foothills. The giant grey slab walls of Dartmoor Prison, built to house Napoleonic prisoners in the 19th century, look brooding in the gloom.

Yet, a mile beyond Princetown the fog vanishes as if I've pushed through a curtain. While the west of Dartmoor is shrouded, the eastern moors and tors are in sunshine. I stop briefly at **Dartmeet**, where the West Dart and East Dart rivers form one band of water. At 9am, I have the beauty spot to myself for gentle riverside strolls, but later in the day this becomes a popular place to park up.

After the 1:5 ascent over Yartor Down, with notable views back of the steep and wooded Dartmeet, the route becomes ever gentler over the gradual descent through the pretty Dart Valley to Ashburton. In little more than a few hours (with a very gentle drive and stops – it can take as little as 35 minutes from Tavistock to Ashburton), I've crossed the width of Dartmoor and witnessed noticeable changes in landscape between the west and east of the national park.

But I'm not ready to leave Devon yet and minutes later, I'm sat beneath a canvas parasol at **Dartmoor Estate Tea**, south of Ashburton. The sun is now flooding light upon neighbouring Chuley Hill, where Red Ruby Devon cattle graze in verdant green pastures.

On the picnic table, grains slip silently through an hourglass, filling its lower bulb as entrancing as soft sand flows between fingertips. A minute later, an empty upper vessel defines exactly the right time for the pot of tea in front of me to be poured. It's a golden moment for a gold-blushed beverage. This is no builder's brew.

While the surrounding hills are typically 'Devon', what's not so Devon-esque is the foreground: a tea plantation filled with row upon row of tea bushes, introduced by owners Jo Harper and Kathryn Bennett with whom I'm drinking. The Dartmoor Golden Vein tea that I sip from a delicate glass cup – its name a

→ Dartmeet (Lorna Munden/Shutterstock)

comparison to the colour of the tannins in the nearby River Dart – has come from the leaves of these very bushes. It's a refreshing, elegant drink, subtle and fragrant.

Seven years ago, Jo and Kathryn knew no more about tea other than the taste of a good cuppa laid in bed of a morning. The couple had acquired 13 acres of land in the foothills of the national park, with a mixture of deciduous woodland and over-grazed pasture on the south-facing slopes of the Ashburn Valley. Having renovated the accompanying house, what to do with the land became the next topic of conversation. A varied selection of small-scale légumes were possibilities, but tea kept stirring in Jo's mind.

Sat mulling over breakfast on New Year's Day in 2015, the conversation turned to tea again. Kathryn issued a decree: stop talking about it and get on with it! Six weeks later, the seed arrived from China and the making of an English tea garden could begin. From those 500 seeds, just thirty plants grew.

There are now some 6,000 bushes handsomely growing in the Devon soil, in five separate tea gardens, and Jo and Kathryn have opened Dartmoor Estate Tea to the public.

It's a beautiful spot to drink tea: at the far end of the plantation, Jo and Kathryn are developing an alternative tea garden, reverting some over-grazed pasture to wildflower meadows. Bluebells and early purple orchids flourish here in late spring and wild cherry trees, mulberry, nuts and soft fruits are being planted alongside the primary crop, so that visitors can see tea growing in a different way.

Once the handpicked harvest has been gathered, the tea leaves are made; Jo and Kathryn make black, green and oolong teas on-site. Visitors to the Tea House

ESSENTIALS

GETTING THERE & AROUND A386 Tavistock to Plymouth; B3417 Plympton to Lee Moor, then rural roads to Meavy & Yelverton; A386 Tavistock to Mary Tavy then rural roads to North Brentor; B3357 to Dartmeet, Hele & Ashburton. Dartmoor Estate Tea is between Ashburton & Buckfast, parallel with the A38.

Coachbuilt motorhomes should use the A386 between Tavistock & Plymouth; the narrow lanes that a sat-nav will take you on are not suitable for this size of vehicle. All other roads on this route are passable for coachbuilt motorhomes. Note, if using the Tamar Bridge between Devon & Cornwall, there is a toll on the Cornwall–Devon side only.

Parking without height barriers: in Tavistock, motorhomes can park in Riverside, a 3-min walk from the town centre. Plymouth is an approximate 15-min journey from Riverside Caravan Park or a 35-min journey via the A386 from Tavistock CCC Site. Coypool Park & Ride has parking bays for motorhomes up to 39ft (12m). However, less than half a mile

(where the tea is made) should not expect rich Devon cream teas, milk and sugar that all mask the subtle flavours. Instead, the tea is served in the simplest of ways so that nothing clutters the experience – simply and slowly, with homemade biscuits that pair well.

I can vouch for that, with the tahini and honey biscuit that accompanies my golden infusion. As for the mesmerising view, it's one over which to ponder a while – with a good pot of tea. Thank goodness Jo and Kathryn run the adjacent campsite, too. I can do exactly that.

from Riverside & 2 miles from the Tavistock campsite is National Cycle Route number 27, otherwise known as the Drake's Trail (see below) for the section between Tavistock & Plymouth, which offers traffic-free cycling along a former railway line. There's a large parking area in Calstock at the quay, but access to the village is narrow and steep. All-day parking (paid) is available at Dartmeet.

ACCOMMODATION I stayed at: Tavistock CCC Site (non-members welcome); Riverside Caravan Park, Plymouth; The Crib CS (CCC members only, though you can join at the site) at Dartmoor Estate Tea.

FIND OUT MORE
Visit Plymouth visitplymouth.co.uk   **Drake's Trail** drakestrail.co.uk
Dartmoor Estate Tea
 dartmoorestatetea.com

↑ Dartmoor Estate Tea (CM)

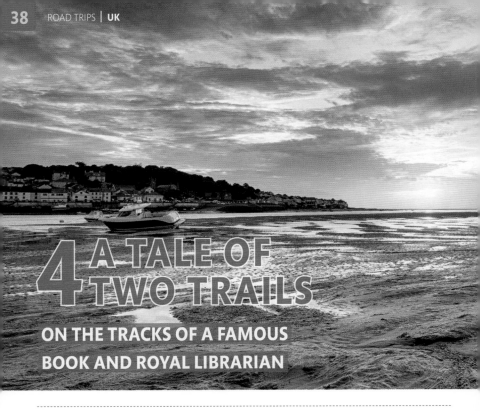

4 A TALE OF TWO TRAILS

ON THE TRACKS OF A FAMOUS BOOK AND ROYAL LIBRARIAN

WHERE	North Devon/Somerset
DISTANCE/TIME	131 miles/7 days
START/FINISH	Bideford/Castle Cary

Tarka the Otter, the well-loved fictional character created in 1927 by writer Henry Williamson, was apparently so named because Tarka means 'Little Water Wanderer'.

Tarka's habitat was that of the 'Two Rivers', the Taw and the Torridge in North Devon. With the opportunity for self-contained motorhomes and campervans to stay overnight in car parks run by Torridge District Council, we can be free spirits to do some water wandering of our own.

Our Friday evening schedule means we're unable to leave home until 9pm, but no matter. Unrestricted by set arrival times at campsites, we creep stealthily into the empty Riverbank Car Park at **Bideford** at midnight. It gives us three complete days in North Devon, rather than an early start and a potentially busy M5 on a Saturday morning. It's wandering freedom already.

Waking to the sound of birdsong, we discover that our overnight stop in Riverbank Car Park has as good a view as any campsite – overlooking Tarka's great River Torridge. It's no less convenient, either, with town centre shops only

↑ Low tide at Appledore, North Devon (Helen Hotson/Shutterstock)

a five-minute walk to collect breakfast treats, and the vast municipal Victoria Park in which children can let off steam.

Bideford has long been nicknamed the 'little white town'. We pass through it and across the ancient, multi-arched Long Bridge to reach the Tarka Trail. This series of footpaths and cycleways covers some 180 miles around North Devon; we make the most of the recycled old railway lines that have become traffic-free cycle routes.

Our first day's route takes us six miles inland from Bideford to Great Torrington. We mix and match walking and cycling, allowing plenty of time to take in the sights as we follow the Torridge's course.

A school project on rivers is greatly enhanced by newfound knowledge of the ecological importance of salt marshes as we leave Bideford behind, crossing the Torridge via an old railway bridge. It's the first of five overland viewpoints we have of the snaking waterway. The trail's views here are by no means the limitless scenes one gets from hilltops, but they make one focus on the microscopic, observing that in front of your footstep in an enclosed, tree-canopied world rather than a wider canvas.

Passing over and under bridges, through damp railway tunnels and past the remains of peculiar follies, we are accompanied on our route by a glorious

combination of wild garlic, violets, bluebells, and celandines, all lighting up the verges of our tunnel-vision cycle route.

There are plenty of opportunities to rest along the way and we select a scenic spot overlooking the tiny riverside hamlet of **Weare Barton** for a picnic lunch before continuing to the Beam Aqueduct. This water carrier was once a part of the Torrington or Rolle Canal (named after the businessman Lord Rolle), which carried coal and limestone from Bideford to Torrington. It features in *Tarka the Otter* as the 'Canal Bridge' and is the very spot where this amphibious creature begins his life. Only a few miles from the coast, all evidence of the tidal Torridge has gone; here it is a quiet, tamed rural river.

By the end of our twelve-mile round trip, our picturesque riverside parking spot in Bideford provides an ideal setting for a Devon cream tea and an afternoon doze on the grass outside the motorhome as we watch the tide roll in.

Keen to compare the various overnight stops, we move onto our next site, the Main Car Park at **Westward Ho!** Once again, the location is convenient, in the centre of town and only yards from the vast sandy beach that stretches for three miles along the North Devon coastline. Our evening entertainment is clear.

Having never been to Westward Ho! before, we were unsure what to expect. What we discover is a very pleasant seaside resort, and the only place name in Britain (and, indeed, Europe) to contain an exclamation mark. Actually the town was founded through literary connections: the publication in 1855 of Charles Kingsley's novel, titled *Westward Ho!*, led to a tourist boom on the peninsula, and the founding of the new town by the same name. It is, allegedly, the only case of a novel leading to the construction of a town, which required the building of a railway (now defunct) to serve it.

We are tempted by the prospect of a scenic coastal wander along the South West Coast Path, which passes through Westward Ho! But, with the children eager to continue cycling, we return to Bideford to pick up the Tarka Trail again, this time heading north towards the popular coastal village of **Instow**. Only three miles long, this section of the Trail is very well used. It is far more open as it hugs the tidal section of the Torridge and has a different feel to the inland part of the trail we'd visited the previous day.

There are excellent views of Bideford from its neighbour across the river, East-the-Water. Then past skeletal corpses of boats akin to the ribs of giant dinosaurs slowly sliding into the tidal silt, before passing beneath the towering plinths of the skyward Torridge Bridge.

Lunch is a pleasant picnic on the beach at Instow (John's of Instow, in the centre of the village, provides some excellent picnic fare) and a chance to idle away an hour watching sleeping boats as the rising tide scrapes them up from the soggy estuary floor and brings them alive once again.

↑ River Torridge and the Tarka Trail (North Devon Photography/Shutterstock) ← Wild garlic and bluebells along the Tarka Trail (Devon Camel/Shutterstock)

From our sandy picnic spot, we can nearly reach out and touch our final overnight stop, the charming village of **Appledore** (indeed, we could have caught the tiny ferry that crosses the Torridge between the two villages). And so it is that, rather than continue along the Tarka Trail towards Barnstaple as it begins its route alongside the Taw rather than the Torridge, we return to collect the 'van.

The sight of Appledore from across the river had charmed us and it does not disappoint when we arrive. Our overnight stop is, once again, alongside the river, this time with delightful views of Instow, and right in the centre of the traditional fishing village of whitewashed houses, interspersed with the occasional splash of colour.

A wander through the narrow streets of this hillside village, Appledore-made ice cream in hand, we pass inviting gift shops and hidden taverns, then chance upon a fish and chip shop with a queue that stretches along the street. It suggests we've found a fish supper that is too good to forego. After all, what could be better than the scent of salt and vinegar mingled with the seaside air as we finger-pick our way through a portion of delectably fresh fish on the quay?

The sinking sun, disappearing beneath the sea, transforms the sands at Instow to pumpkin orange as we opt for a late evening stroll to discover more of Appledore. We soon appreciate our seaside surroundings further as we navigate our way along streets the width of a fishing rod, lined with cosy fisherman's cottages, each one named to suggest its connection with the sea. Dreaming up a romantic, idealised

↑ The Taw-Torridge Estuary (Adam Burton/Robert Harding Picture Library/SuperStock)

Famous Five notion of smugglers' adventures as we walk, our story is brought to life when we reach the rocky slipway above which the Old Customs House casts an eye. It is certainly the stuff of mariners' yarns.

With the arrival the following day of a sea mist so solid it belies the golden glow of the previous evening, our walk along the coast path towards the dunes of Northam Burrows Country Park is curtailed. Consequently, we choose to move on from North Devon, passing through the tiny Blackdown Hills Area of Outstanding Natural Beauty to South Somerset, and from one trail to another. Here it's to walk the Leland Trail.

Some 400 years before *Tarka the Otter* was on bookshelves, John Leland was working for King Henry VIII as keeper of the royal libraries. In 1533, he was commissioned by the king to make a search for England's antiquities. The Leland Trail, named in Leland's honour, is a 28-mile route, which follows the footsteps of John Leland as he traversed south Somerset sometime between 1535 and 1543.

The route is traditionally walked in four stages of approximately 6 to 8 miles each; hence it's an excellent 'long distance' trail to fit into a long weekend. And, owing to its not-too-taxing lowland landscape, with the odd hill for a good view, it's a great one to walk with children or those less able to tackle major inclines.

As a one-way route, it requires a little planning prior to setting out. For the first two days, we base ourselves in **Castle Cary**, which is reasonably central for the Leland Trail, staying at a campsite close to the railway station – where lots of taxi firms are located. We reach Alfred's Tower, the start of the trail and a remote location away from any public transport route, by taxi.

The tower, a deep-red turreted folly that can be seen for miles around, poking up from the trees on Kingsettle Hill, is part of the National Trust's Stourhead Estate. On the border with Wiltshire (Stourhead Gardens are in Wiltshire while Alfred's Tower is in Somerset by a matter of yards), at 852ft above sea level, it is one of the highest points of the trail. The 18th-century triangular tower was built at a spot where King Alfred the Great is believed, in AD878, to have rallied the Saxons in preparation for the Battle of Ethandan, in which they defeated the Danes.

With the first wooded descent complete, our walk takes us through flat open countryside, along the ancient drovers' route that Leland also took. We arrive in the very beautiful honey-stone town of **Bruton** just in time for lunch. An initial round of unappealing, squashed sandwiches, eaten overlooking the roofless dovecote atop an ancient pillow mound, is soon surpassed when we wander along the High Street and find At The Chapel. Here is a place where well-dressed ladies who lunch sit amid muddy-booted walkers, both sets of diners appreciating the delicious food.

Bruton is a delightful place to explore further. The ancient packhorse bridge that crosses the River Brue is a notable landmark while Sexey's Hospital, with its courtyard of similar-aged almshouses, looks gracefully down upon the river.

With a climb up and over Trendle Hill complete, we wander through the tiny hamlets of Wyke Champflower and Cole before tramping through orchards and over the ridge of Ridge Hill to descend into **Castle Cary** and back to our campsite – nine miles complete.

Tuesday is market day in Castle Cary, so we enjoy shopping in the Undercroft of the pillared Market House prior to setting off on stage two of the Leland Trail. Though it looks much older, the Market House was built in 1855 when, it was anticipated, the new railway would bring prosperity to the town. Jars of homemade jam from the market are out of the question for our walk, but deliciously flaky sausage rolls and fruit are a must.

Castle Cary sits on top of a ring of hills, so an initial climb is inevitable. However, the views from Lodge Hill are incredible. It's not only the town below us that we can see, but Alfred's Tower from where we'd begun our walk 24 hours previously, along with, in the far distance, Glastonbury Tor sticking up from the Somerset Levels like a giant molehill. Despite the haze, even the Quantocks and the Mendips, Somerset's most well-known hills, are in full view.

Hill-spotting over, we walk due south along old tracks and ancient drovers' routes used by two other long-distance walking trails, the Macmillan Way and Monarch's Way, in addition to the Leland Trail. We thought, therefore, that the countryside would have been awash with walkers. But no, the paths appear solely for our own use this morning.

↑ Bruton, seen from Lusty Hill (Martin Fowler/Shutterstock) → Market House, Castle Cary (Joe Dunckley/Shutterstock)

Conveniently, we arrive in the village of North Cadbury around lunchtime, when a stop at the Catash Inn allows us to replenish our energy prior to continuing the route alongside Cadbury Castle, an Iron Age hillfort. We finish the stage with a pleasant stroll across pastureland into **Queen Camel**, where the taxi collects us outside the pretty church and a row of thatched cottages to drive back to the campsite – a further eight miles complete.

We're sufficiently far along the trail by this point to switch our base from Castle Cary to the Roman town of **Ilchester**, our planned finishing point, from where the taxi transfers us to where we'd left off the day before.

The third stage of the Leland Trail takes us directly out of Queen Camel and through open countryside to another pretty Somerset village, neighbouring **West Camel**, where we meet the River Cam for the first time. Our previous two days of walking had been accompanied by occasional overhead helicopters and now it's our opportunity to see where they're based as our route takes us around the perimeter of the Royal Naval Air Station (RNAS) at **Yeovilton**.

One of the busiest military airbases in the UK, it is home to the Commando Helicopter Force in addition to the Fleet Air Arm Wildcat Force. As we walk alongside the perimeter fence, there's a bizarre juxtaposition of busy manoeuvres on one side and the peaceful trickles of the rivers Cam and Yeo on the other.

We leave the airbase at the village of Yeovilton, where the Fleet Air Arm Memorial Church is, and continue beside some of the prettiest stretches of the walk as we approach Ilchester. This, too, is a charming town, though of a different character to Castle Cary and Bruton. Here are streets full of pastel-painted houses, traditional coaching inns, and the 11th-century Ilchester Bridge, which crosses the River Ivel.

↑ Thatched cottages in Queen Camel (Martin Fowler/Shutterstock)

With only five miles covered, there's an afternoon off from walking and we spend it at RNAS Yeovilton, looking around the Fleet Air Arm Museum. It's not a cheap museum to visit (though the ticket is valid for 12 months), but there's an impressive display of aircraft, activities in connection to the Fleet Air Arm and the opportunity to experience life on an aircraft carrier, complete with simulated rides. There are viewing points behind glass too, though they do not compare to those in the sheep fields we'd passed through that morning along the Leland Trail.

Staying at a small CS beside The Masons Arms in **Lower Odcombe**, a tiny village close to Yeovil, our final day of walking is planned through the picture-perfect village of **Montacute** and the Montacute Estate. Therefore, we park in the National Trust car park of Montacute House where a taxi takes us to the start of stage four of the Leland Trail, where we left off in Ilchester.

The final day's walking is the most rural, with no villages encountered for the first four miles. Indeed, it's not until we enter Montacute Park that we really see civilisation. But what a reintroduction.

The views of Montacute House, with all its golden-honeyed Elizabethan splendour, are sublime seen from the trail. The walking route then passes through the village before climbing past the near-perfect circle of St Michael's Hill, an Iron Age hillfort, and up Ham Hill and Hamdon Hill Country Park. The views are equally as impressive as those we'd seen elsewhere along the trail, but none more so than our finishing point by the War Memorial at the northern edge of the escarpment. Here we can survey much of Somerset.

It's possible to wander down Ham Hill into the village of Stoke-sub-Hamdon to catch a bus back to Montacute, but with a very pleasant sun-filled day, we opt to wander back the way we had come, celebrating our 28-and-a-bit-mile walk with lunch at Montacute House.

↑ Abbey Farmhouse at Montacute (Loretta Damska/Shutterstock)

A visit to the house and gardens, therefore, is inevitable. The interior of the house matches the splendour of the outside stonework and, upstairs, is a royal collection of portraits from the National Portrait Gallery. It seems rather fitting to be standing in front of the portly paunch of King Henry VIII, as if, like John Leland, we're reporting back our findings.

We cannot leave Somerset without visiting the Haynes Motor Museum, four miles southwest of Castle Cary. The museum was formed from a collection by

ESSENTIALS

GETTING THERE & AROUND Bideford is on the A39 & A386. B3236 to Westward Ho! B3236 east to Bideford/A386 north to Appledore. A39/A361/A38 to Wellington then rural lanes through Blackdown Hills to A303 at Buckland St Mary/A303/A37/B3153 to Castle Cary (Brook House Inn).

A371/A359/A303/B3151 to Ilchester. B3151 south/A37 west/A303 south then A3088 east. Rural lanes to Odcombe. Rural lanes to Yeovil, A359 to Sparkford (Haynes Motor Museum).

While the main roads are fine, extra care is needed through the villages where on-street parking often turns the roads single-lane.

Parking without height barriers in Somerset (for North Devon, see *Accommodation* below): at Alfred's Tower (start of Leland Trail) there's a small parking area, although road to the tower is not suitable for large coachbuilt motorhomes. There is a car park on Ham Hill (end of the trail) but, again, access is not good for large vehicles. Taxis & public transport are the better option. In Castle Cary, try the station car park, if not staying overnight at Brook House Inn. Parking in the main part of Ilchester's High St is not suitable for large vehicles. There is a small car park at the southern end of this little town, but it's only suitable for campervans no bigger than an MPV. We found an off-road parking area at the north end of the town, off the B3151 by St Andrew's Church, where we could park safely for the day.

For the Leland Trail, use OS *Explorer* **maps** *OS129* & *OS142*.

The **taxi** firm we used was Mum's Private Hire; ✆07711 572038; ✆taxiatcastlecarystation. co.uk. Sue Dixon, who runs the cab, was very obliging and happy to run us back and forth to various locations along the Leland Trail.

ACCOMMODATION Our overnight sites in **North Devon** were: Riverbank Car Park, Bideford, EX39 2QS; Main Car Park, Westward Ho!, EX39 1LG; Churchfield Car Park, Appledore, EX39 1RL.

Overnight motorhome parking is available at the car parks we stayed at, along with a further 2 car parks at Holsworthy (Manor Car Park) & Great Torrington (Sydney House Car Park). All specify overnight parking as being from 6pm to 10am. We had no problems

John Haynes, founder of the famous Haynes motoring manuals, and provides a magnificent showcase of vintage and classic motors and motorcycles, with sleek, sporty numbers lined up alongside giant American classics. Our collection of choice is the Red Room – a sea of gleaming, glossy red and chrome from which to pick a favourite.

Leaving Somerset, we pass by Alfred's Tower once more. It seems a very long way from Ham Hill.

parking either during the day or overnight. We did check, prior to setting off, that it is acceptable to purchase a ticket to stay overnight (max 2 nights at each site) and then a further ticket to park during the day, so that there's no need to move the vehicle. Use the RingGo app to pre-register a vehicle and pay for parking online, otherwise, simply purchase a ticket at the car park pay & display machines.

The prospect of a holiday in a car park does not sound overly idyllic or restful, and for a week's exploration (or for security) campsites may be the better option. But for the sense of freedom, arriving or leaving when you wish and the opportunity to grab a last-minute, inexpensive weekend break without the need to book a pitch well in advance, plus the convenience of their central locations, these 'sites' certainly do the job. We paid overnight fees that are a fraction of a large campsite or even some 5-van sites.

Alternative **campsites** for tents and those that prefer not to stop overnight in a car park: Westacott Farm Camping, Abbotsford; Knotty Corner CS, Bideford (CCC members only; page xiv); Marshford Camping, Northam; Seabreeze CL, Appledore (CAMC members only; page xiv).

In **Somerset**, we stayed at Brook House Inn Touring Park, Castle Cary; The Masons Arms, Odcombe.

FIND OUT MORE
The Tarka Trail ⊘ tarkatrail.org.uk
Torridge District Council (for overnight parking) ⊘ torridge.gov.uk
Visit North Devon
⊘ visitdevon.co.uk/northdevon/explore

Leland Trail ⊘ visitsouthsomerset.com/listings/walking/the-leland-trail-.htm
Visit Somerset ⊘ visitsomerset.co.uk

TOP TIP: EXTEND THE TRIP To extend this tour, spend a couple of days exploring the Blackdown Hills Area of Outstanding Natural Beauty, on the Devon/Somerset border. The pocket-sized AONB spans less than 15 miles in each direction yet is big on vistas from its steep wooded ridges and high plateaux. Culmstock Beacon and Staple Hill, the highest point in the Blackdown Hills, are go-to sites for views. So, too, the Wellington Monument, on Wellington Hill.

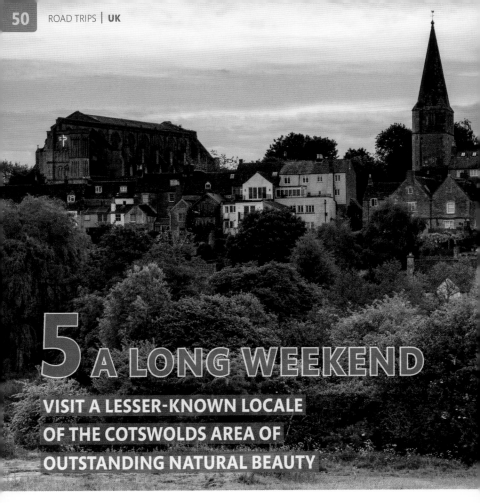

5 A LONG WEEKEND

VISIT A LESSER-KNOWN LOCALE OF THE COTSWOLDS AREA OF OUTSTANDING NATURAL BEAUTY

WHERE	Wiltshire
DISTANCE/TIME	120 miles/3 days
START/FINISH	Malmesbury/Dyrham

'Climbing up on Solsbury Hill,' it's not musician Peter Gabriel's city lights that I can see. Rather the city of Bath bathed in early morning sunlight close to the finger valleys of the southern Cotswolds. As skylarks sing above the hilltop fort, views along the Limpley Stoke Valley to the south, the By Brook Valley to the east and the gnarled undulations supporting St Catherine's Brook to the north appear infinitely long. The roar of traffic along the A46, bringing commuters into Bath, cannot be heard above the tuneful clamour of the skylarks as I examine the western skyline and the Cotswold escarpment northwest of the World Heritage city. 'I was feeling part of the scenery.'

↑ Malmesbury, Wiltshire (stocker1970/Shutterstock)

Having grown up in and been a lifelong resident of the north Cotswolds, I've become accustomed to the coachloads of tourists that step off for a quick selfie in Bourton-on-the-Water, Stow-on-the-Wold and Moreton-in-Marsh. And for many people, it's these oh-so-pretty Gloucestershire towns of golden stone and the surrounding villages that are anticipated as 'The Cotswolds'.

Yet overall, the Cotswolds is a much larger region than this triptych of hyphenated beauties. Indeed, the Cotswolds is, in part, defined as an Area of Outstanding Natural Beauty (the AONB management board is aiming to make it Britain's newest national park, too). It covers some 787 square miles, swallowing up the bulk of the Cotswold escarpment and hills further east.

It can come as a surprise, therefore, that Wiltshire and even the odd fragment of Somerset also dip into the Cotswolds. It's here that I venture in search of the attributes deemed to make the Cotswolds unique: the vernacular architecture created with oolitic limestone; the 4,000 miles of drystone walls (longer than the Great Wall of China); the ancient woodland and unimproved grassland; and archaeological sites and specific settlements associated with the area's longstanding wool and textile trade.

I begin my tour in **Malmesbury**, a gateway town on the fringes of the AONB that has a fraction of the tourists of its northern counterparts and is all the prettier for it. The vernacular architecture is here – ribbons of Cotswold stone cottages that 200 years ago housed millworkers producing silk in the neighbouring mill beside the River Avon. But these pretty, terraced slopes are insignificant by comparison to the dominant building of the town – Malmesbury Abbey.

The hilltop abbey is only a third of its original size. Bits of masonry, including a tower once taller than that of Salisbury Cathedral, have dropped off over the centuries and never been replaced. The once-resplendent stone monks in the elaborate doorway have become faceless as they succumb to the Cotswold weather. But one Malmesbury monk, Eilmer, is written into the history books for his 11th-century stunt. Inspired by the jackdaws that roosted in the abbey, Brother Eilmer strapped wings to his limbs and 'flew' from one of the abbey towers. The unsuccessful attempt led to the 'Flying Monk' being banned by his abbot from making a second attempt and, instead, became a distinguished scholar. It's the Abbey's magnificent decorative manuscripts, for which it gained a European reputation, that are on display today.

SOUVENIR

Caroline Mills is the author of *Slow Travel: The Cotswolds*, also published by Bradt Guides: ⬧ bradtguides.com/shop.

One of the best places from which to view the Abbey is the neighbouring Abbey House Manor. Considered some of the finest gardens in the world, there is year-round interest and when I visit in early summer, swathes of tulips mingle with topiary in the knot garden in front of the manor, while wooded slopes leading down to the River Avon at the rear provide a tranquil setting upon which to dawdle. The gardens are being reimagined over the next few years; hence, work may well be taking place in certain areas of the garden on a visit.

Malmesbury is a foodie town. The High Street is filled with window seats aplenty upon which to ponder over a panini or delve into a vat of coffee. The Summer Café, a tiny deli-style eatery on the High Street, is my choice. But there are bistros, gastro pubs, cosy wine bars, numerous cafés and, when buying for eats back in the 'van, a traditional butcher's shop and bakery.

By evening, I take a stroll through the water meadows along the Avon, from where there are gratifying views of the town. It's possible to make a circular tour that takes in many of the old town streets.

I move on to **Castle Combe**, 11 miles south of Malmesbury. Not so much a hidden secret as a Cotswold treasure, the view from the bridge across By Brook in Castle Combe is one of the most photographed in the Cotswolds.

Superlatives and 'chocolate box' have long been used up to describe the village, which, as its name tells, is situated within a steep-sided, wooded valley. But, once pictures of this preposterously pretty village have been taken, the tearoom has been frequented, you've oohed-and-aahed at the complimentary combination of dwellings *and* had lunch in the Castle Inn overlooking the old Market Square, take a wander along the public footpath to the west of the inn.

Along a sunken lane, visitors pass by yards of Cotswold drystone wall, sinking beneath a sea of ivy, to arrive in the middle of the Manor House Hotel Golf Course. There one can appreciate, still on the public footpath, the prettiness of the 'hidden' valley without the hordes of tourists in the village. It's possible to either reverse the route or continue a very attractive circular walk that brings walkers back to the village along the southern aspect of the combe.

A hefty shower of rain forces me back to the 'van but I arrive in nearby **Biddestone** as the sun re-emerges. One of the most sought-after Wiltshire villages in which to live, Biddestone has everything that more-frequented Cotswold villages have – except the crowds. Sat beside the village pond, with a flotilla of baby moorhens, coots and ducklings for company, I find it a pleasant way to spend a lunch break. It affords time to enjoy this desirable village with its broad village green and agreeable houses.

Leaving the village ducks to their afternoon snooze, beak-under-wing, I move on for a brisk walk around another of the Cotswolds' unsung market towns, **Corsham**. On the fringe of the AONB, like Malmesbury, Corsham also has the

← Castle Combe, a Cotswold treasure (vichie81/Shutterstock)

attributes that make a handsome Cotswold town without the well-worn path of umbrella-led tourists. I aim straight for Corsham Park, the landscaped parkland that accompanies the decoratively embellished Corsham Court.

The Court houses a reputable collection of fine art, but it's the landscape 'art' of Lancelot 'Capability' Brown and Humphry Repton that helps me walk off lunch. Abutting the town centre, the sheep-grazed meadows are a lovely place for a wander, with views of Corsham Court and its neighbouring church.

By late afternoon I'm aboard the MV *Barbara McLellan*, a narrowboat run by the Kennet and Avon Canal Trust that takes visitors along the canal from **Bradford-on-Avon**. Strange as it sounds to have a canal in the hilly Cotswolds (there are two, including the gradually restored Cotswold Canal at Stroud) the Kennet and Avon Canal runs through the southernmost end of the AONB, along the Limpley Stoke Valley from Bradford-on-Avon to Bath. My relaxing two-hour trip is soothingly therapeutic; the slow pace towards the Avoncliff Aqueduct provides a chance to get to know the contours of the Cotswolds, smothered here with bluebells and wild garlic.

Bradford-on-Avon I consider one of the prettiest of Cotswold towns. Its industrial past – with former textile mills lining the banks of the Avon – prevents it from being overly twee. And the captivating collection of tightly knit houses on the valley slopes, from tiny gabled cottages to grand Georgian statements, into which is added the town's vast 14th-century tithe barn and gorgeously diminutive Saxon church of St Lawrence, is a very pleasing mix. It's quite a climb from the town centre and requires a few minutes of effort on foot, but there are fabulous views from the tiny pilgrimage of St Mary Tory. Here I can see much of the town and, with clear skies, across to Salisbury Plain, the White Horse at Westbury and the Mendip Hills.

It's an early start next morning to follow the Limpley Stoke Valley by road, cross into northeast Somerset and head for **Little Solsbury Hill** on the outskirts of Bath. Immortalised by Peter Gabriel in his song *Solsbury Hill*, the Iron Age hillfort takes advantage of the natural lie of the land and is an opportunity to see a tiny patch of the calcareous unimproved grassland, rich with wildlife both on the ground and in the air, for which the AONB is renowned.

The tiny lanes north of Little Solsbury Hill, from Batheaston to Marshfield and Cold Ashton are not suitable for motorhomes, but I urge anyone to park up and cycle these tiny lanes or walk the Limestone Link footpath that follows St Catherine's Valley. These hills and valleys are some of the best secrets of the hidden Cotswolds, with the most contorted folds in the hills plastered with wildflowers. Tucked among them you'll discover one of the most beautiful of Elizabethan houses, St Catherine's Court, and the prettiest of Cotswold churches, ornamented inside with decorative tiles and mosaics.

With my walks at Solsbury Hill over, my next stop must be Marshfield Ice Cream on the Wiltshire/South Gloucestershire border. The farm's ice-cream parlour is open over summer weekends, but prior arrangements can be made to purchase tubs direct from the farm during the week. It's well worth the visit to sample the creamy delights and I chance upon some of the farm's newborns.

I'm nearing the end of my trip around the southern Cotswolds, but I have one final stop to make – magnificent **Dyrham Park**, owned by The National Trust. To reach the house on foot from the car park, I venture out on the 45-minute

ESSENTIALS

GETTING THERE & AROUND B4040 Malmesbury to Acton Turville, then B4039 to Castle Combe. B4039 southeast/A420 west then rural lane to Biddestone. Rural lane south Biddestone to Corsham. B3109 Corsham to Bradford-on-Avon. A363 to Bathford. Rural lanes Batheaston to Solsbury Hill & St Catherine (see opposite). A46 north to Dyrham Park.

Parking without height barriers: Malmesbury is not easy for motorhomes (van conversions & campervans will get into the central car park in Cross Hayes). I recommend stopping overnight at Burton Hill (see opposite) within 10mins' walk of the town centre. For Castle Combe, do not approach from the south by motorhome; the road is too narrow for vehicles to pass safely. Approach from the north (the B4039) where there is a large accessible car park. It's a 700yd walk downhill into the village. There is no parking within the village. At Corsham, motorhomes may not park in the grounds of Corsham Court and therefore need to find roadside parking in town (of which there is plenty). In Bradford-on-Avon, the best place for motorhomes to park

↑ View towards Bristol from Dyrham Park (Anetta Zalewska/Shutterstock)

Prospect Walk, which provides extensive views over the Severn Valley. I can even see the Brecon Beacons and Black Mountains in Wales.

While there's an interesting exhibition on the conservation work taking place in the house, the interior is a little disappointing with minimal viewing available. But the gardens 'out back' offer a bucolic spot to sit beneath the trees in the perry orchard or beside the pond. Amid the tulips and late-flowering daffodils, I can mull over all that I've seen of the southern Cotswolds in a long weekend – without once seeing a coach brimming with tourists.

is the Kennet & Avon Canal visitor car park south of the town. From here it is a 5min walk to the town centre. For Little Solsbury Hill & St Catherine's Valley, motorhomes under 8ft 2in (2.5m) high can park in Batheaston, otherwise taller 'vans should park at the northern end of Swainswick Ln or in Cold Ashton (both off the A46). Either way, anticipate multiple miles walking or cycling. At Dyrham Park, there's a large parking area suitable for motorhomes.

ACCOMMODATION I stayed at: Burton Hill Caravan & Camping Park, Malmesbury; Stowford Manor Farm, Wingfield (nr Trowbridge).

FIND OUT MORE
Malmesbury ⬨ discovermalmesbury.life
Corsham ⬨ corsham.gov.uk/visit
Bradford-on-Avon
⬨ bradfordonavon.co.uk

Barbara McLellan Canal Trips
⬨ katrust.org.uk
Dyrham Park
⬨ nationaltrust.org.uk/dyrham-park

6 LEAGUE OF DIAMONDS

EXPLORE MARITIME HERITAGE ON THE SOUTH COAST BEFORE A HOP TO A DIAMOND ISLE

WHERE	Hampshire/West Sussex/Isle of Wight
DISTANCE/TIME	155 miles/6 days
START/FINISH	Southbourne (West Sussex)/Adgestone (Isle of Wight)

The sky is a battleship grey, the Royal Navy's modern-day flotilla merging into its overcast background; the only sense of colour, a Union Jack aloft a frigate is all the brighter for its monochrome setting. I'm in **Portsmouth** to learn some maritime heritage, and if there's one place to understand how Britannia has ruled the waves, this city is it.

My first port of call, to gather my bearings, is to hit the heights of the Spinnaker Tower, an icon of the south coast with its sail-like structure, rising from Gunwharf Quays shopping and entertainment complex. At 560ft high, there should be giant views from the tower of the Solent, the Isle of Wight and even the coast of France – on a good day. I have not picked a 'good day' so, once the high-

↑ Spinnaker Tower and Portsmouth Harbour (Julian Gazzard/Shutterstock)

speed elevator has catapulted me to the first of three viewing platforms in a mere 28 seconds, my sights are restricted to the immediate vicinity of Portsmouth Harbour, neighbouring Gosport, and a faint line in the sea that, mirage-like, I take to be the Isle of Wight.

The views at my feet, however (and they can be *under* the feet for those who care to walk across the glass floor 350ft in the air) are no less impressive and, with the aid of the pictorial diagrams, I manage to pick out Portsmouth Cathedral, Henry VIII's Southsea Castle, the site where his flagship *Mary Rose* sank (and rose again), witness the comings-and-goings of boats along this busy aquatic motorway and work my way around the Historic Dockyard. It's here that I choose to go next.

Portsmouth Naval Base has Britain's naval history wrapped up. It has been at the forefront of England's defences since 1194 and today is home to two-thirds of the Royal Navy's surface ships. It is a busy, modern working base. Yet, in among the aircraft carriers and destroyers of today, are ships of yesteryear that were once (actually they still are) the pride of the Navy: HMS *Warrior* (1860), the world's first iron-hulled, armoured warship powered by sail and steam – and which never fired a shot in anger during its ten years of sea domination; HMS *Victory*, Nelson's flagship – and his death bed – at the Battle of Trafalgar; and the *Mary Rose*, Henry VIII's first naval warship.

It's forty years since the hull of this magnificent ship was raised from the Solent, and the museum that houses her is a masterpiece worth a full day to appreciate. Sited only 20yds from where the *Mary Rose* was built in 1497 and dedicated to the 500 men that lost their lives when the ship went down, the museum has been designed so that, within the jet-black ship-like cocoon, it houses the half of the hull that was saved and, with a mirror image, positions the 19,000 artefacts that came up with the boat. Truly remarkable, every single item in the museum comes from the *Mary Rose* – the cannonballs, the backgammon board, the pewterware and musical instruments, even the bones of the carpenter's dog, that all miraculously survived under the sea for 500 years.

Adjacent to the Mary Rose Museum is HMS *Victory*, a warship whose rear end looks like a Georgian townhouse, with its sash windows and elegant painted woodwork. Both *Victory* and *Warrior* provide displays of palatial grandeur in the captain's quarters, frightening discomfort in the prison quarters and a sense of day-to-day bustle that would have occurred when both ships were at sea. The history of the two ships is enhanced further by a visit to the National Museum of the Royal Navy, which includes a Trafalgar Experience and an intriguing selection of naval figureheads that once adorned the prows of numerous boats.

There are 11 attractions to visit as part of the entrance ticket to the Historic Dockyard, which includes a 45-minute harbour tour. I run out of time to catch the last trip of the day so opt to take part in 'Action Stations' instead, which provides an insight into today's naval world, with simulators to land a search and rescue helicopter, command a warship and attempt physical challenges that the Royal Marines relish.

Upon leaving, I chance upon the tiny Porter's Garden at the entrance to the dockyard, a delightful hidden haven of calm away from the action of warfare. Appearing to be missed by many visitors, it's worth a few moments to enjoy its scents and beauty.

Leaving the 'van at the campsite for a second day, I take the bus east to **Chichester** for a ramble around this elegant market town. Only two miles inland, it has an alternative atmoscer to that of nearby Portsmouth, and a maritime history of its own.

An important Roman military town, it was at nearby Fishbourne that Emperor Claudius came ashore, in AD43, built a Roman palace and laid out Chichester in

the shape of a cross, with four main streets – North, South, East and West – that remain today. At the interchange of these streets, more Georgian in design now, is the Market Cross from 1501, once used by the poor to sell their wares and one of several landmarks of the town. A greater landmark is the 11th-century Cathedral of Sussex. The building naturally incorporates a Sailor's Chapel – St Michael's – as a memorial to naval personnel from the county.

Entrance to the cathedral is free and it's a very pleasant – and big – place to begin a visit of this compact city. My wanderings take me out of the church via the cloisters and floral-lined St Richard's Walk, where I discover the very attractive Bishop's Palace Garden. It's bordered by the town's Roman ramparts, upon which I wander on a 1.5-mile circular walk 'above' the town to gain one of the best views of the cathedral.

Later, I uncover Chichester's links to the sea with a trip along the **Chichester Ship Canal**. Completed in 1822, the canal once carried coal and later gold bullion, which came from Portsmouth to Chichester Marina and then via the manmade waterway to the River Arun and on to London.

Two hundred volunteers now maintain the canal and my very pleasant hour-long cruise on *Kingfisher* takes me past the spot where William Turner created his famous painting of Chichester Cathedral (now hanging in London's Tate Gallery) and provides the opportunity to spot endless nest-building waterfowl inhabiting the banks. Owing to the low road bridges, built since the canal's heyday, it's not possible to reach Chichester Harbour by boat – for this I feel the need to get on foot.

Chichester Harbour has a unique, undeveloped coastline. Its series of tidal inlets, wide-open expanses and pretty creekside villages provide a haven for wildlife and, understandably, has been designated as an Area of Outstanding Natural Beauty.

My campsite, not only convenient for catching a bus, is also opportune for a network of footpaths and is only a ten-minute stroll from one of the inlets, **Nutbourne Marsh**. Eager to make the most of an elusive ray of sunshine, I set out for an after-dinner walk to find a glorious world of peaceful solitude, uncovering ancient apple orchards, fields of vivid yellow against the harbour backdrop and the first of many pretty villages, Prinsted. It spurs me on for an early-morning rise to walk further.

I'm spoilt for choice the next day – should I circumnavigate Thorney Island with apparently one of the best views of Chichester Harbour or stretch my legs further with a walk to Langstone, a coastal village at the entrance to Hayling Island? Both are accessible on foot from the campsite, but I choose the latter.

Rising with the sun on a blue-sky morning, I leave fellow campers slumbering as I weave my way through the fields to **Emsworth**, another popular village at the end of a finger of water, wedged between Hayling and Thorney Islands.

↑ Bishop's Palace Garden and Chichester Cathedral (Julian Gazzard/Shutterstock) → Chichester Harbour (CM)

Emsworth also has its own maritime history with *The Echo*, which was built there, once being the largest sailing fishing vessel ever built in England. The village, though, is more renowned for oysters, with a once-mighty industry which, at its height towards the end of the 19th century, employed 400 people and sent more than 100,000 oysters a week to market in London.

As the tide is out, I step out around the causeway wall for a beachside walk along the edge of the harbour to Langstone. With its proximity to the water, here I can sit outside The Royal Oak and dangle my toes into the harbour while watching the passing traffic head across Langstone Bridge to Hayling Island.

I return to the campsite via the tiny hamlet of Warblington, with rural views of the South Downs, impressive remains of a castle and a rare example of a grave-watcher's hut – used to guard against the selling of bodies for dissection in the 19th century. Collecting the 'van, I drive to **Hayling Island** for a short road tour. Avoiding the tourist trap of South Hayling, popular with sand lovers on sunny days (my day has long since clouded over), I take a drive around North Hayling, a charming rural route – narrow in places – that includes a magnificent lime tree avenue.

Running out of time to uncover all the creekside villages (Bosham, Chidham and West Itchenor, to name a few) that I'd like to look at, I opt to leave them all behind and instead drive to Pagham Harbour south of Chichester. The huge, sheltered bay is an RSPB nature reserve that's filled with migrating waterfowl. It provides a peaceful walk around the harbour edge – that is except for the sound of tweeting and chirping that swell the reserve hedgerows.

My time has been well occupied, but I leave Portsmouth for the Isle of Wight feeling that I've not seen everything I'd like to. There are plenty more stories of the south coast to discover on a return visit. For now, though, I stand on the top deck of my ferry, heading out of Portsmouth Harbour watching a flotilla of weekend yachters, and it feels as if I'm travelling abroad.

Look on any map and one can see where this precious diamond-shaped stone of an island was once neatly tucked up against mainland Britain before it tore away, creating The Solent in its wake. Hence, despite my sense of leaving for foreign shores, once there I realise just how much a part of the British Isles the **Isle of Wight** is. I call it 'Little Britain' for the island has virtually every natural characteristic that its larger neighbour has.

It's what makes it such a wonderful place to walk, especially for first timers – all the scenery, without the massive distances to cover on foot. That is, unless you wish to tread every inch of the 67-mile circular Coastal Path.

I've been to the island several times before but not for a long while so this feels like a first-time experience. Hence, I decide to circumnavigate the island by road initially to see exactly which parts to walk. It's perfectly possible to tour much of

↑ Langstone (CM) ← Limerstone Down, Isle of Wight (Loz Baker/Shutterstock)

the island in a morning by car and, except for the occasional narrow stretch of road, I have no problems touring with my motorhome.

On foot (or cycling) is best though, and with more than 500 miles of marked footpaths and half of the island designated as an Area of Outstanding Natural Beauty, I am truly spoilt for choice of places to walk.

I plump for a short stretch of the Coastal Path, in the southwest of the island between **Freshwater Bay** and **Brighstone Bay**, to begin. It's an area of the island that doesn't fail to impress with stunning views along the coastline, and inland. From the clifftop path around **Compton Bay**, these views stretch to the dazzling white cliff faces along Freshwater Bay. Surfers below are pummelled by rolling seas – the bay is a popular spot with those who like to ride waves.

And if taking yet another step feels like a dinosaur stride on an island where Jurassic footprints are well known, there's always the lure of the shimmering sands of Compton Bay for feeling the grains squelch between toes and a cool off in the sparkling waters.

Of course, I find the lure of an ice-cream van in the distance encourages further walking towards Brighstone Bay, too, but not without halting progress occasionally to enjoy the scenery. The views of the more northerly downs, Brook Down and Brighstone Down, at 702ft high, offer some of the best views of the island. On as a clear day as I'm fortunate to have, the length and breadth of the island can be seen. The springtime wildflowers, such as the shocking pink cushions of sea thrift, are dazzling, too.

ESSENTIALS

GETTING THERE & AROUND
Chichester CCC Site is on the A259. Owing to the convenience of the campsite location, I was able to leave the motorhome on-site and take the Coastliner 700 bus to Portsmouth & Chichester (the bus, departing directly outside the campsite entrance, also goes to Worthing & Brighton).

A259/A27 to Langstone from campsite. A3023 south then circular route to Northney, North Hayling, Tye, Fleet, Stoke & back on A3023 to Langstone. A259 east/A286/B2201/B2145 to Pagham Harbour Reserve. Reverse route to campsite at Southbourne. A259 west/A27/M275 south/A3 to Wightlink ferry terminal (Portsmouth).

Isle of Wight: ferries run from Southampton to East Cowes (Red Funnel), Portsmouth to Fishbourne (Wightlink) & Lymington to Yarmouth (Wightlink). There's also a passenger-only (no vehicles) hovercraft between Southsea & Ryde (Hovertravel). Journey times for car ferries are between 30mins & 1hr.

A3054 west Fishbourne to Yarmouth. A3055/B3395 Yarmouth to Bembridge. B3395/B3330/A3055 south/Lower Adgestone Rd to Adgestone CCC Site. Rural lanes to Godshill & Chale then A3055 northwest to Compton Bay. B3399 via Brook to Brook Down then

This part of the coast, within the AONB, is also designated as a heritage coastline – selected for its historical importance. Really, it is pre-history that dominates. Heading down to the beach around Brighstone Bay, where the cliffs change from chalk white to take on a sandy pink glow, I follow in the footsteps of giants, searching for prehistoric life. While the evidence is here, I can't find it on this occasion and my own footprints, embedded in the soft sand, seem to be erased from history in a much shorter time with the incoming tide.

Taking in a few miles of clifftop coastline while I soak up the early summer sunshine feels perfect. But, staying at Adgestone Camping and Caravanning Club Site, I discover another stupendous place for a stroll, within walking distance of my pitch – the Yar River Trail.

Flowing past the campsite yet minuscule in size, the Eastern Yar River (not to be confused with the Western Yar that flows out to sea at Yarmouth) is the island's longest river. It gurgles from its source in the village of Niton to Bembridge Harbour, an ambling distance of 19 miles. The waymarked trail is split into four sections that run through beautiful countryside.

I only manage a small portion either side of the campsite in the time I have available, but even in these few miles, I encounter dragonflies dancing across the marshes, watch birds looking for an evening supper and uncover a posy of unusual wildflowers. Informative nature boards highlight what to look out for on the walk.

More than anything, though, is the enjoyment gained from the serenity of the trail, immersed deep in a rural idyll with only the natural world for company.

B3401 east to Calbourne & Lynch Ln south to Brighstone Down. B3401 to Newport then Brading Rd east to campsite.

Parking without height barriers: at Pagham Harbour Nature Reserve, there's a large pay car park. Jubilee Ln Car Park is on Lynch Ln for Brighstone Down. For Portsmouth, use Coastliner bus (see opposite) as the Park & Ride has a barrier (6ft 10in/2.1m).

For walking in the area around Chichester Harbour, I recommend taking OS *Explorer* **map** *OL8 Chichester* with you. *OL29 Isle of Wight* covers the whole island.

ACCOMMODATION I stayed at: Chichester CCC Site, Southbourne; Adgestone CCC Site on the Isle of Wight.

FIND OUT MORE

Visit Portsmouth
✎ visitportsmouth.co.uk
Chichester Ship Canal
✎ chichestercanal.org.uk

Chichester Harbour Conservancy
✎ conservancy.co.uk
Visit Isle of Wight ✎ visitisleofwight.co.uk

7 FOOTSTEPS OVER THE WHITE CLIFFS OF DOVER

MAKE TIME TO FIND KENT'S HIDDEN CORNER (BEFORE CROSSING THE CHANNEL)

WHERE	Kent
DISTANCE/TIME	42 miles/4 days
START/FINISH	Dover/Sandwich

I'm as guilty as the other thousands of motorists who point their nose south on the M20 through Kent, drive on board a cross-Channel ferry in Dover with minutes to spare before the ship leaves port and barely give a second thought to what landscape might lie around us.

I may glance up at the **White Cliffs** for a second – and, of course, they're always there to greet us upon a return to England – but Dover and its surrounds I deemed, naively, to be one of those port towns to simply depart from and arrive at without investigation – until now. Oh, what I have missed over the years!

I begin a long weekend with a dawn rising atop Britain's famous White Cliffs just to the east of Dover, with views of neighbouring Dover Castle and not-so-nearby France. It feels strange not to be among the ant-like stream of vehicles in the ferry port below, but thoughts immediately turn to my two-mile coastal walk along

↑ White Cliffs of Dover (GlennV/Shutterstock)

the clifftop, crammed with wildflowers, to the National Trust's South Foreland Lighthouse. This is where the first international wireless transmission took place in 1898 and tours of the lantern are available (plus Mrs Knott's vintage tearoom is very good). The walk is a magical introduction to White Cliffs Country, and I'm immediately hooked.

Back in **Dover**, I choose to explore the town on foot, following the self-guided Bluebird Trail, indicated by bronze pavement markers and linking 31 of Dover's historic buildings, sites and monuments. I make my way first to Dover Museum to discover the fascinating – and significantly important – history of the town. The museum is laid out chronologically and one of the most notable exhibits is the Bronze Age boat, the oldest known sea-going vessel in Britain that was discovered yards from where it is now displayed.

The lure of the 'beach' is too much to remain indoors, and I wander along Dover's seafront, a combination of Victorian villas, floral gardens and recently redesigned award-winning promenades. I'm mesmerized by the blueness of the water; not mucky or filmed with ferry residue from the neighbouring port but

azure blue. Dover's open-water swimmers are in training, watersports lovers are stand-up paddle-boarding or kayaking (with equipment hire from Dover Sea Sports), and families picnic on the pebbly beach. But I'm booked onto a Dover Sea Safari for a thrill-seeking view of the White Cliffs. What a trip!

The boat ride on a RIB leaves Dover's marina, passing giant cruise ships and ferries docked in port, to whizz at speed along the Kent coast towards the charmingly photogenic town of **Deal**. It's not all about fast-paced action though, and our skipper and tour guide cuts the engine at appropriate moments to provide an animated history, geology and geography lesson, telling the story of the White Cliffs. If there's one must-do experience in the area, this is it.

I've barely made inroads at everything to do in Dover but, having seen the surrounding landscape from the sea, I'm eager to explore further along the coast the following day. Deal, nine miles from Dover, has one of the most scenic seafronts in England while its High Street has won awards, including High Street of the Year for its characterful collection of independent shops.

The historic town is a warren of smugglers' cottages full of personality and grand merchants' houses, and even has its own castle. Plus, there's a fabulous choice of quirky and chic places to eat. I take a stroll along the 1,026ft pier for superb views of the seafront and a magnificent breakfast in the award-winning glass and timber-framed Deal Pier Kitchen at the pierhead. It's well worth the walk.

So too is a visit to Deal's Maritime and Local History Museum. Friendly volunteers run the museum, which has an ad-hoc collection of hoarded maritime relics displayed with abandon. There's everything here from an old fishing vessel used during the D-Day landings and colourful figureheads from ancient ships to a highly ornamented drum used by the Royal Marines, who have connections with the town.

I also make time for a visit to the unique Timeball Tower Museum on the seafront. The displays explain the importance of the building to ancient mariners while a climb to the top of the tower is well rewarded with views over the rooftops of Deal's town conservation area.

On the edge of Deal is Walmer Castle, the official residence of the Lord Warden of the Cinque Ports. The Lord Warden is a ceremonial title now but relates to a collection of once-important historic seaports along the Kent and Sussex coast, to which Dover, Deal and Sandwich belong.

The 1st Duke of Wellington, whose defeat of Napoleon at the Battle of Waterloo remains legendary, was one such Lord Warden. His story is one of many told along the self-guided tour of this remarkable defensive coastal castle. The pretty gardens and grounds are a must for families, too.

As the evening descends, I make my way to **St Margaret's Bay**. This tiny village has a secluded bay approached by a winding road down the cliffside. The bay is surrounded by exclusive villas clinging to the cliffs, one of which was the home of

SOUVENIR

If you are planning on crossing to France from Dover, you can continue your journey with this book's sister guide, *Camping Road Trips: France and Germany*, by the same author. Pick up a copy from ♂ bradtguides.com/shop.

actor and playwright Noel Coward and, latterly, Ian Fleming whose books about secret agent James Bond (and *Chitty-Chitty-Bang-Bang)* are largely inspired by the area.

The tiny St Margaret's Museum houses displays about the village's notable residents together with the history of the White Cliffs area relating to World War II. Opposite is The Pines Calyx garden where, among the six acres of trees and shrubs, are wonderful views of the White Cliffs.

Witnessing another majestic sun float up from the sea the following morning, I make my way to Betteshanger Country Park, situated between Deal and Sandwich. Located on the site of the former East Kent coalfield, the 250-acre landscape overlooking the Kent coast has been transformed into a major visitor destination providing numerous outdoor activities including walking, running, cycling, archery and geocaching. I opt for a walk around the varied landscape of open heath and woodland, but on several occasions I pass visitors enjoying both the 6 miles of mountain bike trails through the woods (with bikes for hire on-site) and the 2-mile traffic-free tarmac track for speed cycling.

My walking doesn't stop when I reach **Sandwich** either. This magnificent town is regarded as one of the best-preserved medieval settlements in Britain – and one of the prettiest in England, I warrant. A wander along the Historic Town Trail, through the remarkable streets where there are reputedly more half-timbered houses than anywhere else in England, reveals it so. My climb of the medieval tower of St Peter's Church further verifies the beauty of the town and its medieval architecture.

My exploration continues as I wander along the extensive boundary path that encircles the old town, including Rope Walk where ships' ropes were made when Sandwich was once the largest port in England. I drift from street to street admiring the eclectic mix of architectural features and the plethora of charming independent boutiques before making my way to Sandwich Guildhall Museum.

Built during the reign of Queen Elizabeth I, the Guildhall, with its impressive wood-panelled Court Room and Council Chamber, is a magnificent building. The museum that the Guildhall now houses includes no less impressive exhibits, incorporating Roman finds and fragmented copies of both the Magna Carta and the Charter of the Forest dating from around 1300.

↑ Ham is a hamlet on the outskirts of Sandwich (Sarah Bray/Shutterstock)   → The Guildhall, Sandwich (CM)

From the Guildhall, I venture across town to The Salutation Gardens. These four-acre riverside gardens are the accompanying grounds to an anomaly within medieval Sandwich – an early 20th-century property built as a country retreat. The celebrated architect Sir Edwin Lutyens designed both the house (now a hotel) and gardens with the property becoming the first 20th-century building to be granted a Grade I listing. The gardens are open to the public and represent a secret, colourful gem.

It's not difficult to find something tasty to eat in Sandwich (yes, it was the 4th Earl of Sandwich who is credited with inventing the eponymous snack of two filled slices of bread) and I'm tempted this way and that by numerous independent pubs, cafés and restaurants for lunch. For picnic treats, The No Name Shop, opposite the Guildhall, is a worthwhile stop for a spectacular selection of French cheeses, charcuterie and deli items.

Sandwich, though once the largest port in England, is now two miles from the sea owing to the silting of the land and shifting landscape. I end my day with a gentle river cruise on board the *River Runner*. The boat trip drifts through scenic countryside to the River Stour estuary at Pegwell Bay, a National Nature Reserve, to observe wading birds and resplendent common seals basking in the salt marsh.

Pegwell Bay is also of notable historical importance. This is where Julius Caesar came ashore with his Roman army in 54BC. Hengist and Horsa, leaders of Anglo-Saxon invaders, came ashore here in AD449, as did St Augustine, who founded Canterbury Cathedral.

↑ Seals are a common sight at Pegwell Bay (Iwona Fijol/Shutterstock)

I drive to Pegwell Bay Country Park where I pick up a tiny stretch of the England Coast Path towards Ramsgate. Along the way, walkers come across the Viking ship, *Hugin*, a replica ship gifted by the Danish Government to mark 1,500 years since the Viking invasion of Britain in the 5th century. There is, indeed, much history as well as wildlife here!

Ramsgate is recognised as the only royal port in England, the title bestowed by King George IV as he journeyed through on his way from England to Hannover in Germany. The town provides a mix of traditional seaside holiday, with stalls selling bucket-and-spade sets and candyfloss by the town's sandy beach, alongside an upmarket arty café culture surrounding the Royal Harbour.

There are some magnificent Georgian, Victorian and Art Deco buildings. Perhaps the most striking element of all within the town is the huge and ornate brick Royal Parade, which descends to the harbour. Beneath the road, harbourside, multiple archways are utilised by attractive cafés, chandlers and artisan craft studios.

It's unique, and a drink here – overlooking the harbour – is a very fine, maritime, way to end a trip along Kent's coast.

ESSENTIALS

GETTING THERE & AROUND White Cliffs Country Park to Maison Dieu Car Park: Upper Rd/Castle Hill Rd (A258)/A256 using one-way system. A258 to Kingsdown Camping then Kingsdown Rd to Deal. A258 south/rural lane to St Margaret's Bay. Rural lanes to Solley's Farm CL. Rural lane to Deal then A258 to Betteshanger Park & Sandwich. A256 then Sandwich Rd to Pegwell Bay Country Park or Hugin Green at Cliffsend. Reverse route to Sandwich Leisure Holiday Park.

Parking without height barriers: in Dover there's Maison Dieu Car Park; at St Margaret's Bay, the beachside car park is accessed from a steep, narrow & winding cliffside descent; in Deal, try Tides Park Car Park; in Sandwich, there is Gazen Salts Car Park; Pegwell Bay Country Park has a height barrier, but there's parking at the picnic area in Hugin Green (Sandwich Rd) – better suited to motorhomes than attempting to park in Ramsgate.

ACCOMMODATION
Kingsdown International Camping Centre, Kingsdown; Solley's Farm CL, Deal (CAMC members only; page xiv); Sandwich Leisure Holiday Park, Sandwich.

FIND OUT MORE
White Cliffs Country ∂whitecliffscountry.org.uk
Visit Kent ∂visitkent.co.uk

8 POP & FIZZLE

TOUR THE VINEYARDS OF SURREY, KENT & SUSSEX TO DISCOVER A WORLD OF VINES & WINES TO RIVAL CHAMPAGNE

WHERE	Surrey/Kent/Sussex
DISTANCE/TIME	204 miles/5 days
START/FINISH	Leith Hill/Rathfinny Estate

Jim loves a tidy vineyard. Tell Jim that the vineyard he oversees at **Gusbourne Wine Estate** looks cared for (it does), and you'll make his day. It helps that the neat and trim vines at this boutique winery have a rather lovely outlook, with views overlooking Romney Marsh.

As I wander among the vines, each row adorned with the blush of a white, red or pink rose – more on that later – I wonder whether the vines appreciate the view as much as I do, and whether the grapes, and the wine, taste all the better for it. Apparently, I'm told by vineyard tour guide Sue, they do. With Gusbourne's vineyards only six miles from Kent's south coast, the minerally maritime influence can be tasted in the wine. I look forward to my tasting.

Our Gallic friends across the Channel would love us to believe that their famous monk, Dom Pérignon, invented sparkling wine. Apparently, the British drink more champagne than any other country outside France. Perhaps, if only subconsciously, we love a glass of fizz because it was actually an English scientist, one Christopher Merrett from Winchcombe, in the heart of the Cotswolds, who, 400 years ago (and 20 years before Dom Pérignon introduced champagne to the world) invented the technique of secondary fermentation – the process by which quality sparkling wines are made today, otherwise known as 'the traditional method'.

Merrett also helped to revolutionise glass production in England so that bottles could be made capable of withstanding the huge pressures of secondary fermentation; before then bottles would explode, rendering the contents undrinkable.

It's perhaps little wonder then that, along with a warmer climate, English sparkling wines are making notable headway on the world stage to rival some of the very finest fizz. Regardless, a tour of Surrey, Kent and Sussex, linking up a collection of English vineyards, makes a very enjoyable trip indeed.

I begin my tour, not heading for the first drink on offer, but with an early morning stroll up **Leith Hill**. At 965ft, it's the highest point in Surrey and the second highest in southeast England, making it a good vantage point from which to view the landscape over which I'll be venturing in search of vineyards. The cool canopy of pine and birch as I climb gives way to a summit of views: The Shard and London's city skyline to the northeast, and a patchwork of glorious countryside to the south.

Not content to visit just one of the viewpoints that make up the heavily wooded Surrey Hills Area of Outstanding Natural Beauty, I move on to **Box**

← Chardonnay grapes ripen at Denbies (CM)

Hill, ten miles north on the outskirts of Dorking. The hill's Zig-Zag Road is famous for cyclists wincing their way up the sharp incline of the chalk slopes. The hill's western slope is also a great place from which to look down upon Britain's second-largest single-estate vineyard, **Denbies**. You can't miss the rows of vines on a wander along the National Trust signposted 'Hill Top Stroll'; autumn, as the vine leaves turn golden, is one of the prettiest times to take in the view.

These are not the only superlative views to be had, though, as a tour of Denbies offers an alternative. I catch the little vineyard train (must be pre-booked) that departs from the dominant winery building at Denbies for a tour of the vineyards. Indoor tours are also available, but the leisurely tour by train, complete with a commentary on the vineyard, is particularly pleasant.

The train winds its way through the rows of vines and woodlands on Ranmore Hill to give outstanding views of Box Hill, Leith Hill and the Mole Valley – it's as good if not better than any vineyard vista you'll find. I'm taken aback by the beauty and number of wildflowers bursting with colour between the rows of vines on the slopes.

At the top of the hill, the train stops for 15 minutes and there's a theatrical pop of the cork as a glass of Denbies' Whitedowns Seyval Blanc sparkling wine is served. It's a lovely spot to enjoy some fizz – and a celebratory introduction to a tour of English vineyards. Accompanying children receive a glass of non-alcoholic grape juice; the whole experience is ideal for families.

It's just over an hour's drive to **Chapel Down**, my next vineyard and the first of a series I visit in Kent. It belongs to a collection of privately owned vineyards marketed under an umbrella organisation, the Wine Garden of England, which can organise personalised tours. There are seven member vineyards: Chapel Down, Hush Heath Estate, Simpsons Wine Estate, Gusbourne, Squerryes, Domaine Evremond and Biddenden. Each vineyard offers visitors exciting tours, wine tastings and events.

Chapel Down is the largest wine producer in the UK, with an output of more than a million bottles a year. That's almost half of all UK production, with a thousand acres under vine.

It's possible to take a self-guided walk along the Red Vineyard Trail but I'd thoroughly recommend a guided tour here. Tom, our tour guide and wine-tasting expert for the afternoon, is outstandingly knowledgeable and explains the history of wine production in Britain: what did the Romans ever do for us? They introduced vineyards!

Thereafter, we're taken on a short tour of the vines and, at weekends when employees in the winery are not working, a brief tour to see the wine presses and shiny steel vats, with technical details given about viticulture.

↑ Leith Hill (Ant Cooper/Shutterstock) → Autumn at Denbies vineyards (CM)

But much of the afternoon is taken up with a tutored tasting in The Wine Sanctuary, a stylish contemporary building with huge glass doors overlooking the vines. Tom is not just a tour guide. He takes us on a tour of the wine glass, explaining how to taste wines as the wine trade does. The systematic, step-by-step tasting is very educational, with the reward of six or seven wines to taste.

Those not dining at the two-AA-rosette Swan Restaurant on-site can visit the estate shop and pick up a chilled bottle along with some locally sourced gastronomic supplies for a picnic on the lawn.

The countryside in this central part of Kent, in which Chapel Down is situated, is some of the most charming of the county. There are fruit orchards in abundance, lines of hop bines reaching for the clouds, brick oast houses aplenty, and picture-perfect towns and villages such as Tenterden, Cranbrook and Goudhurst, all of which offer a little tea room, a delightful pub, or a village pond to sit by.

They're all worthwhile for exploration in between vineyards. I love **Goudhurst**, which, as one of the highest villages in the Kent Weald, has some beautiful views. Head along the little footpath beside the war memorial and you'll come out into open countryside in a matter of yards, with a hilltop panorama as just reward.

After a restful overnight stay at Tanner Farm Park, I continue on to my next Kentish vineyard, **Hush Heath Estate**. I'm not sure what to expect as I traverse the Kent countryside to reach it, but I leave with a sense that this could be my favourite vineyard. It's a place you can certainly spend a full, leisurely day at.

The Balfour family bought 400 acres of land by accident! Of that, 100 acres are designated ancient woodland with private footpaths to wander – a bonus for those that like to work up an appetite for lunch. It's one conservation aspect that the Balfour family are committed to – a guided tour will take you past 20 acres of wildflower meadows, perfect for pollinating bees that gather nectar for the estate honey and to pollinate the 30 acres of apple orchards, used to make a delicious sparkling cider.

But it's the 150 acres of vines and the winery building, completed in 2018, that can't fail to impress most of all. Take a stroll through Nanette's Vineyard, a young parcel of vines, for views back that rival Épernay's Avenue de Champagne. Equally impressive are the views over the vineyard from the balcony of the winery, where I sit for a tutored tasting and a sharing platter lunch of exceptional Kentish charcuterie, cheese and crudités. Inside the building, a mezzanine overlooks the 'champagne' bar below and the huge winery where you can watch the wine-making process.

It's a shame to have to make a definitive choice from the six wines tasted of the 27 wines made at Hush Heath, but Balfour's Brut Rosé is the flagship wine of the estate. It consistently wins gold medals at the International Wine Challenge, was

↑ Chapel Down sparkling wine (Eugene Regis/Shutterstock) ← Goudhurst, Kent (Andrew Fletcher/Shutterstock)

the first English sparkling wine to be served in British Airways first-class cabins and is also served on the *Venice Simplon Orient Express*. It has some pedigree!

I could happily stay in the area for longer to visit cultural gems such as Scotney Castle, Sissinghurst and the National Pinetum, but Kent's backroads, and the little villages along them, are worthy of exploration too, as I go on my way to another Wine Garden of England vineyard, **Simpsons Wine Estate**.

My route takes me east towards Canterbury, cross-country via scenic villages such as Charing, but none prettier than **Barham**, the little village on the North Downs Way in which Simpsons Wine Estate sits.

The entrance to the smart, timber-clad winery is directly opposite the pretty village church, a typical Kentish one made of flint under a green copper spire, which can be seen from the estate vineyards. Visitors on a vineyard tour stroll through the churchyard, under the lychgate, past cottage gardens crammed with scented roses and along an old, leafy Roman road to reach one of two vineyards belonging to the estate.

It's a very peaceful spot and a gorgeous suntrap for growing vines. Much like most of the vineyards of Southeast England, Simpsons grow Chardonnay, Pinot Noir and Pinot Meunier – the three 'noble' grapes used to make champagne. The geology of the North and South Downs is the same as under the Channel, the Paris Basin and the Champagne region, and the similar soil and terroir, coupled with good amounts of sunshine, has proven to generate excellent growing conditions for English sparkling wine.

The owners, Ruth and Charles Simpson, know a thing or two about making wine – the couple also own a vineyard in the Languedoc region of France. They created Simpsons Wine Estate in Barham from scratch in 2012, planting 85

TOP TIP: THE BEST VINEYARD FOR...

Offering technical knowledge on wine: Chapel Down
Informality: Gusbourne
Views: Rathfinny
Walks: Rathfinny/Denbies/Hush Heath
Tutored tastings: Chapel Down
Organic production: Sedlescombe

Families: Denbies
Lunch: Hush Heath/Rathfinny
Afternoon tea: Sedlescombe
Conservation: Hush Heath/Rathfinny
Pretty villages: Simpsons
Wine: That's up to you!

Other recommended vineyards to visit: Kingscote (East Sussex); Nyetimber (set open days only; West Sussex); Squerryes (Kent); Biddenden (Kent); Domaine Evremond (Kent); Bluebell Vineyard (East Sussex); Greyfriars (Surrey).

acres of vines. Their first harvest was in 2016 and, having planted vines based upon certain rootstocks and clones from Burgundy, they found they could make excellent still English wine too, including a Pinot Noir rosé and a Pinot Noir red, with a light clarity similar to that of a good burgundy.

Tastings are fun rather than pompous. The tasting room sits above the winery – and guests can leave via a curly slide! At other times, guests taste the wines in the pressing room, beside the giant grape press and a showcase shelf of oak wine barrels.

It's a scenic drive through the Kent Downs AONB to my overnight campsite, though I wish I'd left more time to enjoy the pretty villages of Exted, Elham and Ottinge en route. They offer typical Kentish architecture that's exceedingly attractive.

I stay overnight at Daleacres, a tidy campsite between the Kent Downs and the coast, and a good mid-way stopping point between Simpsons and Gusbourne, the last of the Kent vineyards I choose to visit.

One tenth of the size of Chapel Down, **Gusbourne Wine Estate** is one of the smaller vineyards on my tour, though its focus is on outstanding quality, not yield, pitching itself within the top 2% of English wine production and selling to outlets such as Selfridges, Harvey Nichols and Berry Bros & Rudd, along with a

↑ Wine barrels at Simpsons Wine Estate (CM)

selection of very special still wines only available direct from the vineyard due to the small quantities.

A visit is refreshingly informal; Sue and Matt, tour and tasting guides for the morning, are quickly on first-name terms with visitors as we sit beneath a large canvas canopy overlooking the vines and the winery. Tall, purple *Verbena bonariensis* sway in the sunny breeze, and thyme and rosemary perfume the air. As we wander among the vines, Sue talks of the staff – vineyard manager Jim, winemaker Charlie, sommelier Laura and tractor driver/frost-buster Darren – all as important as each other to the quality of the resulting wines.

For anyone whose ampelography skills are unremarkable, a visit to Gusbourne makes life easy. In a nod to French tradition, where roses are planted in the vineyard reputedly to indicate signs of potential disease, the owner at Gusbourne has planted a rose bush at the end of each row: a white rose for Chardonnay, red rose for Pinot Noir and pink for Pinot Meunier. If the vineyard butterflies that are unrelentingly sipping nectar from the roses are anything to go by, they recommend a bottle of Pinot Meunier! Though, at the tutored tasting led by Matt, it is Gusbourne's Blanc de Blanc (100% Chardonnay) that is 'the vineyard wine', the wine which expresses the vineyard and its maritime location best.

I take a short break from touring vineyards and, crossing the border into East Sussex, stop in the historic inland port of Rye. My route there is no less scenic than anywhere else I've been, through the pretty villages of **Appledore** and **Stone**, and alongside the Royal Military Canal and River Rother, which sparkles in the sunshine.

But the hilltop town of **Rye** perhaps tops all this for its charm. It's a tiny town of narrow streets and overhanging brick and timber buildings. My favourite is the peace of Church Square and the surrounding cobbled streets, where tiny front gardens bloom. The town has a wealth of coffee shops and places to eat; The Fig, at the top of the High Street, is particularly good for brunch and lunch. For afternoon tea, though, the place to visit is **Sedlescombe Organic Vineyard**, the first of my Sussex vineyards.

Sedlescombe is reputedly the oldest organic vineyard in Britain, begun in 1979 by Roy Cook, a pioneer in organic wine production who latterly was moved to use biodynamic methods. These are principles which are still in use throughout the vineyard. Sustainability is in evidence across the estate, from the recycled materials used in the attractive visitor building to the ground source heat pump that sits beneath the vines to heat them.

Sat in the sunny courtyard dappled by giant oak trees and crab apples, it's a restful spot to sample the vineyard's organic wines and discover the biodynamic methods used here, including utilising the lunar cycle to dictate when certain activities are carried out on the vines.

→ Rye (CM)

If that all sounds a little bit fanciful, spending time over a ploughman's lunch or afternoon tea with a glass of organic fizz will soon bring you round. My choice is a still Riesling-like Old Vine wine, made from a 32-year-old Rivaner grape, a variety otherwise known as Müller-Thurgau that's widely used in German and Swiss wines.

There are plenty of cultural diversions around Sedlescombe, including the National Trust's Bodiam Castle nearby (where the vineyard also has some vines) and Bateman's, the former home of writer Rudyard Kipling. I decide to go further back in time, to 1066 and the Battle of Hastings.

With places like Bayeux Cottage and Battle Gate, it's obvious what went on in the town of Battle. While the town of Hastings lies on the coast, William the Conqueror's battle with Anglo-Saxon King Harold took place in fields north of Hastings. You can visit the battlefield site, follow the trail, and see where the future of English rule was decided. Access is part of the Battle Abbey and grounds, owned by English Heritage.

Take a wander around the town, too. There are plenty of little eateries (the Battle Deli and Coffee Shop offers a good frothy coffee) and independent shops for browsing.

I opt for an overnight stay at Battle Normanhurst Court, a campsite set in the grounds of a 19th-century garden packed with magnificent trees. It's all within a vast parkland estate, through which there's a fabulous walk to the nearby village of Catsfield. Keep a look out for the avenue of giant western red cedars – you can't miss them.

There can be few more picturesque brick buildings in the whole of Britain than Herstmonceux Castle, and few older; it is regarded, built in 1441, as one of the oldest brick buildings in Britain. The castle's moated setting certainly has a wow-factor as visitors approach down the long drive.

It also provides another cultural interlude from vineyard touring and I spend a lovely morning wandering the 300 acres of woodland and themed gardens. The woods are noted for their 300-year-old chestnut trees with portly trunks, while the more formal gardens, where vivid peacocks strut amid the rose bushes, offer plenty to occupy a few hours.

But I'm eager to visit the last vineyard on my road trip, the **Rathfinny Wine Estate**, situated within the South Downs National Park, just a mile from the idyllic and very popular village of Alfriston.

For views, it's evident I've saved the best until last. Climbing up from the vineyard entrance, a turn of a corner and over the brow of a hummock, suddenly there in the distance is the most incredible view of the Cuckmere Valley leading to the English Channel. It is a view that must be impossible to tire of and one needs a moment to stand and stare to appreciate its beauty. If one does tire of it,

↑ Herstmonceux Castle (CM) ← Battle Normanhurst Court CAMC (CM)

no matter; turn to the northeast and there is a no-lesser view of the South Downs on which sits the Long Man of Wilmington chalk figure. Turn to the west and you'll come across views of the South Downs stretching as far as the eye can see.

The Rathfinny Wine Estate has in recent years become the largest single-estate vineyard in Britain, overtaking Denbies in the acreage of vines planted. It truly is vast – and a remarkable estate – it takes the best part of a mile to reach the winery and estate shop from the entrance, having passed by acres of vines to get there.

Guided estate tours are possible, as are self-guided tours of the estate, along permissive footpaths that make up the Rathfinny Trail. I anticipate a half-hour walk but such is the beauty of the estate that I spend two hours wandering and watching, for the biodiversity is extraordinary.

ESSENTIALS

GETTING THERE & AROUND From Leith Hill/Etherley Farm rural lane/ B2126 to Ockley, then A29/A24 to Dorking & Box Hill/Denbies. A25 towards Sevenoaks then A21/A262/A28 to Goudhurst & Tenterden/B2082 to Chapel Down Vineyard. Reverse route to Goudhurst then B2079 to Tanner Farm Park; rural lanes to Hush Heath. Rural lanes to Headcorn & Charing Heath, A252 to Challock & Chilham, then A28/A2 & rural lanes to Barham (for Simpsons). Rural lane & A20 to Elham, Ottinge & West Hythe (for Daleacres). B2067 west to Kenardington/rural lane south for Gusborne, then follow Royal Military Canal from Appledore to Rye. B2089 west to Cripps Corner & B2244 to Sedlescombe. Rural lanes to Battle. A271 to Herstmonceux Castle. Rural lane south to A27 west then rural lane south (at Drusillas roundabout) to Alfriston for Rathfinny Estate.

Parking without height barriers: all vineyards & Herstmonceux Castle have parking suitable for motorhomes & campervans. Leith Hill has 2 small car parks, but they involve

↑ Picnics at Rathfinny Wine Estate (CM)

Rathfinny is not just about vines. There are fields of arable crops and acres left for nature. I spend much of my time distracted by clouds of butterflies that refuse to sit still to have their picture taken. Within just a small area of the estate I come across fifteen species, each feeding off the extensive assemblage of wildflowers.

I could wander for far longer, with direct access to the South Downs Way and its magnificent chalk grassland. But the vineyards call – and my tummy is chattering with anticipation at the choice of eatery options to quell the hunger of eager visitors alongside pre-ordered picnics served in the vineyard.

English sparkling wine is known to accompany a good old-fashioned portion of fish and chips exceedingly well. Sat overlooking the vines and the South Downs, they taste even better!

narrow lanes & tight turns unsuitable for large coachbuilt motorhomes; I walked from Etherley Farm campsite. At Box Hill there's a large car parking area (NT: pay & display). In Rye, use Riverside Parking on Winchelsea Rd. The English Heritage car park on Park Ln in Battle is free to EH members (otherwise £4/day; no dedicated motorhome spaces).

ACCOMMODATION I stayed at: Etherley Farm, Ockley, Surrey; Tanner Farm Park, Marden, Kent; Daleacres CAMC, Hythe, Kent (where they also offer glamping in yurts); Battle Normanhurst Court CAMC, Battle, East Sussex.

FIND OUT MORE
Wine Garden of England
⌀ winegardenofengland.co.uk
Denbies ⌀ denbies.co.uk

Visit Kent ⌀ visitkent.co.uk
Visit Surrey ⌀ visitsurrey.com
East Sussex ⌀ visit1066country.com

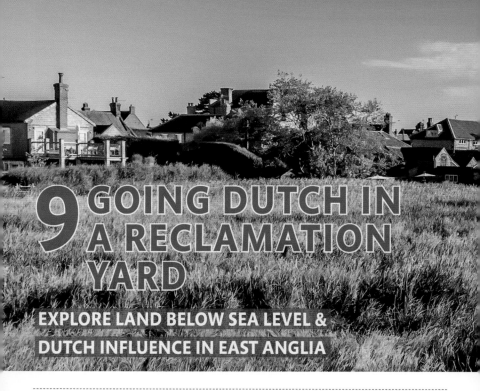

9 GOING DUTCH IN A RECLAMATION YARD

EXPLORE LAND BELOW SEA LEVEL & DUTCH INFLUENCE IN EAST ANGLIA

WHERE	Cambridgeshire/Lincolnshire/Norfolk
DISTANCE/TIME	319 miles/8 days
START/FINISH	Wicken Fen/Hickling Broad

The Netherlands, for me, conjures up images of windmills, fields of flowering bulbs – tulips, and daffodils – bicycles, waterways, and flat, *very* flat land. All true. Except that I thought visiting Holland required a trip across the North Sea.

At least that is until I visit the Lincolnshire Fens in which one finds the district of South Holland. Here – and across the fens of Cambridgeshire plus along the coast of North Norfolk – I come across Britain's Dutch relation, with an area of land that reflects a link across the water. The Norfolk coast is, after all, as close to the Netherlands as it is to London – and quicker to reach!

My tour begins at **Wicken Fen**, a 2,000-acre national nature reserve in the Cambridgeshire Fens, which showcases the very special landscape across much of East Anglia. Once uninhabitable and unusable swampy marshland, the Fens were drained by creating a series of water channels in the 17th century to develop

↑ Cley-next-the-Sea (Nicola Pulham/Shutterstock)

very fertile agricultural ground. One of the main protagonists was Dutch engineer Cornelius Vermuyden.

His drainage scheme, however, did not account for the layers of peat that lie across the English fens; the draining of the land made the peat contract and thus the land levels lower, allowing the fens to flood again. It was not until the creation of windpumps – inspired by Dutch engineering – in the 19th century, to aid water drainage and keep the fields free from flooding, that the network of drains and irrigation channels became successful. The last remaining working wooden windpump in Cambridgeshire is on display at Wicken Fen.

I take a short guided boat tour, run by The National Trust, along Wicken Lode. The whisper-quiet *Mayfly* glides peacefully through the narrow channel, our heads brushing against the overhanging reeds, passing by floating waterlilies. A coot scurries across the surface of the water, as if using the ripples created by the boat like stepping stones.

Our skipper explains the precarious nature of the fenlands – less than 1% of Britain's wetland habitat remains – the importance of the layers of peat for both soil fertility in the surrounding agricultural fields (more than 80% of the UK's lettuces are grown in the Cambridgeshire fens) and for its role as a carbon store. The serene experience over, I drive north to **Ely**, the capital of the fens, through which the River Ouse provides ample entertainment for messing about in boats. The town-sized city – once an island of high ground surrounded by swamp until the fens were drained – boasts a monumental cathedral with an octagonal tower that dominates the skyline.

I continue my drive northwest through the fen landscape, sometimes following alongside and at other times crossing numerous water channels, each ruler straight. My camping base in **Whaplode Drove** is central to the South Holland area, where lanes and waterways criss-cross the landscape like a chequerboard. The most horticultural of the fenlands, here the Netherlands appears at its most influential.

Even the bus driver transporting me to Spalding is of Dutch stock, with a Rembrandt moustache to boot. I have to pinch myself. In Spalding, the Chatterton Water Tower, in fetching pink, includes a stuccoed tulip; the entrance to the neighbouring town of Holbeach illustrates tulips on its name plate; and the ever-eager Spalding United FC are nicknamed The Tulips. Sadly, these may be the only tulips you'll see in the area today. Tulips in Spalding market really are from Holland – the Dutch one.

Until thirty years ago, the South Holland district had a thriving tulip industry. Dutch companies with world-recognised brand names bought into the rich, fertile loams of the Fens, with much of the countryside, like the Netherlands, beneath sea level. Unfortunately, most of this industry that, like a Dutch spring, transforms the land into rainbow stripes, has now gone. A significant number of tulips are still grown under glass in the area, for sale as bulbs. Millions of gladioli and an increasing bunch of cut flowers are grown too, but again these are cosseted in glasshouses away from the tourist's gaze.

What I come across, though, in a haze of golden yellow, is a blossoming daffodil industry. Keen to see these fields, and true to the Netherlands, I set out on a bike to explore.

Lincolnshire's South Holland is flat. The only incline observed is a molehill, the furry creature's earthworks accentuated by the uniformity of the surrounding land. It means cycling is a doddle, and I can stretch my legs for miles without the need to change gear or catch breath.

The Fens don't have roads; they have Droves and Gates – and there are hundreds upon which to ride, with only the occasional passing tractor. Better still, I pedal along a grid of traffic-free tracks, pencil-straight lanes and bridleways, often right alongside the many waterways. In the sunshine, with a picnic harnessed upon my back, it proves the ideal way to potter about this Anglo-Dutch landscape and soak up the yellow hues of the numerous daffodil fields that I come across.

→ Ely Cathedral (CM)

If there's one issue with the Fens being so flat, it's that you *can* cycle for miles without realising – until your legs tell you that they need to turn back. Ache? Mine needed to be forcibly removed from my bed the following morning.

And so I opt for a bus ride into South Holland's main town, **Spalding**. Past more daffodil fields, and crates piled high with bulbs, the Dutch-driven bus drops me at Spalding bus station, beneath the tulip-clad water tower and adjacent to The Tulips' home ground. At first glance, Spalding is an unremarkable town. Once the epicentre for all things floral, it looks to have lost its way in recent times. But head to the River Welland, which runs through the town centre, and on show is another side, a riverside idyll of elegant town houses festooned with weeping willows and blossoming cherry trees.

I hop on Spalding's water taxi, which plies the River Welland and the much wider Coronation Channel between the town centre and the Springfields Festival Gardens and Outlet Shopping Centre. The 35-minute ride provides a great opportunity to see the town from the river, engage with wildlife (one male swan, wings adrift, takes it upon himself to hold a duel with the boat) and relax, once again, on the region's waterways.

Out of town, past the riverside Ayscoughfee Hall – Spalding's most attractive visitor attraction, with its decorative 15th-century architecture and graceful gardens – we navigate our way along the Coronation Channel.

My destination is the 15-acre Festival Gardens. The spiritual home of the Springfields Horticultural Society, the gardens boast more than 150,000 flowering bulbs in tribute to the industry that once was and, to a certain extent, still is.

The daffodils appear in the gardens first, around February and March, alongside the crocuses and hyacinths, followed later by tulips towards the end of April. Free to visit, the interconnected gardens have been designed by several well-known gardeners. There are formal layouts, woodlands strewn with springtime colour, wetlands and thematic spaces with modern sculpture and futuristic plantings based upon the effects of climate change.

To explore the area further, I take a circular tour in the campervan. My first stop is the pretty village of Moulton, two miles east of Spalding. Here, I'm obliged to look skyward; at 100ft high the 200-year-old Moulton Windmill is the tallest in Britain.

On to **Holbeach**, South Holland's centre for the continuing bulb industry, with several bulb fields seen just off the main A17. I continue to Holbeach Marsh, close to The Wash, and the tiny hamlets of Holbeach St Marks, Holbeach St Matthew and Gedney Drove End. This is perfect for cycling and, I determine, would be better explored by bike.

Crossing back through this reclamation landscape via Sutton Bridge, where the once-dangerous-to-traverse River Nene has long been tamed with a striking

↑ Spalding with the River Welland in the foreground (Steven F Granville/Shutterstock) ← Crocuses in bloom at Springfield Gardens (CM)

burly looking rivet-encrusted bridge, I finish my visit of this Dutch-inspired region in **Crowland**. Lying on the southernmost border of Lincolnshire (and South Holland), Crowland's centrepiece is the ruin of its Benedictine Abbey. Naturally, with the lie of the land, it stands out for miles as a momentous structure. Up close, its vast hanging archways and pigeon-topped columns appear gargantuan.

Much of the demised abbey's stone reappears in the walls of cottages and houses around the town, which is worthy of an extended stop to enjoy its historic buildings and location close to the River Welland. Besides the abbey, Crowland's significant other is Trinity Bridge, a three-pronged affair with knobbly stone steps that lead to nowhere in particular. Of 14th-century origin, it once provided a crossing point over the River Welland, now half a mile or so to the west, and its tributaries.

By morning, I cross into Norfolk to begin a tour of the county's northern coastline, utilising the many wondrous estates and parks for outdoor activity and discovering further connections to its neighbour across the North Sea.

My first stop, slightly inland southeast of The Wash, is Oxburgh Hall. The magnificent medieval moated hall highlights the wealth and status of the family owners at the time, for it was built in brick, a building material that was usually reserved for royalty. It's not for the interior of the house that I've come, but for a good walk around the 130 acres of Grade II listed parkland and woodland, which is filled with huge ancient oaks and thick stumpy chestnuts with twizzled bark. There's a ten-year project underway to restore the lowland meadows, with evidence of historic irrigation channels.

I drive cross country to **Sandringham**, past fields of onions in straight rows of silty soil, via the villages of Eastmoor, Grimston, Congham and West Newton. One after the other, each village offers north Norfolk characteristics of houses made from flint and edged in brick. But at West Newton, an estate village connected to Sandringham, I see the unusual building method of brick-quoined houses infilled with courses of teeny slivers of ironstone.

The Sandringham Estate extends over thousands of acres of organic farmland and, while you cannot stomp all over it, there are 600 acres of royal parkland to explore on foot, by bike or by road. The forest – of Scots pine and birch, infiltrated by endless rhododendron bushes – is wonderful to wander through, with waymarked trails, an orienteering course and wide grass avenues for picnicking. I choose also to visit the gardens where there are further woodland walks and lawns with colourful flower borders around Sandringham House. My overnight camping pitch is within the royal parkland, scented by the surrounding pine trees, and less than a mile from royalty.

In the morning, I see more brick and miniature ironstone buildings as I pass through Dersingham, Ingoldisthorpe and, by far the prettiest, Snettisham on my

↑ Tulips growing in a Norfolk bulbfield (Kev Gregory/Shutterstock) → Sandringham CCC site (CM)

drive to the 12th-century village of Old Hunstanton before I turn east destined for Holkham Hall. But that's not before a stop at **Thornham** – where the ironstone vanishes, replaced by flint – and **Brancaster Staithe**. Both villages offer Norfolk beauty. The tide is out when I reach the latter, with boats perched at a precarious angle against squelching mud, their anchoring ropes and chains vanishing into the mire. On a coastal walk, alongside the complex network of natural rivers and streams that race at a snail's pace to the sandy foreshore, there's evidence of manmade drainage, like that in the Fens.

Each village in turn thereon proves prettier as I pass through Burnham Deepdale, Burnham Overy Staithe and the estate village of **Holkham** where Dutch influence in the form of crow-stepped gables appear on the old brick cottages.

Like Sandringham, the estate at Holkham is vast, and incorporates the north coast beach, Holkham National Nature Reserve, woodland, extensive parkland, and farmland. Visitors pay a nominal charge to park all day and can then wander at will through the parkland. There are options to hire a bike (or to bring your own), or a rowing boat on the Capability Brown lake, to try out the woodland ropes course or take a tractor-and-trailer ride through the park. On my cycle ride, it's not the imposing Palladian bulk of Holkham Hall that draws my attention, but close encounters with some of the 400 fallow deer that roam freely throughout the park – and into the lake.

On my way to the campsite at West Runton, I stop again, at Morston Quay for a short walk over the salt marshes and extraordinary views of Blakeney Point and the appealing Old Lifeboat Station, home to the coastal rangers that look after the national nature reserve here. There's a fresh, coastal breeze blowing that masks the sunshine warmth as I watch the sails of traditional clinker-built Norfolk fishing boats glide by along the creeks. There's also a very popular boat trip to see the common and grey seals that live on Blakeney Point.

It's getting too late to stop and see everything worth looking at before dusk so, the following morning, I backtrack to **Cley-next-the-Sea**, a charming village with more Dutch gables and a windmill overlooking the coastal marshes and sand dunes. The Norfolk Coast Path passes through the village and across the marsh, but I continue by road to Wiveton Hall which, over a frothy coffee and cooked breakfast, offers some of the best views of the sea. It's a rare glimpse, for touring along the coast road there are few moments to see the sea because of the dunes. But an outdoor table at the rustic café, connected to a Jacobean house with more curvy Dutch gables, is a lovely place to sit and enjoy the view.

I turn inland, through the flint villages of Langham and Binham, to Hindringham Hall. The privately owned house and gardens are open to the public two half-days a week from spring to autumn and a visit is well worth it. The exquisite, moated Tudor house – all gables (crowstepped, of course) and

↑ Rowing boat hire at Holkham Hall (CM)   ← Hindringham Hall (CM)

chimneys, is surrounded by a series of garden rooms, with an adjacent collection of medieval fishponds overlooking flat Norfolk meadows.

I return to the coast through **Holt**, a fine Georgian town with an attractive High Street, first to Sheringham Park and latterly to Felbrigg Hall. On a hillside (yes, there are hills in flat Norfolk), the 1,000 acres of gently undulating landscaped parkland at Sheringham – regarded as some of the finest in England by the celebrated local landscape gardener Humphry Repton – offer views across the coast from numerous waymarked trails, including some suitable for wheelchairs and pushchairs.

Felbrigg Hall, three miles southeast of Cromer, also offers excellent walks through its wonderful parkland, with lakeside and woodland walks and, as created by The National Trust, the Norfolk Mountain Walk, a 16-mile trek with a combined gradient of a small mountain. For a shorter, contained walk with plenty of colour, Felbrigg's walled garden is exceptional, dominated by its 18th-century octagonal dovecote and with many unusual plants. The West Garden provides a less formal wander under the canopy of trees.

As if the 520 acres of Felbrigg Hall is not enough, I move on to the 4,600-acre Blickling Estate, also in the hands of the National Trust, and with plenty of Dutch gables on the notable brick mansion to marvel at. Closest to the house are the formal gardens, including a bosquet with symmetrical paths for gentle strolls.

↑ Morston Quay (Andy333/Shutterstock)

In addition to waymarked walking trails, there's also bike hire for exploring the wider estate.

It's only a short drive from Blickling to meet up with the Norfolk Broads at **Coltishall**, passing through the Broads National Park from west to east and crossing the River Ant as I go.

As naturalistic as the Broads appear, this incredible landscape is manmade, the broads and meres the result of peat extraction for use as fuel in medieval times. The subsequent holes flooded, creating shallow lakes more than 600 years ago. I drive to the far eastern edge of the national park, on Norfolk's east coast. Here, it's impossible to see the sea without climbing the dunes, defences that prevent, like the Netherlands, the North Sea from reclaiming the land.

I stop at Horsey Mere and Horsey Windpump, an historic structure that gives an idea of how land in the Broads has been managed. Like the Fens, it's a wetland marsh – the village of Horsey was, like Ely, an inhospitable island village cut off by the marsh with limited access. Windpumps, like that at **Horsey** and many others that dot the landscape, have helped to keep water levels stable, preventing the wetland areas from drying out and contracting while keeping the land suitably drained.

On my final morning, I rise to blue skies and make the short journey to **Hickling Broad**. The largest of the 63 broads, together with the surrounding wetland

↑ Blickling Hall (CM)

↑ Hickling Broad (Helen Hotson/Shutterstock)

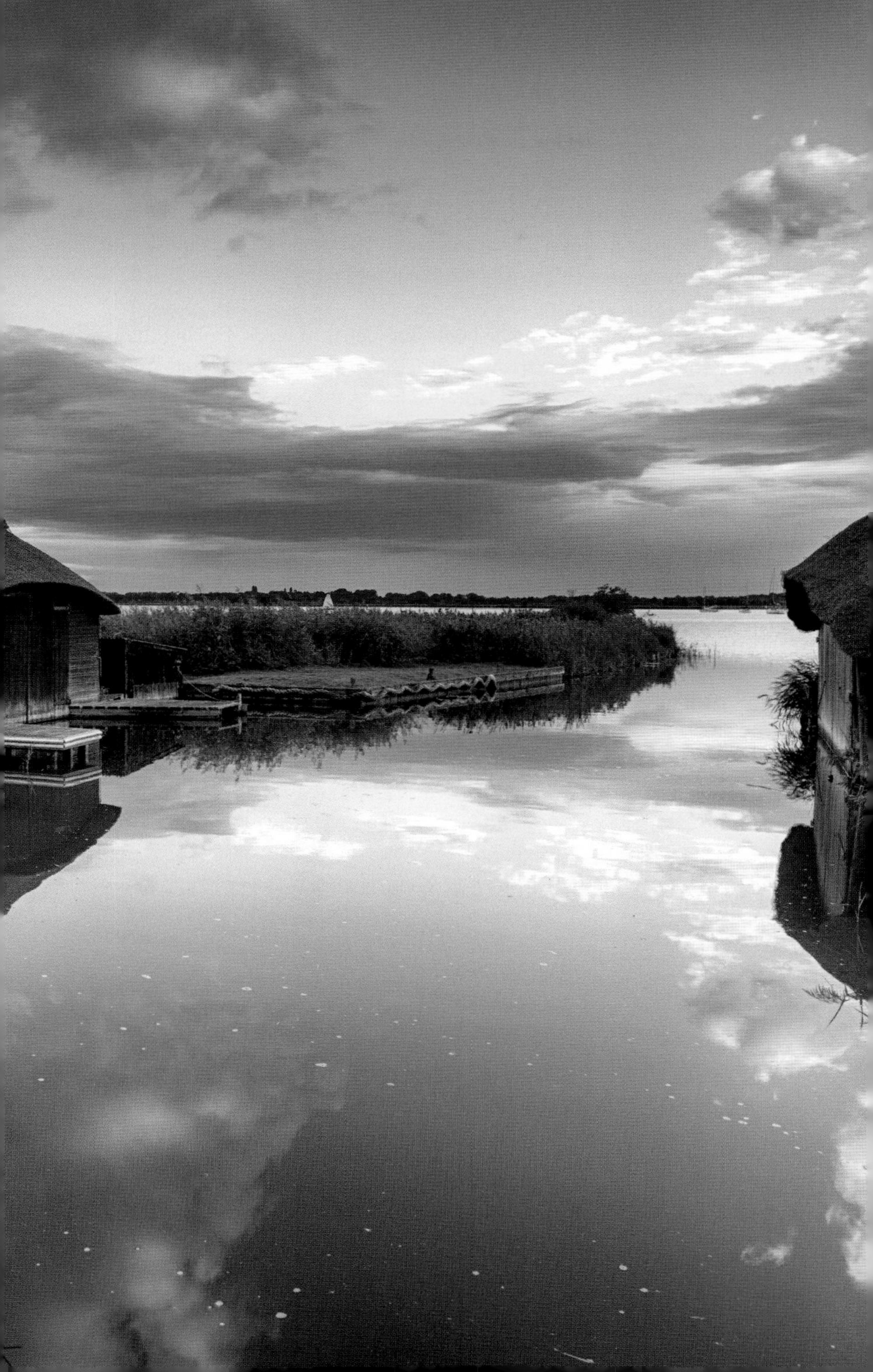

landscape, it is owned by the Norfolk Wildlife Trust and protected as a national nature reserve.

While the Broads at Wroxham and Potter Heigham heave with watercraft, jostling for position like fairground dodgems, at Hickling Broad there's a converse serenity. I step on-board *Swallowtail*, a 12-person flat-bottomed boat that's owned by the wildlife trust. It's barely visible in a narrow backwater hidden by reeds and David, the skipper for myself and four fellow passengers, gently guides the boat through the undergrowth, parting the stems topped by iridescent tufted peacock feathers as if a ship breaking ice.

On the open broad, we see few boats but plenty of birds. During the trip, we are taken through hidden narrow channels that no boat other than *Swallowtail* can venture along and taken to two bird hides, inaccessible except exclusively on this boat trip.

In an incredible two hours, I see godwits, ruff, ringed plover, avocets and lapwings. I see rare cranes flying overhead, a marsh harrier whose menacing presence makes the peaceful birdlife explode across the surface of the water, witness Konik ponies grazing the marsh and, through binoculars, watch a Chinese water deer emerge through the reeds to drink on the edge of the mere.

We're guided to a lookout tower in wetland woods where, above the oak treetop canopy our view is extensive: across Hickling Broad to the coast and

ESSENTIALS

GETTING THERE & AROUND A1123 west/A10 north from Wicken Fen to Ely. A142 to Chatteris then A141 north to Ring's End. B1187/B1166 to Whaplode Drove. B1166 west/Eaugate Rd & B1357 north to Moulton (5 miles east of Spalding). A151 to Holbeach. Rural lanes to Holbeach St Marks, Holbeach St Matthew, Gedney Drove End & Sutton Bridge. Rural lane south (alongside River Nene) to Tydd Gote & Tydd St Mary. B1165 west/B1168 south/B1166 west to Crowland. Return to Whaplode Drove via B1166. B1166 east to Wisbech. A1101/A1122 to Downham Market & Stradsett. A134 south then rural lane east to Oxburgh Hall. Rural lanes north to Narborough then B1153 & B1440 to Sandringham. B1440 Dersingham & A149 north to Old Hunstanton then east to Holkham Hall via Brancaster Staithe. A149 east to West Runton via Cley-next-the-Sea. Reverse route to Blakeney then rural lanes south to Hindringham Hall via Langham & Binham. Rural lane east to A148 then northeast to Holt, Sheringham Park & B1436 south to Felbrigg Hall, B1436 north/A148 & Tower Road to West Runton (campsite). A148 east/B1436 south/A140 south/rural lane to Blickling Hall Estate. Rural lane to Aylsham then southeast to Horstead. B1354 to Wroxham & A1062 to Ludham then rural lane north to Sutton & Stalham. Circular route using rural lanes to Horsey Windpump the dunes, to Horsey Mere and the River Thurne. The striped lighthouse at Happisburgh is in view, too. Though discussion is more about the effects of drought witnessed in the treetops, and on the wetland birds. As we climb back on board the boat, a fellow passenger enquires, 'Do you see many grass snakes in the reserve?' An affirming yes, rounded off that they should be called water snakes for the number seen swimming in Hickling Broad, makes me leap into the boat rather faster than I had intended. I'm not sure whether to look down into the water on guard, or up at the birds flying overhead as we return through the reeds to the hidden jetty.

My mile-long walk from the water's edge back to the visitor centre is occupied with thoughts of the birds I've seen, in some instances for the first time. It's too early for swallowtails, Britain's largest butterfly that's restricted to the Norfolk Broads such is its rarity, so my eyes are fixed down at the footpath rather than looking ahead.

I stop at a pathway junction to determine the route back. I see him first, then, looking up, forked tongue flicking forward, he sees me. His curled-up body, like a stack of hoops, unravels and weaves its way between the reeds deftly. My encounter with the grass snake is limited to seconds. The remainder of my walk back through the nature reserve, checking every reed along the footpath edge, is slow and methodical. Would I could be a swallowtail at this moment in time.

via Sea Palling, returning via West Somerton. North on A149 to Sutton then rural lane northeast to Hickling (for Norfolk Wildlife Trust Hickling Broad Visitor Centre).

Parking without height barriers: for Ely, use Newnham Street or Brays Lane car parks. In Spalding, there's parking off Winfrey Avenue (if not using the bus from Whaplode Drove). Cley-next-the-Sea has a large free car park beside the village hall. There were no problems with motorhome parking at any of the visitor attractions mentioned.

ACCOMMODATION
I stayed at: Meadow View Campsite, Wicken; Ashleigh Lakes, Whaplode Drove; Sandringham CCC Site, Sandringham; West Runton CCC Site, West Runton; Bush House Certificated Location, Sutton (motorhomes/campervans & touring caravans only; CAMC members only; page xiv). Alternative for tents & glamping is Hickling Campsite, Hickling.

FIND OUT MORE
Visit Ely ⚭ visitely.org.uk
Visit Lincolnshire ⚭ visitlincolnshire.com
Visit Norfolk ⚭ visitnorfolk.co.uk

Norfolk Broads National Park
⚭ visitthebroads.co.uk

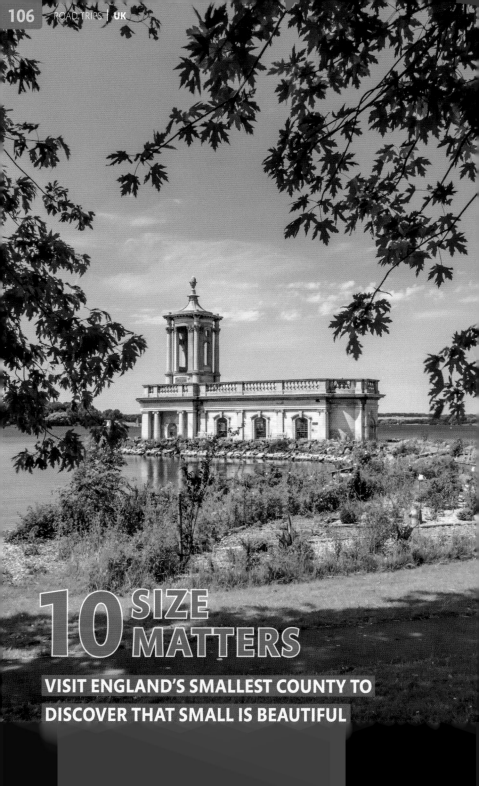

10 SIZE MATTERS

VISIT ENGLAND'S SMALLEST COUNTY TO DISCOVER THAT SMALL IS BEAUTIFUL

WHERE	Rutland/Lincolnshire
DISTANCE/TIME	67 miles/3 days
START/FINISH	Clipsham/Lyddington

Multum in Parvo is its Latin motto – 'Much in Little' – and the county is true to its word. Silent, elegant and understated, Rutland is full of surprises – whether it's the undulating landscape, the attractions that it packs in or that Rob Waddington, drummer from the famous 1980s rock band New Model Army, now teaches fly fishing on Rutland Water.

At just 17 miles long and 18 miles wide, Rutland is England's smallest historic county (there are other administrative areas now smaller). It makes the county ideal to explore in a weekend although, as I discover, it would be easy to stay for a week, such is the attractiveness of the area. At its very heart is Rutland Water, England's largest manmade lake (by surface area rather than capacity) and a beautiful, bizarrely 'natural' looking spot that has become home to a significant wildlife population.

Essentially rural, Rutland is made up of a collection of charming, peaceful villages and a couple of small towns – Oakham, the county town, and Uppingham a half-dozen miles further south. To the east is Stamford, officially in Lincolnshire but right on the border. I visit all three, but not before taking a turn in the countryside.

Approaching Rutland along the Great North Road, following the line of the Roman Ermine Street, my first place to visit is **Clipsham**, a tiny, picturesque village in the northeast of the county. Clipsham's great attraction is a vast 200-year-old yew tree avenue, the remnants of a great estate, where each of the 150 yew trees is clipped into shape. As far as the eye can see – it was once the carriage drive to neighbouring Clipsham Hall – the yews form great artistic perspective; reach the end and antlered deer roaming the vast parkland can sometimes be spotted.

Weaving in and out of the yews of this empty avenue, I meet an elegantly dressed elderly lady. Hunter-clad and carrying a tipped walking stick, she's perfumed and lipsticked to walk her pooch. We begin chatting about the avenue and, frankly, I could have spent my entire time in Rutland listening to her enthralling in-depth knowledge of the county.

'Do you know the area?' she enquires. 'No,' I say, 'I thought I'd spend a few days in the county to explore.' With the conversation suggesting that Rutland is a forgotten destination, her eyes light up with excitement, as if delighted that someone is taking the trouble to visit *her* county. 'Oh,' she says, 'I think you'll like it.' I already did – and I'd only been in the area an hour.

From Clipsham, I drive to discover enchanting villages, one after another, each worthy of a wander on foot – Pickworth, Greetham, Thistleton, Market Overton and Langham.

← Normanton Church and Rutland Water (Peter Jeffreys/Shutterstock)

My last destination of the day is **Oakham**. To match the size of the county, the county town is pleasantly small. The centre clusters around the High Street, the market square with its fine buttercross situated outside the entrance to prestigious Oakham School, the soaring spire of All Saint's Church and the grounds of Oakham Castle.

All that exists today of this fortified manor house are earth mounds and the impressive 12th-century Great Hall, which displays more than 200 horseshoes (the county symbol of Rutland), each one given to the Lord of the Manor by passing royalty or peers of the realm.

With a great collection of independent shops and eateries, Oakham is a rewarding county town; in preparation for supper, I opt for some award-winning sausages and a pork pie from Leeson Family Butchers on the High Street.

Rutland has numerous campsites, but my choice is the aptly named Rutland Water Campsite. Right beside the southern shore of this vast reservoir, it's a basic site. But its location, with views over the lake from some pitches, more than makes up for its lack of facilities. Just behind the HQ for Rutland Sailing Club, the campsite is also alongside the 25-mile off-road cycle trail and footpath that circumnavigates the lake, which I make full use of.

Rutland Water is a must for watersports enthusiasts, with sailing, boat hire and fishing possible. But, with the weather struggling, I choose to make the most of some off-road cycling. Irritated at first by the lack of sun and clear sky, I begin to enjoy the strange and evocative coloured light – like a midnight blue on a moonlit night – that the hanging mist creates as I pedal along the shore, taking pleasure in the company of wigeons, grebes and mute swans. It makes the 'sea' – for this is a big piece of water – seem even bigger, because I can't establish where the mist begins, or the water ends.

Rutland Water was created at the expense of now submerged villages. Normanton Church, Rutland Water's most famous landmark, almost succumbed too. It was saved and is now a scenic spot upon which to stop for a breather on the circular cycle route. I've brought my own bike, but there's a huge bike shop and bike hire venue at Edith Weston, where day-trippers can also park up.

The southwest corner of Rutland Water is a vast nature reserve that's managed by Leicestershire and Rutland Wildlife Trust. A great place to witness the comings and goings of migrating wildlife is at the Anglian Water Birdwatching Centre at Egleton Bay. My timing is poor, however, so I opt to visit their other site, the Lyndon Visitor Centre on the south shore of the Reserve. For this is at the very heart of the Osprey Project, these enormous birds of prey having been successfully introduced to the area in 1996.

A gentle and extremely peaceful stroll from the visitor centre takes me through waterside meadows to a bird hide where I can sit and watch the breeding pair

↑ Oakham buttercross (Gordon Bell/Shutterstock) ← Ospreys can be seen on Rutland Water (Edwin Godinho/Shutterstock)

tussle in their telegraph-pole nest and hunt over the waters of the lagoon. It is a magical sight. The ospreys are generally in residence between March and June.

I begin my final day with a visit to the outstanding town of **Stamford**, of which the very fringes press against the county boundary. A period piece, Stamford is one of those must-visit towns whose collection of attractive listed buildings and streets is so close to perfection, it's almost impossible to comprehend. The town is greater enhanced by the pretty River Welland that flows through it. Beyond lies vast Burghley Park and sumptuous Elizabethan Burghley House.

However sumptuous, Burghley Park will have to wait till another day; I have Rutland to explore. I drive to Ryhall, another of Rutland's pretty villages, on the River Gwash where ducks smile on the riverbank. This is followed by a stroll in Exton, just north of Rutland Water, a village no less attractive. Like its neighbouring counterparts, **Exton** is peacefully idyllic and my stroll of the Exton Park Estate allows me to see parts of the county inaccessible by road – such as Fort Henry Lake and its neighbouring Lower Lake, the site of the medieval village of Horn and the unique lakeside setting of Fort Henry, an 18th-century Gothic summerhouse.

↑ Stamford (John New/Shutterstock)

Close to Exton is Barnsdale Gardens. The collection of 38 gardens were transmitted into millions of homes during the 1980s and '90s during the BBC's *Gardeners' World* television series, when the presenter and garden owner, Geoff Hamilton created many of his notable TV gardens.

Now run by his son Nick Hamilton, the award-winning gardens are open to the public, and still maintained using Geoff's organic principles. I visit early in the gardening season, when spring bulbs are at their best but other areas of the gardens still come across as winterised.

I have two more places I'm keen to see before leaving Rutland. The first is **Uppingham**. Like Oakham, this delightful little market town is a pleasure to wander around, its main streets filled with small independent retailers and some great places to stop for a coffee or enjoy a pub lunch.

My final stop is **Lyddington**, a long ribbon village that is equally as appealing as, if not prettier than, all the other Rutland villages that I've visited. Of note is Lyddington Bede House, a mighty medieval wing of a palace that once belonged to the important and wealthy Bishops of Lincoln, but latterly – in Elizabethan times – became an almshouse.

I'll have to wait to view the house another time, for I realise that, however small Rutland might be, I still have much of it yet to explore. *Multum in Parvo*? Most definitely.

ESSENTIALS

GETTING THERE & AROUND Clipsham is 1.5 miles off the A1 in the northeast corner of the county. Rural lanes to Pickworth, Greetham (using A1 north/B668 southwest), Thistleton, Market Overton & Langham. A606/Barleythorpe Rd to Oakham. A6003 south then rural lane east to campsite. Rural lane northeast/A606 to Stamford. A6121 to Ryhall. Rural lane west/A606 west/rural lane north to Exton. A606/A6003 to Uppingham. Rural lane to Lyddington.

Parking without height barriers: use Kilburn Rd Car Park in Oakham & Bath Row Car Park in Stamford. At Lyndon Visitor Centre, access is single-track but there is a large gravel car park next to the entrance. Uppingham has North St East Car Park.

For walking or cycling, I recommend OS *Explorer* **map** *234 Rutland Water*.

ACCOMMODATION
I stayed at: Rutland Water Campsite, South Shore, Rutland Water.

FIND OUT MORE
Discover Rutland discover-rutland.co.uk
Visit Lincolnshire visitlincolnshire.com

11 THE HIDDEN COTSWOLDS

SEARCH HIGH & LOW AMONG THE COTSWOLD HILLS

WHERE	Gloucestershire/Oxfordshire
DISTANCE/TIME	61 miles/3 days
START/FINISH	Stinchcombe Hill/Kelmscott

If you mention the Cotswolds, many think of Bibury, Chipping Campden and languid villages like the Slaughters – all magnetic for tourists by the busload. But what of Hatherop, Chalford, Fairford, Amberley, Nailsworth and Dursley? Or the delightfully named Filkins? I've explored every square inch of the Cotswolds, researching for another travel guide, *Slow Travel: The Cotswolds*, and I would deem that all these lesser-known Cotswold towns and villages are equally as heavenly and more unspoiled. Now, days before my son Dominic heads off for secondary school, he and I are taking a few days away together in some of those same square inches.

I ask Dominic where he'd like to go. 'Winstones Ice Cream,' is his reply. At the rate he eats a Winstones – one of the creamiest ices you could imagine, based on Rodborough Common south of Stroud – I reckon I'd have a matter of seconds to

↑ The Slad Valley (PJ photography/Shutterstock)

spend with him. His plan, of course, is to eat more than one, so we strike a deal; ice cream interspersed with some hearty walks.

We begin our trip striding out on Stinchcombe Hill, a mile southwest of **Dursley**. The long-distance Cotswold Way national trail, which runs for 102 miles between Chipping Campden and Bath, ambles along the High Street of Dursley, not your average-looking Cotswold town, and up on to Stinchcombe Hill. Here, to make the most of the escarpment, with its pleat-like creases and folds, the Cotswold Way loops around the hilltop from where there are excellent views across the Severn estuary and beyond, into Wales and the Forest of Dean.

It feels surreal as we, enjoying the gentle pace of our walk, peer out from Drakestone Point to watch M5 traffic speeding at a seemingly jet-propelled pace, and watch an ensuing storm roll across the vale. Dominic's preamble is in search of lost golf balls from the wayward shots of golfers who also walk the hilltop. I fear there may be one or two putters still looking for their dimpled orb that never make it to the 18th hole.

On our return to the main road (the lane to Stinchcombe Hill is narrow but quiet, with passing places) we stop in Twinberrow Woods, where there's a sculpture and play trail beneath the beech trees to exercise the imagination. With rumbles of thunder funnelling overhead, the woods are atmospheric, but with the prospect of an electric clear light once the storm has passed, we move northeast running along the ridge of the Cotswolds' most westerly escarpment.

We are not disappointed. The storm clears the air, and the colours of the landscape are as vivid as the hues of the broadcloth once dyed around these parts – Uley Blue, Stroud Scarlet and Billiard Table Green – the plump hills surrounding the attractive village of Uley looking every bit the lush green of a billiard table.

Coaley Peak, seven miles to the northeast of Stinchcombe Hill, is our next stop. At first it seems the view remains much as before. Then again, it doesn't. For as the escarpment twists and bends, alternative vistas come into view and, with the visibility now limitless, we can see the Malvern Hills, Sugar Loaf Mountain in Wales and the Severn Bridges.

Our impatience for more of the same spurs us on north to make the most of the panoramas that the escarpment affords, stopping at Selsley Common. The area around **Stroud** is known as the Five Valleys, and Selsley Common has a quintet of views: west across the Severn; north over Stroud plus the Painswick and Slad valleys; and east over the top of the Nailsworth Valley. It's only the Toadsmoor and Frome valleys that are out of sight, hidden from view by the vast expanse of neighbouring Minchinhampton Common.

On the western edge of Selsley Common, where the Cotswold Way continues its march, there's evidence of the ferocious gradient of the escarpment. And we, in a now equally ferocious heat, choose to traverse this slope. Against a backdrop of gasps from nearby dog walkers – gasping at the view rather than our absurd desire, for there are others of similar mind – we begin the descent.

With each footstep we see a changing light over the landscape, a different perspective on the disused mills of Stroud and the hills beyond. Our draw – or mine at least – is the distinctive-looking church at **Selsley**. Far from being quintessentially English in style, its tall saddleback tower is based upon a church in Austria, and it glows iridescent at times when the surrounding landscape is in shadow. The stained glass windows are distinctive too, being the first major commission for the 19th-century designer, and founding member of the Arts and Crafts Movement, William Morris. His Pre-Raphaelite friends Dante Gabriel Rossetti and Edward Burne-Jones also had a hand in the work, as the trio did in many places throughout the Cotswolds.

Dominic's draw, other than hurtling down the hillside, is the Stroudwater Canal, one of two Cotswold canals that together linked the River Severn with the River Thames (the other being the Thames and Severn Canal). Much of the 36-mile

↑ View from Coaley Peak (chrisatpps/Shutterstock) → The church at Selsley (CM)

SOUVENIR

Caroline Mills is the author of *Slow Travel: The Cotswolds*, also published by Bradt Guides: ⏚ bradtguides.com/shop.

stretch between the two rivers is now defunct, although there are conservation efforts to bring the canals back into use. The section in Stroud is already in existence, but we don't make it. With two reasonable walks already under foot and the heat of the sun soporific, we turn and walk – at a considerably slower pace – back up the escarpment and onto Selsley Common. I succumb to the purchase of two ice creams, but they don't make the ache in our feet any better, so we retire to the first of our two sites, Sallywood Farm, overlooking the Nailsworth Valley.

With the sun bouncing off the cushioned hills around the farm we rise early the following morning, our feet recovered and feeling lighter in spirit once again. A clean light makes **Nailsworth** glow in the distance, and we take to the streets while the car parks are quiet.

I love Nailsworth. Unlike the aforementioned towns and villages of the north Cotswolds, which can feel prettily twee (it was these that made all the medieval money from wool, the buildings and churches a result of serious Middle Age wealth), Nailsworth has a grittier industrial beauty to its buildings. This particular part of the Cotswolds has connections to making cloth; tiny back-to-back weavers' cottages and giant mills clogged with windows, yet all made from characteristic Cotswold stone.

Ready for our next walk, we take the campervan up the 'W', an impressive hairpin road from Nailsworth to **Minchinhampton Common**. Our mission for the rest of the morning is a treasure hunt – a four-mile walk around the common, taking in the beautiful villages of Amberley, Box and Minchinhampton, while looking for clues, based upon a pre-set path offered by Treasure Trails.

Rare-breed cows and golfers mingle on the common, so we dodge both as we take in yet more glorious views and explore each of the three settlements. Striding into Minchinhampton looking for treasure, we hear that inimitable jingle that sends children into a frenzy. For one beginning to comment about tired feet, Dominic seems to find a hurried spring in his step racing towards the ice-cream van – a Winstones van no less. As we stroll on, watching the seller sample his own produce, Dominic announces that he has found his ideal career a few days short of his secondary education – selling ice cream.

Post-lunch we venture onto **Rodborough Common**, a finger of high ground touching Stroud and parting the Nailsworth and Frome Valleys. Here is where Winstones is based and where blackberries and cream – frozen in a cone – never

→ Cotwold stone cottages in the village of Minchinhampton (John Corry/Shutterstock)

tasted so good. Few ice cream sellers, inland at least, can offer such glorious views while devouring such loveliness.

We take a brisk detour along the **Slad Valley**, so exquisitely depicted by Laurie Lee in *Cider with Rosie*, and a glance into the beech trees in Buckholt Wood at **Cranham**, a National Nature Reserve, to exit the Five Valleys along the Frome Valley. This is also known as the Golden Valley due to the amount of wealth it generated in the textile industry and one of the best places to see the old mills and old weavers' cottages is in **Chalford**, clinging to the gorge-like hillsides above the River Frome. Some mills are now luxurious apartments or offices, in others the fabric of the buildings is disintegrating as fast as the industry they represent.

En route to our night-time pitch at Lechlade, we stop in **Fairford**, a gloriously attractive town that sits on the River Coln, in my humble opinion one of the prettiest of Cotswold rivers. The town has a stunning High Street and Market Square, topped with one of the most impressive Cotswold 'wool' churches, built

↑ The Plough Inn, Kelmscott (CM)

off the industry's wealth. Understandably, Dominic is not remotely interested that the church is renowned for its medieval stained glass windows, but finds interest looking for the grave of Tiddles, the church cat.

Our final day is 'heaven on earth', on the banks of the mellifluous River Thames, in the satisfyingly idyllic dead-end village of **Kelmscott**. The village is the spiritual home of William Morris, where he once lived at the Manor House, and here he gathered inspiration for his famous textile designs like the Strawberry Thief and Willows. He described Kelmscott as 'heaven on earth', and indeed it is.

A visit to the house provides plenty of motivation for creativity but first we venture out on a trek along the Willow Way, a four-mile circular walk that takes in a good stretch of the Thames Path and is supposedly a walk that William Morris and his artistic friends would often tread. The Thames is serene, the walk delectable as we chat and enjoy the company of the river's resident wildlife, including the shimmering flash of a kingfisher, while inhaling the sickly sweet scent of the invasive Himalayan balsam. We stop for coffee and cake in Buscot, a tiny hamlet owned by the National Trust on the fringes of the Cotswolds, before heading back to Kelmscott.

On our way along the banks of the Thames, Dominic makes a bark boat with a twig for a mast topped with a sticky burr plus two water snails and a slug as passengers (boys will be boys). We find the perfect spot to launch the boat on its maiden voyage. I think it's passing under London Bridge about now.

ESSENTIALS
GETTING THERE & AROUND
B4066 northeast from Stinchcombe Hill to Stroud/A46 south to Nailsworth. A46 north, via Stroud/rural lane to Cranham. B4070 to Birdlip/A417 to Cirencester & Lechlade-on-Thames. B4449 & rural lane to Kelmscott.

Parking without height barriers: try the Old Market at Nailsworth, although potentially troublesome for coachbuilt motorhomes when the town is busy. The alternative is Common Rd, Minchinhampton Common (allow plenty of time for a steep walk via The 'W'/The Ladder to Nailsworth). There's on-street parking at Fairford.

ACCOMMODATION We stayed at: Sallywood Farm, Horsley (tents only); Rough Grounds Farm, Lechlade.

FIND OUT MORE
Cotswolds AONB
⌀ cotswoldsaonb.org.uk
Cotswolds Tourism ⌀ cotswolds.com

Treasure Trails ⌀ treasuretrails.co.uk

12 HEAD FOR THE HILLS

EXPLORE WORCESTERSHIRE FOR FAMILY-FRIENDLY, CROWD-FREE PLEASURES

WHERE	Gloucestershire/Worcestershire & the Malverns
DISTANCE/TIME	80 miles/4 days
START/FINISH	Tewkesbury/Worcester

'They don't look that big,' remarks 12-year-old daughter Kate, as she spies the bony ridge of the Malvern Hills from the comfort of our motorhome. She and I are edging ever closer to the point of execution, that is to say, the point from where we begin our hill climb on foot, the full nine-mile length of the hills stretched out ahead of us as we approach from the east. I disagree with her, undoubtedly not for the last time as Kate fast approaches her teenage years. To me, the Malverns look high enough.

Our first glimpse of the hills comes during the journey to Worcestershire for a long weekend. They appear a mere streak on the horizon as we descend from a Cotswold escarpment. I feel they look momentous, for the bizarre range appears to erupt against a scenic foreground of the Severn Valley that lies between us and them.

It's this plain that we decide to explore first, beginning in the small riverside town of **Tewkesbury**, officially in Gloucestershire but right on the county boundary.

Our first stop is Tewkesbury Abbey, the centrepiece of the town since Norman times. That this enormous structure still stands intact is remarkable; not because

↑ The Ham, Tewkesbury (Martin Bache/Alamy)

of river floods from recent years, but because, if Henry VIII had had his way, Tewkesbury Abbey would have fallen during the 16th-century Dissolution of the Monasteries. Fortunately, the townspeople bought it from the king, and we can now enjoy the seriously chunky stone columns that prop up the roof and the magnificent webbed ceiling of garish vermilion red and lustrous blue.

Tewkesbury has had a grisly past, with fields to the south of the abbey witnessing the penultimate battle in the Wars of the Roses in 1471; many of the defeated Lancastrian soldiers looked for sanctuary in the Abbey grounds but were executed nearby. You can walk The Battle Trail but, opting for something a little less gruesome, we decide to visit The John Moore Museum, offering a natural history collection, housed in one of the many medieval half-timbered buildings that make the town so attractive.

John Moore was a 20th-century writer (he founded the now-famous Cheltenham Literary Festival) and naturalist living in Tewkesbury. He was passionate about the countryside, using fiction to write about his home town and his observances of a changing rural landscape. The tiny museum pays homage to his work but also provides many fascinating displays and information about country life.

To some visitors, it could be as gruesome as the town's battle-scarred past, with many stuffed animals (albeit beautifully presented). But it's not often that

you can stroke a mole, feel the prickles of a hedgehog, or view the iridescent colours of a kingfisher so closely. At the back of the museum is a minute but lovingly cared-for garden where we sit enjoying restful sunshine while admiring the unique view of the abbey's tower, reputedly the largest Norman tower in Europe.

Having nipped into the neighbouring Merchant's House (also part of the museum) for a quick snoop at a medieval cottage, we decide it's time for lunch. Tewkesbury has plenty of eateries, from old coaching inns and coffee shops to places from which to select picnic bits for a park-bench feast. Our choice is Miss Muffet's Deli, on Church Street, for its freshly made sandwiches.

We explore the bulging River Avon and its larger partner in crime, the River Severn. Both have been known to wreak havoc on the town, and though they're creeping too far up the banks for the daily boat trips, we can at least walk over the footbridge to the Ham, a large island meadow between the two rivers. It's a lovely place for a peaceful walk along the riverbanks; on the northern side, there are pretty views of the town and the Cotswold hills beyond. We catch another glimpse of the Malverns, too. They appear even bigger.

That evening, pitched up at the Tewkesbury Abbey Caravan and Motorhome Club site with its prime location next to the cathedral-sized church, we listen to the evening bellringing practice as darkness falls. By morning, Tewkesbury becomes a memory as we drive north to our next location, Upton-upon-Severn.

While high river levels had cancelled boat trips at Tewkesbury the day before, after a night of receding water **Upton** comes up trumps. Our boat, a little self-drive craft hired from Severn Expeditions at Upton Marina, allows us to get in tune with the pace of the river, watching the wildlife and scenery unfold. No experience is necessary – tuition is provided before you set off– though there are skippered boats for those who prefer to hand over responsibility to someone else. At the Heritage Centre, there's insight into the torment that the Severn can hail over Upton residents: the water can rise by 25ft in winter and, on occasions when it bludgeons its way into riverside pubs, by up to 38ft.

We find plenty to do for a few hours in Upton, with a town heritage trail available from the tourist information centre. The Pepperpot, Upton's most famous landmark (and which houses the Heritage Centre) is a must on the itinerary. A must for Kate is a visit to Sweet Daisy on Old Street to select from eye-popping numbers of old-fashioned sweetie jars, while I have to indulge my passion for maps by visiting The Map Shop; heaven on earth with more than 55,000 worldwide maps and guides in stock.

Choosing where to go next from the collection is almost impossible. Except, of course, the Malvern Hills are on the agenda – but not before a trip to Clive's Fruit Farm a mile from the centre of Upton.

← The Pepperpot, Upton-upon-Severn (Jo Jones/Shutterstock)

As we arrive at the fruit farm, a Worcester Pearmain apple is thrust into Kate's hand and the sweetest Victoria plum into mine for us to try. As if we need any encouragement to pick fruit, we find ourselves running for the orchards.

There's usually something to pick all year round, and if there isn't there's always homegrown apple juice, cider and other local produce to purchase in the farm shop.

From the fruit farm, the Malverns appear close enough to touch and we shouldn't really put off our acquaintance any longer. But with the cloud thickening over an otherwise blue-sky day, and the light beginning to fade, we determine it would be foolish to begin our walking ascent immediately so choose to wait until the following day.

Instead, we take a little driving tour on the roads that ring-fence the series of hills, each with its own name. And thereby comes my joy-of-joys discovery. For all the while that I had been peering at this seemingly mammoth ridge from afar, I had anticipated that it would be necessary to climb on foot from the very base of the ridge. There is no need! For the roads do much of the work, and we find that we will be well on our way uphill with the use of the throttle and a few gear changes. Such a helping hand seems fraudulent, however, as we return to our overnight base camp in Upton, though feeling lighter in step ready for the next day.

We decide from our driving tour the previous evening that the West of England Quarry Car Park is the easiest place for motorhomes to park, on the west side of

↑ Malvern Hills (CM)

the ridge. So, boots on, we begin our ascent from here. The climb is far easier than either of us had imagined, along well-worn paths. We see cyclists, walkers carrying babies and someone pushing a buggy up the hill, in addition to the stunning views over Herefordshire and the Welsh mountains. Our initial destination is the Worcestershire Beacon, the highest point on the Malverns at 1,394ft, before having a good mooch around the hilltops admiring all that's laid out below.

We take a late lunch in the 'van on Castlemorton Common, where there are some excellent walks on the flat for those who don't enjoy climbing hills yet still appreciate the closeness of them. An early evening is spent feeding ducks on the pond at Kings Green Caravan Park.

Our final day takes us to **Worcester**, nine miles north of the Malverns. With its industrial heritage, it's not always considered the most picturesque of cities. But

SOUVENIR

The Worcester Pearmain is a traditional heritage variety of apple from the local area with a sweetly scented flesh. It is just one of 15 varieties of apple tree that are grown at Clive's Fruit Farm.

Forget buying bottled water. Around the Malverns there are several waterspouts supplying fresh mineral water straight from the hills, including at Hayslag on the western side of the ridge. Anyone is allowed to fill a bottle.

↑ Worcester Pearmain apples (WalterL/Shutterstock)

we find much to occupy our time, including a look around the cathedral, where the tomb of King John lies, and the Museum of Royal Worcester, showcasing the city's porcelain heritage.

I'm not a massive fan of overly ornate porcelain and china (the museum determines the differences between the two) and I anticipate the exhibition might be a little old-fashioned. But the commentary is fascinating, exploring social history and etiquette through the fragile exhibits. There are numerous family activities, too, including pottery painting and ceramic workshops.

The Worcester City Art Gallery and Museum provides good insight into the industrial past of the area, including Worcestershire Sauce. But a big hit with us is The Commandery, a beautiful half-timbered building with Civil War connections (it was the Royalist Headquarters during the Battle of Worcester in 1651) and a tranquil garden beside the Worcester and Birmingham Canal.

The city is, of course, also synonymous with the composer Sir Edward Elgar. His birthplace museum, The Firs, lies four miles west of Worcester at Lower Broadheath, where we discover his love for cycling the country lanes around the Malverns, composing tunes in his head as he pedalled. It's an unassuming and unpretentious Victorian brick home and a world apart from our final visit at Spetchley Park Gardens, to the east of Worcester.

The vast formal gardens that surround the imposing Georgian mansion are displaying late summer colour from some of the very rare species collected over the years, and nectar for a kaleidoscope of butterflies. Elgar was reputedly inspired to write *The Dream of Gerontius* here; he loved to fish in the lake.

ESSENTIALS
GETTING THERE & AROUND
A38/A4104 Tewkesbury to Upton-upon-Severn. Upper Hook Rd, Upton for Clive's Fruit Farm. Continue west on rural road to B4208 then north & west on B4209. A449 north to Great Malvern, then B4232 south (on west side of Malverns). A449/A4104 to Upton. Reverse route to West of England Quarry Car Park, then B4232/A449/A4104/B4208 south to Castlemorton Common & Kings Green Caravan Park. B4208 north/A4104 west/A449 north to Worcester. A44 west & rural road to Upper Broadheath (for The Firs; note its official address is Lower Broadheath) then A4440 (Worcester ring road) & A44 east for Spetchley Park.

Parking without height barriers: in Tewkesbury, if not staying at the campsite, park in the Gloucester Rd Car Park (next to Marquis Leisure). At Upton-upon-Severn, there's Hanley Rd Car Park. The Malverns have 16 car parks, operated by the Malvern Hills Trust with a flat rate charge per day; none has a height barrier. The West of England Quarry Car Park (on the western side) is the largest and easiest for coachbuilt motorhomes. In Worcester,

Ambling around the water's edge and through the deer park, we're able to take in one last view of the Malverns that we'd 'conquered' the day before. Somehow, their stature doesn't look as formidable as the day we arrived.

Croft Rd Car Park has 4 'oversized' bays for motorhomes; all other city car parks have height barriers. NB: it can be easier to park in Great Malvern and take the train from Great Malvern or Malvern Link to Worcester.

ACCOMMODATION We stayed at: Tewkesbury Abbey CAMC Site; Little Fish Meadow Camping, Upton-upon-Severn; Kings Green Caravan Park, Kingsgreen.

FIND OUT MORE
Visit Worcestershire
⌂ visitworcestershire.org

Malvern Hills AONB
⌂ malvernhillsaonb.org.uk

TOP TIP: EDWARD ELGAR'S GRAVE The grave of the composer Sir Edward Elgar (together with his wife and daughter) lies in the churchyard of St Wulstan's at Little Malvern, with spectacular views over the Severn Vale. It's on the busy A449; there is a tiny car park, or parking in the lay-by opposite the church.

↑ Half-timbered buildings on the River Avon at Tewkesbury (BBA Photography/Shutterstock)

13 THE REAL DOWNTON

PUT ON A PAIR OF WALKING BOOTS TO STRIDE OUT ACROSS NORTH HEREFORDSHIRE

WHERE	Herefordshire/Shropshire
DISTANCE/TIME	72 miles/3 days
START/FINISH	Ludlow/Kington

The weather is not unkind; it's cruel. Torrents of rain deluge the ground. Grey clouds hang around hilltops – and hill bottoms. Roads are flooded, ploughed fields run into the paths of passing vehicles, precious soil silts up the byways, and rivers rampage through the valleys. Innocent streams don't gurgle, they gush.

Arriving for a walking tour, I'm all for turning around and heading home. But it has been a summer of persistent wet and I'm determined not to be beaten.

My first stop, on the Herefordshire/Shropshire border, is Ludlow. Not to explore the town on foot – it's far too sodden for that – but to buy wellies and a beefier waterproof (I've only packed a lightweight cagoule), followed by a trip to the celebrated Ludlow Farm Shop to stock up on comfort food; something to enjoy with a cuppa while the rain beats against the windows of the campervan.

Ludlow Farm Shop, the retail side of the vast 8,000-acre Oakly Park Estate, in Shropshire is worth a road trip alone to visit. On the outskirts of Ludlow, in

↑ Hergest Ridge (SuxxesPhoto/Shutterstock)

Bromfield, the farm shop sells everything local – 80% of its produce comes from Herefordshire, Shropshire, Worcestershire or Powys, with most of the food from the estate or within a 50-mile radius. There are large plate-glass windows around the edge of the shop floor to watch the production of cheese, coffee being roasted and bread being made.

Stocked up with treats, I cross the River Teme at Leintwardine and drive to **Aymestry**, arriving just as the rain begins to let up. Smug with the purchase of my new raincoat, I tog up and march off on foot to see what I can find.

Herefordshire, I find, is full of lumps and bumps. Aymestry huddles its few houses and church together in the Lugg Valley, surrounded by several of these lumps and bumps, many of which were used as natural defences by Iron Age civilisations.

I follow the Mortimer Trail, a footpath named after a large dynastic family who ruled these parts for centuries, which runs alongside the River Lugg. My new coat is keeping me dry, but the riverbanks are not; the Lugg is a raging torrent to rival the finest falls, bulging through wooded slopes. Passing a small orchard, I suddenly grasp the smell of cider apples; windfalls that have been crushed against the road. Climbing up into Pokehouse Wood, east of the village, I can nosey down on to Aymestry and get my first peek over the hummocks at what else Herefordshire countryside offers. It inspires me to move on.

I hop back across the border to stop overnight in Shropshire, in the picturesque village of **Bucknell**. A useful place to stay, there's a tiny railway station here for the Heart of Wales Line with services to Craven Arms and Shrewsbury to the north or Knighton and Swansea to the south, with ample opportunity to take the train a mile or two and walk back to the village along the Heart of Wales Line Trail.

The Norman family of Mortimers, mainly associated with the village of Wigmore and residing at an impressive castle there that is still just about standing, were not the only important residents in these parts. The Harleys, significant players in the English Civil War, have been based at Brampton Bryan, four miles north of Lingen, since 1294 and their name is given to Harley's Mountain between the two villages. The Harley family and the Mortimers of Wigmore also gave their names to two of London's most well-known thoroughfares, Harley Street and Wigmore Street.

Rising early, there is the faintest glimmer of sunshine and, keen to make the most of it, I drive to nearby **Lingen** to start another walk. My plan is to climb Harley's Mountain and it does indeed feel like a climb, and then to climb some more. At 1,266ft, the views from the top across several counties are rewarding, even if *my* view is to watch a vast band of rain heading my way. To return to the village I descend along the Herefordshire Trail, an ancient barrel-shaped sunken pathway between old meadows. I'm treading on history, imagining workers and farm labourers using this pathway in centuries prior, heading to work from their cottages. My mind begins to overthink, though, and I also imagine highwaymen. I run the last few yards back to the 'van.

The rain sets in again and I'm fed up with it. So I take a drive to the National Trust's Croft Castle, which, according to the website, can offer miles of woodland walks through the 1,500-acre estate. No, thank you. What I need is a roaring fire and to put my feet up. As it happens, the castle obliges. Welcomed by a cheery naturalised carpet of cyclamens at the entrance, some of the estate wood is crackling in the hearth and visitors can settle down on old comfy sofas in the drawing room as they learn about the Croft family. I could have settled down all afternoon but, once the rain subsides, I'm eager to visit a place I'd seen on my way through **Brampton Bryan** earlier in the day.

The village, filled with half-timbered properties, has a magnificent ancient, knobbly yew hedge that continues for yards along the roadside, encircling the church and castle remains. Appearing to drip like melted icing over the church wall, it's impressive but so too is Aardvark Books. In a converted barn on the road to Lingen, the bookshop has over 50,000 second-hand titles to browse including

↑ Views above Lingen (CM)   → Roadside produce at Brampton Bryan (andreac77/Shutterstock)

a mammoth travel section. With a log-burner and small tearoom located in the centre, it is easy to lose a rainy day here.

Stopping back in Bucknell, the rain continues to fall the next day too but I no longer care. I plan for getting wet and set out on a walk from Leintwardine to explore the Teme Valley, a wispy mist drifting silently through treetops. I walk for ten miles and see no one, yet come across a surreal other world of minuscule hamlets that give life to a handful of residents, which all seem so far removed from busy real-life Britain.

On the Herefordshire Trail, I walk through the real Downton Estate (the TV programme *Downton Abbey* is filmed at Highclere Castle, Berkshire), and right past Downton Castle, only visible when on foot.

A fairy-tale castle, the building and its surroundings are exactly like a 17th-century imaginary landscape painting. Indeed, influenced by key European landscape painters, Richard Payne Knight built and landscaped the place in the late 18th century to look just like a painting. He was a major figure in the Romantic 'Picturesque Movement', whereby country estates were landscaped to

↑ Downton Castle (Lavinia Lawson/Shutterstock)

emulate classical artworks. Very Romantic in style, one can easily imagine the place to be the setting for a Byron poem or a gothic novel.

Driving on to **Kington**, an old drovers' town, I arrive late afternoon and venture along the High Street to find it eerily quiet. In today's world of 24-hour commercialism, I'm surprised to find a town that still adheres to half-day closing – and I have arrived on that day.

Under a pale autumnal sky the following morning, I set out for one last walk, to climb neighbouring Hergest Ridge – pronounced 'harghest'. This is perhaps my hardest climb but the views from the Offa's Dyke Trail, which runs along the ridge, into Wales and further Herefordshire hills more than make up for the ache in my legs.

The wild ponies stand with their backs to the wind and even the woolly-coated sheep look cold. Fog is blown along the ridge and I know it's time to leave, safe in the knowledge though that I have seen much more of Herefordshire by keeping my campervan hooked up on site than I ever would have done simply by driving.

ESSENTIALS

GETTING THERE & AROUND A49 northwest from Ludlow/A4113 to Leintwardine/A4110 to Aymestry. A4110 north/A4113 west/B4367 to Bucknell. B4367/A4113 east then rural road south to Lingen. Rural lane south/B4362 east to Croft Castle. B4362 west/A4110 north/A4113 to Brampton Bryan then B4367 to Bucknell. A4113 east to Leintwardine. A4110 south/A44 west to Kington.

It's no good being in a hurry in North Herefordshire; even the A roads, from virtually any direction, take time as they twist and turn with significant frequency. Both A and B roads are fine for coachbuilt motorhomes; smaller lanes between villages are better suited to campervans. Park up and explore on foot.

Parking without height barriers: for Aymestry there's a lay-by just north of the village (on A4110) or a car park at the Parish Hall. In Kington use Mill St Car Park (or stay overnight at Fleece Meadow). There's ample parking next to the church in Lingen. And at Leintwardine, campervans may get into the Community Centre car park, or park roadside.

ACCOMMODATION I stayed at: Chapel Lawn Farm CL, Bucknell (CAMC members only; page xiv); Fleece Meadow Caravan & Camping Site, Kington.

FIND OUT MORE

Visit Herefordshire
⚲ visitherefordshire.co.uk

Eat Sleep Live Herefordshire
⚲ eatsleepliveherefordshire.co.uk

Kington Tourist Group
⚲ kingtontourist.info

14 BEACONS OF LIGHT

TAKE A CIRCUIT AROUND THE GOWER BEFORE CROSSING THE BRECON BEACONS

WHERE	Gower Peninsula (Abertawe)/Carmarthenshire/Powys
DISTANCE/TIME	240 miles/5 days
START/FINISH	The Mumbles/Abergavenny

There is a nursing home that sits close to the cliff's edge at Southgate, its residents sheltered by shrubbery from wanderers venturing along the Wales Coast Path. At its entrance is a tiny, understated plaque. It reads: *Vernon Watkins lived here 1924–45. He and Dylan Thomas wrote many poems in this house.*

Swansea and Laugharne are the focal points for devotees of Welsh poet Dylan Thomas. Heatherslade Residential Home in Southgate is not a pilgrimage site. Yet Thomas spent much of his youth camping on the Gower Peninsula, and visited his great friend, the poet Vernon Watkins, in Southgate regularly. They would wander the clifftop walks around Southgate, Pennard and Three Cliffs Bay, talking about and reciting poetry.

There is much to be poetic about on the Gower, with the entire peninsula designated as an Area of Outstanding Natural Beauty. I begin a tour of it at **The Mumbles**, a small seaside resort with a promenade of terraced villas at the southern tip of Swansea Bay. Here, too, Thomas was often to be found frequenting favourite pubs. My short wander from the rocks of Bracelet Bay takes me past the lighthouse on Mumbles Head to the pier, which is undergoing a long-term multi-million-pound restoration. Its white lace ironwork balustrade draws me out to sea for all-encompassing views of Swansea Bay.

Collecting the campervan, I drive along the south coast, passing first Langland Bay and latterly Caswell Bay, both popular with families being the closest out-of-town sandy beaches from Swansea. My drive climbs and turns inland through the pretty village of Bishopston to Pennard and **Southgate**. Here coffee and cake at the excellent Three Cliffs Coffee Shop, overlooking the sea, pre-empts a walk on the coastal path along the clifftop to Three Cliffs Bay.

Slivers of shiny rock slide towards the sea as the angled cliff faces, one after another, protrude seawards. There are views aplenty, of Pobble Bay and the Three Cliffs, of expansive Oxwich Bay, of Pennard Castle – and of Exmoor and North Devon across the Bristol Channel. The flat, open clifftop is great for picnics before descending to Three Cliffs Bay via mountainous sand dunes.

Continuing my drive west, I hop inland to the viewing point on Cefn Bryn Common, a red sandstone ridge that is the spine of the Gower. It's one of the highest points on the peninsula, from which are views to the south coast and, more so, the stretch of north coast, the Loughor Estuary with its saltmarsh and gleaming sandbanks.

I continue west, through the village of Reynoldston, matching Bishopston for attractiveness, to reach **Rhossili**, the most westerly village on the Gower. It is little

← Sychryd Waterfall, Brecon Beacons (Luke Deakin/Shutterstock)

more than a few white-washed houses but, National-Trust-owned, it's a popular place and, today, there are biblical numbers of visitors (for peace and quiet, don't arrive on a sunny Saturday in August!) enjoying coastal walks on the headland and Rhossili Down, along with, understandably, the three-mile-long beach of Rhossili Bay. This is, arguably, one of the most beautiful beaches in Britain.

As I take the short walk west of Rhossili, people are hanging around the headland. They're waiting for the tide to recede and reveal the causeway that will take them to Worms Head, a small island with a serpent-like rock dressed in an emerald green cloak.

But while the south and west coasts of the Gower are well populated with visiting sandcastle architects, I find the north remains a forgotten idyll. The roads to Burry Green and Llanmadoc, in the northwest of the peninsula, are deserted and the extensive beach of Whiteford Sands, as long as Rhossili Bay, I share with three people. That may be owing to the mile-long walk to reach it from Cwm Ivy but it's a beautiful walk through Whiteford Burrows, a national nature reserve of sand dunes and saltmarsh, pine woods and past the mountainous limestone outcrop, Cwm Ivy Tor.

The seawall was breached here in 2014 and, since then, a new saltmarsh has developed naturally, with a change in landscape that has brought a vast display of new wildlife. With so few people in the vicinity, it's a joy to become lost in the sights and sounds of coastal nature.

Following an overnight stay at Gowerton Caravan and Motorhome Club Site, in the northeast of the Gower, I head further northeast to **Brecon Beacons National Park**. Passing through Brynamman, a large, former coal-mining village of pebbledash terraces, the climb up Black Mountain is immediate. Looking back, there are views to Swansea Bay and, in the foreground, the slopes of the South Wales Coalfield. Coal was extracted here as recently as the turn of the century and a giant lake seen during the climb is one of those open-cast pits.

While coal is the most well-known industry of the Welsh Valleys, Black Mountain has its own history of quarrying, with limestone extracted around the summit. There's a short circular walk to learn about the forgotten lime industry and, I confess, *I've* soon forgotten when the countryside from Black Mountain's north face comes into view. Reputedly, the green pastures are luscious because of the lime from Black Mountain that was once spread on the fields. The sight is astounding.

I'm told that Black Mountain can live up to her name, a dark and bleak landscape. But tonight, sat in a silent meadow at Cosmos Camping, she glows like a chameleon – first a dusky salmon, then rose pink, then flame orange. As a half moon rises, the fickle light highlights every scar where the limestone quarrymen once defaced her, every freckle and dimple, every facial feature.

↑ Rhossili Bay (salarko/Shutterstock)   → Whiteford Burrows (Leighton Collins/Shutterstock)

↑ The Brecon Beacons National Park is an International Dark Sky Reserve (Charles Palmer/Shutterstock)

But these imperfections – if that's what you call them – don't seem to matter. They are what makes her a beauteous sight with the descending sun. Even the woolly coats of the sheep glow like little cosmic constellations against the orange hillside and as car lights come and go following the hairpin bends of the mountain road.

The Brecon Beacons National Park covers 519 square miles of countryside stretching from Llandeilo in the west to Hay-on-Wye in the northeast and Pontypool in the southeast. Its western half – including Black Mountain – is also named as a UNESCO Global Geopark for its important geological structure.

I move north through the gentler foothills of Black Mountain to **Llangadog**. It's a comely village of grey stone and painted houses sitting around the rivers Sawdde and Towy. It's also the start (or end) of the challenging 100-mile Beacons Way which crosses the national park.

Northeast is **Llandovery**, whose painted houses outsmart Llangadog in both number and colour intensity. Those around the marketplace are almost luminous! There's a pleasing view over the town from the ruins of the motte-and-bailey castle. Alongside stands the steel statue of Llywelyn ap Gruffydd Fychan. The 14th-century local braveheart was gruesomely executed here by Henry IV of England for his support of Owain Glyndŵr during the Welsh rebellion and war of independence.

Travelling first east, along the 'top' of the national park, to Sennybridge, I move south again, then east along the 'bottom' of the park, where it meets the Welsh Valleys. Then back north criss-crossing the national park back and forth along its river valleys towards Brecon. With each run north to south, or south to north, are tunnel-like vistas of high hills either side and a band of rocky hills to aim towards.

Approaching Brecon from the south, I set out on foot from the roadside picnic site along the A470 to climb the nursery slopes of Fan Frynych for exceptional views of Corn Du and Pen y Fan, two of Brecon's most famous beacons. So, too, of the tamer-looking Tarell Valley – lusciously green by comparison to the beige sculptured beacons – as it forges its way towards the River Usk and Brecon. The hill appears mine alone on this occasion, but looking towards Pen y Fan those aiming for the summit swarm up the well-worn track from the Pont ar Daf car park like ants.

The summer heat is unbearable by the time I reach **Brecon** and, having climbed a hillside, I'm more inclined to sit a while and rehydrate in one of the many town cafés than waltz around its streets. I'm not alone in that; Brecon is a beacon for many walkers. So, too, for cyclists who begin (or end) their 55-mile journey to Cardiff along the Taff Trail, which begins here, utilising the towpath of the Monmouthshire and Brecon Canal.

Just as the night before, when I'd watched the sun set on Black Mountain, I spend the rest of the afternoon and evening watching the carved and chiselled Pen y Fan, Cribyn and their associates in a detailed chiaroscuro light show from

↑ River Sawdde at Llangadog (CM) → Colourful houses in Llandovery (RogerMechan/Shutterstock)

Cefn Cantref Campsite. I should cook a campsite supper, but I cannot take eyes off my geological neighbours.

I'm reluctant to leave Pen y Fan and co the following morning, but I find I've not left them behind as I traverse the national park north to south again for the last time. Crossing the Monmouthshire and Brecon Canal and, alongside the River Usk, heading towards Pencelli, I retrieve an alternative angle of the two beacons, and I realise I have saved the best until last.

While all of my south-north-south crossings of the national park thus far have been on A roads, I now cross the park along minor roads, turning at Talybont-on-Usk towards the Talybont Reservoir. The large sculpted peaks disappear, replaced by the gentle valley slopes of the Caerfanell River through the Talybont Forest. Then the rushing of water as I approach the foot of a series of waterfalls.

The road makes a short, steep climb through pines and mountain ash to reveal the naked humpback of Craig y Fan Ddu, accessed via a sharp ascent along the Beacons Way. I park at Blaen-y-Glyn Forest for the woodland waterfall walk, to witness the beauty of Caerfanell and her tributary, Nant Bwrefwr, on foot. Both tumbling rivers gift a string of glistening waterfalls to wander beside.

Talybont Reservoir is the first body of water along this route, and I latterly witness Pentwyn and Pontsticill reservoirs through swathes of forest. Pentwyn is revealing its red bottom with only a mirage of muddy puddles left occupying the tank. The larger Pontsticill, with its steep banks of bracken (and bluebells in spring), offers more for the resident sailing club to float upon. As I approach and cross over the dam wall before my descent to **Merthyr Tydfil**, I hear the chug and hollow toot of a steam train; the Brecon Mountain Railway, regarded as one of the Great Little Trains of Wales, follows the water's edge from nearby Pant station deep into the national park.

The landscape changes as I drive east along the famous Heads of the Valleys Road, spying the last remaining open-cast coal mining in the area at Merthyr Tydfil along the route. I meet up again with the River Usk for a short hop north to **Crickhowell**, which I deem to be the prettiest of the towns I visit on this trip. At its foot is the River Usk with views of the iconic flat-topped Table Mountain to the northeast of the town. In the centre, an award-winning Georgian-façaded High Street of black-and-white matched by a riot of floral colour.

It's only eight miles to **Abergavenny** then, my final stop, passing the famous Sugar Loaf Mountain along the way. The town is regarded as a gateway to the Brecon Beacons. I use it as a leaving post but not before sampling some of Abergavenny's hospitality. Self-styled as a gastronomic destination – and with an excellent annual food festival – I find an incomprehensible number of tearooms, cafés, restaurants and bars. Choosing one is nigh on impossible. A climb up Sugar Loaf will have to do. Sweet.

↑ Talybont Reservoir (CM) → The River Usk at Crickhowell (Richard Whitcombe/Shutterstock)

ESSENTIALS

GETTING THERE & AROUND
Begin at Mumbles Head at end of B4433. Road through Mumbles to B4593 west to Caswell then road north to Bishopston. B4436 west to Southgate. Reverse back to B4436 north then A4118 west to Little Reynoldston. Northwest towards Reynoldston then east to viewpoint nr Arthur's Stone. Reverse route to Reynoldston & A4118 then continue west/south to Scurlage. B4247 to Rhossili. Reverse route to Llanddewi, then rural lanes to Burry Green & Llandmadoc. Rural lanes east through Cheriton to Llanrhidian then B4295 to Gowerton. A484 east/A483 north/A48 east/A4067 northeast (unless going through Swansea) to Pontardawe. A474/A4069 to Brynamman, then Llangadog & Llandovery. A40 east/A4067 south at Sennybridge, A4221/A4109 east to Glynneath/A465 to Hirwaun. A4059/A470 north to Brecon. Rural lane to campsite at Cefn Cantref. Back to Brecon then B4558 to Talybont-on-Usk, then rural road to Pontsticill & Merthyr Tydfil. A465 east then A4077 to Crickhowell. A40 to Abergavenny.

Parking without height barriers: on the Mumbles, Bracelet Bay has a large car park suitable for motorhomes. For Three Cliffs Bay, a large National Trust

↑ Mumbles Head (Red Media/Shutterstock)

car park beside Three Cliffs Coffee Shop at Southgate has direct access to Wales Coast Path. There's another extensive National Trust car park at Rhossili. At Llanmadoc, use the field car park just beyond the church at Cwm Ivy. Llandovery Castle has a car park. In Brecon, there's The Promenade car park. Beaufort St car park is in Crickhowell. And at Abergavenny, use the bus station car park.

ACCOMMODATION I stayed at: Pitton Cross Caravan & Camping Park, Pitton Cross; Gowerton CAMC Site, Gowerton; Cosmos Camping, Gwynfe (16+ years); Cefn Cantref Campsite, Brecon (13+ years).

Both Cosmos and Cefn Cantref are for tents and small campervans up to 18ft (5.5m); no motorhomes or touring caravans. They are also both adult-only sites. Alternatives include: Abermarlais Caravan & Camping Park, Llangadog (adult-only; accepts motorhomes); Erwlon Caravan & Camping Park, Llandovery; Pencelli Castle Caravan & Camping Park, Pencelli.

FIND OUT MORE
Gower Peninsula
⌖ visitswanseabay.com

Brecon Beacons National Park
⌖ breconbeacons.org

15 TALES OF WALES

VISIT NORTH WALES IN SEARCH OF A STORY

WHERE	Wrexham/Denbighshire/Conwy/Gwynedd
DISTANCE/TIME	168 miles/5 days
START/FINISH	Pontcysyllte Aqueduct (Trevor)/Betws-y-Coed

Roaming through the jungle of sessile oaks, azalea bushes and sky-high pines with burly trunks as orange and hairy as an orangutan, I step back, camera poised, and almost stumble over a crocodile. Teeth blazing amid its timber jaws, the wooden beast of Portmeirion's woodland momentarily catches me unawares as I focus on the brilliant carmine of a flourishing rhododendron. Beneath a sultry sun and the startling floral pinks and striking reds, the environment feels more Mediterranean, or even tropical, than North Wales coast.

My trip to Wales would, I hoped, be the stuff of storybooks. It had begun the previous day at one of Wales' most significant 'legends', the Pontcysyllte Aqueduct. The work of Thomas Telford, and a masterpiece of the Industrial Revolution, the aqueduct is the longest in Britain and the highest in the world. Together with an 11-mile stretch of the Llangollen Canal, the aqueduct is also designated a UNESCO World Heritage Site. Taking time to explore the canal's beauty, I could understand why its superlatives also make it one of the best in the world.

Leaving narrowboats behind to squeeze along the celestial aqueous tape, I follow the 4.5 miles of canal towpath towards the monochrome world of **Llangollen**. If

↑ Llangollen and the River Dee (Jason Winter/Shutterstock)

the houses of the town are black and white, the countryside of the Dee Valley, along which the canal runs, is anything but: a pastoral idyll of verdant hills topped by ruined castles, gentle pastures filled with dozing sheep and an extravagant catalogue of wildflowers, crowned by canal-side bluebells and a showy display of ramsons.

The canal, punctuated by bridges in multiple architectural styles, makes for a particularly attractive and gentle walk. With a hardstanding towpath all the way to the Horseshoe Falls – Thomas Telford's engineering masterpiece west of Llangollen that provides a water source for the canal – the route is also suitable for pushchairs and wheelchairs.

My arrival in Llangollen coincides perfectly with lunch, which I take in an old railway carriage at the heritage train station where, over soup and a sandwich, I can watch adventurers plunge through the white-water rapids of the River Dee. There's also time for me to step off the towpath, onto a canal barge for a 45-minute horse-drawn canal journey. The whisper-quiet equine excursion is one of two short narrowboat 'cruise' options in the area – the more daring may prefer a crossing of the Pontcysyllte Aqueduct.

Accompanied by abundant broods of ducklings on my return walk, I'm ready for rest at my first campsite in nearby Carrog. This is Owain Glyndŵr territory, where the last Prince of Wales (and a national legend) drew arms against the English. His reputed stronghold, Owain Glyndŵr's Mount, is just about in view from my riverside pitch.

↑ Narrowboat on Pontcysyllte Aqueduct (travellight/Shutterstock)

With a very pleasant drive through Snowdonia National Park, past sparkling lakes and ever-more precipitous hills, by coffee time the following morning I reach **Portmeirion**, where the Llŷn Peninsula begins its protrusion into Cardigan Bay. The Italianate village was designed and built between 1925 and 1975 by the eccentric architect Clough Williams-Ellis as a tourist attraction and to show how a beautiful site could be developed without spoiling the landscape.

Some may see the Mediterranean-style village as a pastiche. But there is an unequivocal charm in both the buildings (all Grade I or II listed structures) and the setting. Many visitors venture no further than the 'village' centre, but there are 70 acres of woodland gardens to explore, much of which is within the Morfa Harlech National Nature Reserve.

I have the run of the woods, taking the circular coastal trail for memorable views of the Dwyryd Estuary, Tremadog Bay and the Llŷn Peninsula. Empty beaches and the wild and lawless colour of the Azalea Trail lure me ever deeper through the trees, as if trekking into a rainforest. Every sense is heightened: blackbirds create a cacophonous din rustling leaves on the forest floor; azalea petals, like delicately crumpled paper, shine brilliantly; the tangle of ancient rhododendron trunks appear like giants and the whirling scent of honeysuckle propels one into a giddy stupor.

Dazed by the enchantment of this legendary village, I could have stayed under its magic spell much longer. But the allure of Snowdonia's mountains is magnetic, too, and I succumb to the temptation of ever-greater views and more legends to unfold.

It doesn't take long. Passing through the rocky and fabled wilderness of the Aberglaslyn gorge, once voted by National Trust members as the most beautiful landscape in the UK, I arrive in the photogenic village of **Beddgelert**. With its compendium of quaint stone cottages lining the Rivers Glaslyn and Colwyn, and surrounded by powerful mountain views, it's easy to become mesmerised by the lilting tune of the bumbling rivers and succumb to the many tearooms and tourist traps.

But Beddgelert has a tragic tale to tell, about the 13th-century Prince of Gwynedd, Llywelyn the Great, and his faithful dog, Gelert. The sad story is revealed at Gelert's Grave, a five-minute walk from the village, and the resonating beauty of its location on my riverside return seems all the more poignant.

The legend of Gelert is not the only tale to be told from Beddgelert. Half a mile from the village is Dinas Emrys, a noticeable tree-lined mound like an upturned pudding bowl. To reach it, I tramp through the boggy underworld of Craflwyn, where spongy moss, dripping ferns and timber serpents combine to create a mythical landscape. Dinas Emrys, as legend tells, is the birthplace of the red dragon commemorated on the Welsh flag. The dragon, allegedly, once

↑ Portmeirion, designed as an Italianate village by Clough Williams-Ellis (EddieCloud/Shutterstock)
← The pretty village of Beddgelert (Adrian Baker/Shutterstock)

lived inside the mountain. With the remote call of a steam engine echoing through the Glaslyn Valley, I'm not going to quibble over telling tales. I have a train to catch.

At 25 miles long, the longest heritage railway in the UK, the Welsh Highland Railway is hauntingly therapeutic. I join the Caernarfon-bound steam train from Porthmadog at Beddgelert Station, where sheep not only graze the bluebell banks behind but roam the railway track too. Fortunately, the train goes at a steady pace, the short distance taking 1½ hours to appreciate the transcendent splendour of the Gwyrfai and Colwyn valleys.

The syncopated, staccato rhythm of the train lull my eyes to focus on the here and now – the oak woods, the young calves and the skittish lambs, the waterfalls and the lakes amid the irresistible industrial scent and sound of coal and steam.

And then, snaking a corner, it's there. Every mountain that passes by, one questions if it's Snowdon. But once seen, you just know. More stately, more resplendent than any other, there is no mistaking its bulk, its piercing, otherworldly summit.

Snowdon may be legendary – its Welsh name, Yr Wyddfa, has legends of its own – but reaching the summit provides stories. Visitors to Hafod Eryri, the UK's highest café, are told that the summit of Snowdon was once under the sea. It's a tall tale, stood at the peak of Wales overlooking the Snowdon massif and the moulded, velvet suede crags. But the receding water has clearly left its mark – and seashells – in the rock.

To reach the summit, I take the gentle option of the Snowdon Mountain Railway. It feels a bit of a cop out, being pushed up the cog railway by the green, steaming beasts of *Enid* and *Yeti* while watching the ant-like trail of mountain walkers putting their all into reaching the same goal. But by the time the train pulls up at Clogwyn Station, three-quarters of the way up the mountain, one or two walkers look dreamily at the railway carriages that pass them by.

The railway stops just short of the trig-topped peak, a narrow circumference of stone that performs as a stage for how many people can fit onto a penny. I leave the crowning glory for those who deserve to be there, climbing the mountain the hard way, and spend my time staring out in reverence at all that was once under the sea.

But, from Snowdon, the sea is in view. And, the azure blue of the day draws me to the coast to visit another natural phenomenon – Great Orme's Head.

This lump of limestone, like a giant dozing tortoise from a distance, sleepwalks its way into the Irish Sea beyond the Victorian seaside resort of **Llandudno**. The town itself has links to Alice Liddell, the real-life heroine of Lewis Carroll's *Alice in Wonderland*. There's a themed Alice Trail to follow, though I forego a stroll through the town (but not a homemade ice cream in the Alice-themed

↑ Snowdon Mountain Railway (Dilchaspiyaan/Shutterstock) → Cable car over the Great Orme, with the 2,295ft Grade II-listed Llandudno Pier in the background (Marso/Shutterstock)

Looking Glass Ice Cream Parlour) in my eagerness to reach the summit of Great Orme's Head.

Other than a steady climb on foot, there are two ways to reach it: by colourful cable car or, my option, the Great Orme Tramway. These historic, fully restored trams glide quietly through the streets of Llandudno from their hub, Victoria Station, before climbing to the top of Great Orme.

Many visitors stay within the Summit Complex but Great Orme's Head is a country park and nature reserve, and provides some fabulous walking. I recommend the mile-long ascent by tram followed by a walk back to Llandudno via the alpine gardens in Happy Valley at the southeast tip of the country park. From here, there are tremendous views of the town, the famous pier and Little Orme on the far side of Llandudno Bay.

Returning to the campervan, it's time to explore the Great Orme in an alternative way, one that becomes a highlight of my tour. Around the base of the limestone headland is Marine Drive, a spectacular 'touring' road. Just four miles long, the toll route is one-way, from the North Shore to the West Shore of Llandudno. There are places to stop and pull across beneath the towering limestone cliffs, or you can park at the summit. My drive, in drenching sunshine, is memorable for the sighting of the Great Orme's fabled wild Kashmiri goats.

Introduced to the Great Orme more than a century ago, these goats roam the headland with limited human intervention. I stop to take in a view of the sea, turn only to find a pair of eyes peering at me... then another, and another. Bathing in the evening sun, they too seem to be enjoying the sea views.

The Great Orme is at the very head of Conwy Bay and it's to the Conwy River that I turn as I drive inland. Close to its banks is the National Trust's Bodnant Garden. The landscape was the vision of one man, Henry Pochin, a Victorian entrepreneur who, in 1874, established the now world-renowned garden.

After much walking in recent days, I anticipate a gentle stroll but it's not to be. The 80 acres of Grade I listed garden, filled with plants collected by famous global explorers, pull me in every direction to follow this path or that amid specimen trees, rose borders, trellises and deep down into The Dell for a long, streamside walk to what's admirably called 'The Far End'. This hidden corner of the garden is assured of my attention; Bodnant's 1880 Laburnum Arch, the earliest such arch to be created in Britain, is legendary.

So far, I've come across mythical landscapes, discovered the stories of folklore, 'climbed' famous mountains, enjoyed the ride on historic trains and trams and explored celebrated Welsh gardens. It's time, I feel, for some legendary Welsh eats. Fortuitously, less than a mile from Bodnant Garden is Bodnant Welsh Food.

The venue celebrates local provenance. The home of the National Beekeeping Centre Wales, there's also a five-star restaurant, cookery school, tearoom and farm shop. Moreover, the food centre has its own dairy on-site, making award-winning cheese and butter, and a bakery with Welsh delicacies like bara brith and Welsh cakes. And, nearing the end of my stay in the area, I can return home with a little taste of Wales – local beef and lamb reared just 300yds from the farm shop.

My final evening is spent in **Betws-y-Coed**. This little village is a legend on an historic route – it was used as a stopping point for horse-drawn coaches on their way between London and Holyhead – though, as a gateway to Snowdonia National Park and tucked amid the vast Gwydir Forest, it remains popular today. With steep, gorge-like valleys and even the appropriately named Fairy Glen, a mystical beauty spot of cascades and waterfalls on the Conwy River, the village has enough legends of its own to fill history books.

I've plenty of tales and legends of my own to narrate as I return home, including the magnitude and splendour of North Wales.

ESSENTIALS

GETTING THERE & AROUND Trevor (parking for Pontcysyllte Aqueduct) should be approached via the A539 & not the A5, where access is over a very narrow bridge. A539 west to Llangollen then A5 to Carrog (campsite). A5/A494/A4212/A470 north/A487 west to Portmeirion. A4085 north/B4410 west/A498 north to Beddgelert. A498 northeast/A4086 northwest to Llanberis. A4244/A55 east/A546 north to Llandudno. B5115 to Rhos-on-Sea (campsite). A470 south to Betws-y-Coed.

All roads in the area that I travelled on are acceptable for coachbuilt motorhomes, though particular care should be noted on the A498 from Porthmadog to Beddgelert & the A4086 Llanberis Pass. Both roads are narrow in places.

Parking without height barriers: At Llangollen, motorhome parking is not particularly easy. I found it easier to park in Trevor (free) & walk to the Pontcysyllte Aqueduct from there. Portmeirion has free motorhome parking. Beddgelert village is compact; there is parking at the railway station but best to pitch up at the campsite & walk to the village. In Llandudno, there are dedicated motorhome bays at Maelgwyn Rd car park, otherwise park at Great Orme summit.

ACCOMMODATION I stayed at: Station Campsite, Carrog; Beddgelert Campsite, Beddgelert; Llanberis Touring Park, Llanberis; Dinarth Hall, Rhos-on-Sea; Riverside Touring Park, Betws-y-Coed.

FIND OUT MORE
Visit Wales ∅ visitwales.com

Snowdonia National Park
∅ snowdonia.gov.wales

Visit Conwy (for Llandudno, Conwy & Betws-y-Coed) ∅ visitconwy.org.uk

16 COAST OF MANY COLOURS

DISCOVER A LAND OF COLOUR ON A CIRCULAR TOUR OF WALES' LARGEST ISLAND

WHERE	Anglesey
DISTANCE/TIME	129 miles/3 days
START/FINISH	Britannia Bridge/Aberffraw

I have recently painted my bathroom. It's a sort of chocolate-fudgy brown colour (it looks much better than it sounds) and the name given to the paint is 'Ynys Môn'. I'm ashamed to say that, until the family decided to take a short trip to Anglesey not long after the latest DIY project, I had no idea that Ynys Môn is the Welsh name for Wales' largest island.

So, no sooner have we crossed over the Menai Strait via the Britannia Bridge, I have my eyes pressed to every bit of rock, building material and sandy beach to see if my chocolate-fudgy bathroom walls bare any resemblance to the colour of Anglesey. I conclude the name must include some artistic licence on the part of the paint manufacturers. We see no such similarity. And yet, what we do find is a land filled with colour that I had not anticipated.

The A55 through North Wales seems to go on forever and yet, suddenly, we're deposited in Anglesey. Unsure what we're doing or where we're going, we dive off at the first exit after crossing the Britannia Bridge. We find ourselves at a viewing point, overlooking the Menai Strait and the famous Menai Suspension Bridge, a graceful relic of the industrial age, built by Thomas Telford in 1826. The scenic backdrop to the bridge is the undulating line of Snowdonia's hills. The swirling

↑ Beaumaris Castle (Tomas Marek/Shutterstock)

waters encircling the charming, whitewashed cottage on Fish Trap Island (it has its own tidal fishing pool) are of an exotic emerald-cum-turquoise green.

Continuing east, following the coastline past Bangor Pier, which all but joins Anglesey with the mainland such is its projection into the Strait, we reach **Beaumaris**. In my humble opinion, it's the island's prettiest town. Upon arrival there is a sense of historical elegance with smart, seaside cottages, yachts bouncing in the bay and the ordered Regency-style façade of Victoria Terrace overlooking the sea.

The moated remains of Beaumaris Castle, built by Edward I in 1295, are tucked neatly to the side of the town's main thoroughfare, Castle Street, where we're able to pick up suppertime goodies and sample a refreshing homemade orange and sea buckthorn ice cream from the Red Boat Ice Cream Parlour. Multicoloured nautical flags flutter along the quayside as we lick away and watch the chosen activity of many – crabbing from the pier.

As a spur-of-the-moment trip, we've not planned where to stay overnight. Looking for a camping spot gives us the opportunity to explore the eastern tip of the island around Llangoed and Llanfaes. We're in luck and find a quiet CL in Llangristiolus, central to the island, with views of Snowdonia. We have the place to ourselves and receive a private glimpse of Snowdon's summit, glowing pale yellow in the late-evening sunshine. Perfection.

The A55 is Anglesey's busiest road. Cutting through the centre of the island, it transports cargo from mainland Britain to the port at Holyhead, and on to Ireland. The A5025 and A4080, Anglesey's other two main roads, link to create a ring around the 276-square-mile island, always within a mile or two of the sea. And, as the island's entire coastline is designated as an Area of Outstanding Natural Beauty, it's this that we choose to focus on for our second day.

↑ Menai Strait (CM)

We begin in the southwest corner near **Malltraeth**, at the nature reserve, where it's possible to walk along the top of the dyke and see Malltraeth Sands stretch out one way and a plethora of wildlife filling the wetlands of Malltraeth Marsh on the other. We watch white wild ponies bathing their feet as sandpipers grub around them to pick out tasty morsels from the pools.

Through Newborough Forest, we drive parallel with the westernmost section of the Menai Strait to the National Trust's Plas Newydd, the traditional seat of the Marquess of Anglesey (who stands aloft on a plinth close to the Britannia Bridge). There are acres of grounds in which to take a wander, right down to the shoreline of the Strait, including an arboretum and a formal terraced garden adjacent to the house where the vivid hues of red, violet and orange cheer up an overcast morning.

On the east coast, we track beaches, first the vast Red Wharf (where we'd heard of quicksand, so avoided) followed by Benllech and Lligwy. All are preposterously busy with summer holidaymakers; visible grains of sand seem hard to come by, so we continue our way, ready to take in the view at Bull Bay, just north of Amlwch. Here we see bright flashes of orange montbretia flaming the coastline against the deep blues of the sea. A wild version of the garden plant crocosmia, the montbretia is an unexpected sight, one which we later see all over the island and seems to symbolise Anglesey.

While the east coast is a buzz of activity, the northern coast is not; it becomes our favourite part of the island. The wild and craggy coastline offers astonishing walking, so we take up a small section of the 125-mile Anglesey Coast Path, which circumnavigates the island.

↑ Coastal path from Crigyll Bay to Aberffraw Bay (Phillip Roberts/Shutterstock)

The tiny town of **Cemaes**, with its own beach, is enchanting, though we prefer the solitude of Cemlyn Bay, to the west. Here we stride out utilising the coast path across the rugged moors, strewn with a purple haze of heather jumbled with mustard and olive-green lichens smothering the protruding rocks. Virulent yellow ragwort clings to cliff edges , contorted leaves of shale mottled silvery grey with a tidal stripe of black.

As we had spent some time driving on our reconnaissance tour the previous day, our last morning demands a bracing beach walk, for which we choose **Aberffraw**. The terrain is surreal – a lumpy, lunar landscape of grassy dunes tinged with purple knapweed and ragwort. Beyond is a vast beach along which we have only our own shadows for company, a mighty contrast to the east coast sands we'd witnessed the previous day.

Wandering back along the tiny Afon Ffraw estuary, we pass electric-blue fishing boats, cast aside by the lack of tidal water, and coloured houses. But not one of them is painted in 'Ynys Môn'.

ESSENTIALS

GETTING THERE & AROUND
A55 Britannia Bridge, A5 & A545 to Beaumaris. B5109 north to Llangoed/rural lanes to Llanfaes. B5109 west/A5114 to Llangristiolus. B4422 southwest/A4080 to Malltraeth/Newborough (Niwbwrch). A4080 to Plas Newydd. A5025 north to Amlwch & west to Cemaes/Llanynghenedl then B5109 southeast to campsite. B4422 southwest/A4080 northwest to Rhosneigr then south to Aberffraw.

Parking without height barriers: Beaumaris Green Car Park is opposite Beaumaris Castle on a large flat grassy park. There's 1 price that covers all-day parking (even if you're only staying for 1hr); perfect if you wish to stay for the day, popping back to the 'van to make a brew etc. Castle Car & Coach Park is a smaller car park just east of the castle, on the B5109 towards Llangoed; easy access. Rhosneigr Pay & Display Car Park on Awel-y-Mor has no height barrier but is small. To the southeast of Rhosneigr is the larger Porth Tyn Tywyn Car Park, with a ½-mile walk along the beach into town. High 'vans should watch out for the railway bridge just north of the town with a 9ft 6in (2.9m) restriction. At Benllech, use Lower Wendon Pay & Display Car Park (it looks as if you're being taking into the centre of a housing estate, off A5025), just a few yards from the beach. Upper Wendon Car Park has a max height of 6ft 6in (2m).

ACCOMMODATION
We stayed at: Cefn Farm CL, Llangristiolus (CAMC members only; page xiv).

FIND OUT MORE
Visit Anglesey ⊘ visitanglesey.co.uk

17 SALT OF THE EARTH

CHESHIRE? PLAIN? NO. BUT 'WICH' PLACES TO VISIT?

WHERE	Cheshire
DISTANCE/TIME	65 miles/3 days
START/FINISH	Macclesfield (Sutton)/Nantwich

'I laid the stone paving path to White Nancy many years ago,' says Mr Bullock, owner of Jarman Farm Certificated Site. He and I are chatting about one of Cheshire's most iconic landmarks that I'm looking forward to visiting following a stay at his riverside farm campsite, and I'm keen to gain local knowledge.

Cheshire has recently been associated with wealthy footballers' mansions and not-very-real housewives. It's not an aspect I've come to the county of cheese and grinning cats to investigate, preferring a solitary walk amid green fields and a heritage that goes back longer than ITVBe's second-highest-rated programme. It didn't take long to find an alternative side.

As a tourist catchment area, Cheshire is extraordinarily underrated. For example, the most eastern locale of the county is situated within the Peak District National Park. It's here that I begin, with a stay at Jarman Farm. I spy

↑ Macclesfield Forest (CM)

walkers on the hill above the CS and, though it's difficult to prise myself away from the soothing murmurs of the River Bollin beside my pitch, I venture on a circular four-mile trek that introduces me to the undulating terrain and views – of parkland meadows, moors and the giant Lovell Telescope at Jodrell Bank – afforded by an evening stroll along Birch Knoll, east of Macclesfield (or 'Macc' as Mr Bullock likes to call it).

It's the hottest day of the year as I approach the coolness of the Dane Valley, Cheshire's border with neighbouring Staffordshire, on a short road trip the following morning. The idyllic wooded dell, with historic stone bridge and microbrewery riverside, coupled with a water's edge footpath, is far removed from the county's Golden Triangle. This is the real Cheshire, where the natural folds of the hills are tight and contorted.

Passing through the remote Peak District village of Wincle, I continue north along the valley to the distinctively named **Wildboarclough**. It's no more than a couple of houses and a pub, the Crag Inn, beside a rocky gorge of red sandstone amid trees. The sheltering canopy of leaves are refreshing but once in open countryside, with the heat rising, I shy away from climbing Shutlingsloe, the 'Matterhorn of Cheshire', despite the magnificent views of Cheshire's Peak District, instead preferring refuge from the sun in Macclesfield Forest.

The forest, of oak and ash, beech, sycamore and larch, is uplifting, and there are footpaths and bridleways aplenty through the trees to explore. But I stand still in

↑ White Nancy and the Cheshire Hills (Stanth/Shutterstock)

bewilderment at the beauty of Trentabank Heronry, a nature reserve managed by Cheshire Wildlife Trust that is, arguably, the most restful spot in the county.

The lake (strictly speaking a reservoir) is surrounded by larch trees used by herons for breeding. Bracken, meadowsweet, wild carrot, foxgloves and willowherb sweeten the air around the banks while herons drift undisturbed beside beds of water lilies.

It is the first of several lake-like reservoirs that I pass on my way to Tegg's Nose Country Park. There's a bruising climb to the summit of Tegg's Nose from its foot in the village of **Langley**, but a gentler option is to start a walk from the car park of the Country Park to reach this distinctively shaped snout. Views are notable, of Macclesfield Forest and the chain of reservoirs in one direction and the jigsaw of Manchester's high-rise buildings in the other.

My miniature road trip takes me north again, between the rounded hills of Cheshire's Peak District towards Bollington and the elongated Kerridge Hill. White Nancy sits at the northern end of the hill; it's possible to approach from the south along the Saddle of Kerridge. Despite the swollen sun, I choose the short but sharp option from Bollington – up the very paved path laid by Mr Bullock.

↑ A wintry scene at Tegg's Nose Country Park (Toby Howard/Shutterstock)

I'm grateful for his efforts for, at the top, White Nancy – a rotund stone obelisk created in 1817 to celebrate victory at the Battle of Waterloo – gives reason to sit for a while and take in yet more of Cheshire's fine views, including the former cotton mills in Bollington, a hint at part of the county's heritage.

Cheshire is a landscape of two halves, with a marked difference. In the east – my first day's travels – are rounded hills, burbling streams and appealing villages made up of stone cottages. It's very rural and feels remote. In the west, the Plain. There's nothing ordinary about it, but the flat, open landscape makes way for wider rivers, canals and brick-built towns rich with industrial history.

I choose to explore the Plain via a trio of 'wiches', three towns that line-up north to south, each with a canal (or two) and an important history of salt production. With an overnight stay at Shrubbery Cottage CS in the village of Comberbach, I take the opportunity of its location for an early evening wander to explore the rural north of **Northwich**. From the CS, it's an easy walk along the North Cheshire Way, through extensive Marbury Country Park and along the towpath of the Trent and Mersey Canal. I pass by the ingenious Anderton Boat Lift, which allows boats to navigate both canal and river – the Weaver Navigation.

The extensive expanse of meadows, woodlands, nature parks, lakes, canals and rivers creates Northwich Community Woodlands, growing on reclaimed wasteland established by the salt and soda industries. The formal parkland avenues of trees and picnic areas surrounding Budworth Mere in Marbury Country Park contrasts with the wild meadows and woods. On my return walk to Comberbach, the child in me finds it a welcome treat to syphon off a pint of milkshake from the Milkbot at Home Farm as I pass by, the very herd of cows that supply the milk in full sight.

Northwich, as its name suggests the most northern of the 'wiches', is a waterside town of converging rivers. While there's a rather shabby looking 1960s market hall building in the centre and a more gleaming riverside glass-and-steel construction at the newly built Baron's Quay (a pleasant place to sit for a drink), there are plenty of black-and-white timber buildings for which Cheshire is notably renowned. A brief history is gleaned with visits to the Weaver Hall Museum (the town's museum, housed in a former workhouse) and the Lion Salt Works, in the suburb of Marston, on the edge of town.

Cheshire is famous for its exceptional rock salt and there were once many mines around Northwich and the surrounding area. Lion Salt Works, the last open-pan salt plant left in the UK, harks back to a hot and sweaty industry as depicted throughout the museum. The collection of brick and timber buildings beside the Trent and Mersey Canal, along with a series of flashes (lakes that swallowed up former mines as they collapsed beneath the water), offer an attractive glimpse at a not particularly appealing occupation.

↑ Shropshire Union Canal at Middlewich (CM)

My final day in Cheshire is experienced canal- and river-side, first in **Middlewich**, where the Trent and Mersey Canal and the Middlewich Branch of the Shropshire Union Canal merge.

There's not a great deal to keep a tourist in Middlewich for long, unless the day is spent walking the towpaths – by no means a bad way to spend the day, particularly along the Shropshire Union Canal, which appears the more appealing of the two. But beyond a short browse of Middlewich's High Street (taking in the Art Deco façade of the former Alhambra cinema) my preference is to spend the greater amount of time in **Nantwich**, the most southerly of the three 'wiches'. In my humble opinion, I'd left the best of the three towns until last.

There's a goodly assemblage of monochrome timber buildings, a café culture within the pedestrianised centre (including an excellent bookshop-cum-café) and an impressive parish church. There's also the three-mile Nantwich Riverside Loop, a circular walk that takes you out of town along Welsh Row, a historic street of Georgian merchants' houses, before bringing together the Shropshire Union Canal and River Weaver, which flow either side of the town.

I spend 72 hours in Cheshire. I'd happily spend many more, especially if they happen to be at my final stop of this trip, Snugburys Ice Cream. There's a selection of 30 or so flavours to be indecisive about at the farm ice-cream parlour and my eventual choice is one of the creamiest, most delicious ice creams I've ever had, made all the tastier while wandering through the wildflower meadows on the farm. Honeycomb or Cherry Blizzard? Hmmm, now there's a decision to be made.

ESSENTIALS

GETTING THERE & AROUND A537 Macclesfield; rural lanes around Sutton, Wincle, Wildboarclough, Macclesfield Forest & Langley to Tegg's Nose Country Park. Then north to Rainow & Bollington. A523 to Macclesfield; A537 to Knutsford; A556 then A559 & rural roads to Comberbach. A533 to Northwich & Middlewich; A530 & B5074 to Nantwich. (Snugburys Ice Cream is a detour, 3 miles north of Nantwich on the A51.)

Parking without height barriers: at Northwich, there's parking at Victoria Club Car Park, Weaver Hall Museum & Lion Salt Works. On-street parking available everywhere in Middlewich. At Nantwich, try Snow Hill Car Park or Lakeside Parking.

ACCOMMODATION I stayed at three charming CS (CCC members only; page xiv): Jarman Farm, Macclesfield; Brook House Farm, Middlewich; Shrubbery Cottage, Northwich.

FIND OUT MORE
Cheshire Tourist Board visitcheshire.com

18 PEAK FITNESS

PUT SPRING IN YOUR STEP & WALK YOUR WAY TO FITNESS IN THE PEAK DISTRICT

WHERE	Derbyshire Peak District
DISTANCE/TIME	70 miles/4 days
START/FINISH	Chatsworth/Upper Derwent Reservoirs

I'm on a mission. Once a keen and active sportswoman, I'm now, dare I say it, plump. While my children's athleticism continues to grow, I, as a taxi service to their sporting fixtures, am far from the peak of physical fitness.

I know walking in the Peak District is not the most original idea, but the area passed me by for many years, with no particular reason why. So, with the national park filled with skipping lambs, I set out for a few detox days and an opportunity to rejuvenate the body and spring-clean the mind.

I begin with a picturesque but leisurely three-mile wander around the Chatsworth Estate. A slight incline at the start to get leg muscles working again affords incredible views across this 1,000-acre Lancelot 'Capability' Brown parkland. With woods and hidden valleys one way, the eyes are naturally drawn to the sheer scale of Chatsworth House on the opposite side of the River Derwent, dominating the landscape, with East Moor as an imposing backdrop.

The hillside opposite is certainly one of the best places from which to view the overall layout of the Duke of Devonshire's residence, the formal gardens and mammoth fountains. Passing a herd of antlered deer, I drop down into the estate village of **Edensor**, with its dusty-blue colour scheme that attractively links every

↑ The Pennine Way at Mam Tor (Pajor Pawel/Shutterstock)

building. A cut across towards Chatsworth's main entrance brings the gigantic house to the fore, before ambling back along the riverbank to the campervan, with feet intact and lungs refreshed.

By mid-afternoon, and with a snack purchased from the multi-award-winning Chatsworth Estate Farm Shop in Pilsley, I'm ready to tackle another walk. Again, this is on the level, a riverside walk through Wye Dale and Chee Dale. This is no ordinary river valley though, with the sparkling River Wye – little more than the width of a hop, skip and jump – hemmed in by razor-sharp hillsides that touch the sky above.

The gorge, in addition to carrying the river, carries the **Monsal Trail**, which utilises a disused railway that connects Buxton with Bakewell. At eight miles long it's considered one of the prettiest off-road cycle- and footpaths in the area, with the option to walk one way and hop on the bus back.

With day one a success, I choose to pitch up by noon the following day at Hardhurst Farm, with reason. Situated in the **Hope Valley**, the sheep farm campsite is within a few hundred yards of Hope railway station, allowing me to hook up the motorhome and see the sights of Edale without having to negotiate the all-too-narrow (for a large coachbuilt) road to the village.

But first, I set off on foot to engage with the vicinity of the campsite. A circular route little more than a mile or so takes me over the railway and up a gently sloping lane to the tiny village of Aston, where I can cut back across sheep fields and over the footbridge at Hope station. Perfect timing. The walk provides the opportunity

to get to know Win Hill atop which sits Winhill Pike. This miniature volcano-like peak is a significant landmark in this part of the Peak District, and I have plenty of time to view it with admiration. 'One day, I'll climb that,' I tell myself, looking at the closely knitted contour lines of its form on the Ordnance Survey map.

My short railway journey to **Edale** feels as if I'm entering another universe as the sun explodes onto the horizon from behind a cloud, splintering rays of light across the rumpled terrain. Arriving in the remote and surreally deserted village (on this occasion at least – of a weekend, the masses descend), I'm greeted by a sheep and her lamb hogging the road; upon my approach they trot nonchalantly through the lychgate of the tiny church as if to pray for redemption due to breaking away from the fold.

My redemption from too little exercise in recent years continues as I take my first steps on the Pennine Way, one of Britain's most popular long-distance National Trails. It begins – or ends – in Edale, with a smooth well-worn flagstone path that leads the walker into the distance like a lure, coaxing even the weakest walker to follow. And the scenes, with a heavenly panorama as the Vale of Edale opens before you, prevent any cry of aching muscles when, latterly, climbing Jacob's Ladder.

In truth, the start of the Pennine Way is not taxing. I only cover the first few miles to reach Kinder Scout and it really is one of those items to put on a 'must do before you die' list.

Back at the station, with a moment to sit entranced on the platform while the sun gently touches my face, I switch my mobile to silent to relish the landscape without interruption, other than the calling of a lamb or the swish of a bird on the wing. For those who regularly commute this line and are accustomed to the outlook from their railway seat, ears plugged into a device, forgive my enthusiasm, for I have not seen such beauty from a railway carriage for a long time! Such moments provide gratification for being alive.

Avoiding the temptation of the many tearooms and eateries in the ever-popular village of **Castleton**, I find myself on another mission by morning. Like a giant landslip, the 1-in-5 gradient of Winnats Pass is a mere nothing to my lungs now as I sidestep the entrance to Peak Cavern. The giant, gaping hole is affectionately known as The Devil's Arse, so why on earth would I wish to enter such a place on a trip like this? Heaven knows I didn't need to be reminded of such things!

Instead, I make a beeline for **Mam Tor**, its craggy northern slopes introduced to me across the Vale of Edale on the previous afternoon. Mam Tor – or the Mother Hill – seems apt and I'm eager to witness the view from the top. Once an Iron Age hillfort (the earthworks are visible from Edale), Mam Tor is not for those whose hair has just been styled in an expensive salon; Mam Tor will do that for you, but not necessarily in desirable fashion. At 1,696ft above sea level,

↑ Road through the Peak District (Daniel_Kay/Shutterstock) ← Chee Dale (Andy J Billington/Shutterstock)

SOUVENIR

Derbyshire Oatcakes are the perfect teatime snack after a long walk in the Peak District. Completely different from Scottish oatcake biscuits, these are best described as a cross between a savoury pancake and a large, very flat, pikelet. They're made from oatmeal and have a delicate flavour that's enhanced with a smear of salted butter. Serve warm, with jam to make a sweet treat, or as a basis for savoury breakfast and teatime snacks.

You'll find them in shops and bakeries throughout The Peak District, including the Chatsworth Estate Farm Shop.

the hill gives inactive legs a very good workout. Incredible scenes appear, once again, along the length of Edale and the skyline hilltops of neighbouring Hollins Cross and Lose Hill.

Now feeling lighter in step – or giddy with wonder at the spectacle before me – I descend Mam Tor, cross the road, and take a leap on to **Rushup Edge**. This is not a hill to rush up; the long ridge creates quite a climb to reach its highest point – higher than Mam Tor. But the multi-directional views – whether north across Edale and on to the Kinder Massif, or south towards Wye Dale from whence I'd come – are something to marvel at, if you can stand up in the wind long enough to appreciate them. Paragliders leap off Rushup Edge; little wonder with the lift achieved.

With hair restyled, I feel ready to try out another part of the Peak District, travelling northwest to the edge of the national park, south of Glossop. Finding a lay-by with direct access onto High Peak, I venture onto Chunal Moor, the first of many moors that make up this mammoth area. My aim is to reach the trig point at Harry Hut, not as high as I'd already 'climbed' but this is different ground. The massif is indeed too massive; the burnt heather and scrub at this moment appears inhospitable and uninviting. I feel vulnerable – birds with a call I've not heard before cackle as if mocking my every footstep.

I thought I might see a grouse. Names on the OS map suggest so, but the only one I've seen so far adorns the sign of the neighbouring forlorn-looking (and long-time closed) Grouse Inn. Then, just as I climb the giant-sized steps up and over the wall, returning to the 'van, there appears a copper-bronze flash in duo. And then they're gone, a part of the bronzed crisp and brittle heather topping, and I know not whether, like an oasis in the desert, too much fresh air has gone to my head.

Climbing back into the national park over Snake Pass, my final walking place is to be the Upper Derwent Valley. Like a giant finger prodding its way into the upper moorlands of the Peak District, the valley comprises three reservoirs, which between them hold ten billion litres of water. Ladybower is the first approached by road. With a hard-surfaced walkway alongside and across the dam, it's accessible countryside for wheelchairs and pushchairs, overlooking the Woodlands Valley and, once again, Winhill Pike.

I, though, am moving 'inland', up the valley to the Upper Derwent Reservoir. The water is treacle black immediately behind the dam walls, its towers looming like medieval fortresses along a drawbridge. The weather is not great; mist hangs over the tops of the moors and, as I wander along the shore, the water appears like a mysterious, opaque glass that swallows up villages – a strange, almost eerily serene presence. I had not intended to walk for long. But the smell of the pines alongside the 'lake' (reservoir sounds far too technical a word for somewhere with such unnatural beauty), its character and the company I keep draws me further, and further, along its banks.

My company is purely natural: soft, lime green mosses and the odd crunch of a pine cone beneath my feet; birdsong and the echo of a woodpecker hacking at a tree trunk, which resonates across the lake as if sending ripples over the water; three barnacle geese that tear at the grass and who grow less curious the more time I spend with them (we walk together); and the sound of a shepherd calling from a distant hillside.

Looking up from the thick pile of moss, I notice a ewe peering inquisitively at me from behind a tree. She stares me out but, as I move sideways, there curled in the nook of two tree roots is a pair of lambs. I had just missed the birth but have the privilege of watching them take their first tentative, wobbly steps. 'Well done,' I say, and leave the new family to their first precious moments together.

↑ Upper Derwent Reservoir (JuliusKielaitis/Shutterstock)

ESSENTIALS

GETTING THERE & AROUND
B6012 Chatsworth to Pilsley (for farm shop) then A619/A6 west towards Buxton for Monsal Trail & Staden Grange. A6 north/A623 to Sparrowpit, then rural road to Hope via Winnats Pass (1:5). Reverse route to Mam Tor then rural roads west to Chapel-en-le-Frith; A624 to Hayfield & Chunal Moor. A624 north to Glossop & A57 Snake Pass then rural road to Fairholmes (visitor centre).

Parking without height barriers: I had no problems either parking or driving a large coachbuilt motorhome within the area. There are plenty of parking areas to pull off-road close to Mam Tor & Rushup Edge, plus lots of car parks (with room for motorhomes) around the Chatsworth Estate. For my walk here, I parked at Calton Lees Car Park, while for my walk along Wyedale & Cheedale I parked at the pay & display Wyedale Car Park, just off the A6. The national park operates 48 parking areas, which are suitable for medium-sized motorhomes.

↑ Ladybower Reservoir (Paul K Martin/Shutterstock)

The road to the Upper Derwent reservoirs is well maintained and wide enough for 'vans. For Ladybower Reservoir, it's possible to park roadside on the eastern edge nr Heatherdene. However, for the Upper Derwent & Howden reservoirs, park at Fairholmes; I don't recommend travelling in a vehicle beyond the dam walls for the Derwent Reservoir as the road then narrows; beyond Fairholmes, the road is closed to motor vehicles at weekends & bank holidays from Easter to Oct. For walking, I used the OS *Explorer* **maps** *OL1* & *OL24*.

ACCOMMODATION
I stayed at: Staden Grange, Buxton; Hardhurst Farm Caravan & Camping Site, Hope; Hayfield CCC Site, Hayfield.

FIND OUT MORE
Visit Peak District
⌖ visitpeakdistrict.com

Peak District National Park
⌖ peakdistrict.gov.uk

19 FLYING HIGH

80 YEARS ON FROM THE DAMBUSTERS RAID, DISCOVER THE AVIATION HERITAGE OF NORTH LINCOLNSHIRE

WHERE	Lincolnshire
DISTANCE/TIME	112 miles/4 days
START/FINISH	Cranwell/Lincoln

'That's not Barnes Wallis,' I ponder as I silently hum the theme to *The Dambusters*. I am, of course, looking at a photograph of the real Barnes Wallis during a visit to RAF Coningsby in Lincolnshire and, like many, much of my historical knowledge of the Dams Raid comes from watching Sir Michael Redgrave portray the bouncing bomb inventor in the 1955 black-and-white movie.

With May 2023 being the 80th anniversary of the Dams Raid by 617 Squadron (the 'Dambusters'), I feel it appropriate to sort fact from fiction and learn something more of Bomber Command and the part they played in World War II. Hence, my son Dominic and I approach Lincolnshire, the county of aviation, with excitement.

It seems appropriate to start at the beginning – **RAF Cranwell**, where the Royal Air Force was formed in 1918 and the site of the Royal Air Force College, which opened in 1920 as the first military air academy in the world. Today, it still remains the base where many personnel begin their initial flight training with the RAF. We begin at the Heritage Centre, a mile or so from the airfield, but with views across the base.

Though not directly linked to 617 Squadron, Cranwell has a significant history of its own, with Sir Frank Whittle, the inventor of the jet engine, being one of its most noteworthy pupils. Whittle's developments, which changed the entire nature of aircraft design and the way we fly today, began as his college thesis. This led to the airfield being used for several record-breaking flights including the 1941 maiden flight of Britain's first jet aircraft, the Gloster E.28/39, followed in 1943 by the Meteor, Britain's first operational jet fighter.

While I'm engrossed in the history, Dominic begins his own flight in a Jet Provost (used as a jet training aircraft until the 1990s) simulator and educates himself about the aerodynamics of propeller design. Riveted by what we had learned within the first hour of our trip, I feel compelled to discover more.

It's possible to drive right through the airbase at Cranwell, as we did, Dominic eagerly watching uniforms going about their daily business and craning his neck skywards to the sound of engines while I appreciated the architecture of the striking College Hall, a building inspired by Sir Christopher Wren.

Our next stop was going to be RAF Digby, which houses the Lima Sector Operations Room, where many of the orders and plotting of movements by both enemy and British wartime aircraft took place. Unfortunately, the room is only open on Sunday mornings, so we venture on, along the Lincoln Edge escarpment and through the picturesque limestone villages of Navenby and Boothby Graffoe,

← The Red Arrows are based in Lincolnshire (Svitlana El/Shutterstock)

to **RAF Waddington**. Prior permission is required to visit the heritage centre on the active airbase, so we head to the specific Aircraft Viewing Enclosure on the A15. It's right at the end of the runway, with superb views of aircraft manoeuvres and, when in situ, the iconic-shaped static Vulcan bomber – active from RAF Waddington during the Falklands War –which is currently being restored. There's a café to top up with a bacon butty at the viewing enclosure, too. As the new home for the RAF Red Arrows, there's a good chance of seeing this extraordinary and well-loved aerobatic display team in training; we chance upon witnessing new recruits practising take-offs, circuits and landings.

We progress to the village of **Tattershall** to visit the National Trust castle. While the building lives up to its title as 'the finest medieval brick-built castle in England', we're visiting for ulterior motives. Six floors high and with open battlements, the skyline view is impressive, not just of the neighbouring Collegiate Church and Lincolnshire countryside, but also of **RAF Coningsby**, home of Typhoon fighter jets. As we climb the stairs, the roar of the jets echoes through the 15th-century brickwork, the juxtaposition of medieval castle as both historic and modern lookout post.

It's in the town of **Woodhall Spa**, our overnight stop, that we begin to pick up traces of Dambuster sites. The 617 Squadron, which was formed in 1943 specifically for the Dams Raid, was first based at RAF Scampton, three miles north of Lincoln. After the initial raid, the squadron moved to RAF Coningsby and then RAF Woodhall Spa.

Naturally, the town played an important part in the lives of the servicemen and the imposing Petwood House Hotel was used as the Officers' Mess for the squadron. A large memorial to all the airmen involved in the Dams Raid commands a central position at the town-centre crossroads.

A Georgian spa town, Woodhall Spa continues to provide a welcoming retreat, its parade of shops and eateries, and town centre woodland walks, offering something different from the infusion of aviation fact-finding.

The following morning, we drive to **RAF East Kirkby**, no longer an active airbase but home to the Lincolnshire Aviation Heritage Centre. Here, two brothers, Fred and Harold Panton, lovingly created a living memorial to their brother, lost during raids in Germany, and all 55,500 aircrew of Bomber Command who lost their lives during World War II.

The centre is very educational, with exhibitions on the Home Front and an Escape Museum, highlighting the work of the Resistance, in addition to authentic displays of briefing rooms, billet huts and the original control tower. The displays are also incredibly moving, showing last letters home, notifications of missing loved ones and reports of extreme bravery, as well as the silence-inducing mangled metal of once sleek and graceful aircraft. Inside the main hangar is an original

↑ Petwood House, Woodhall Spa (Avalon Licensing Ltd/SuperStock) → Memorial at International Bomber Command Centre (Jason Wells/Shutterstock)

Barnes Wallis bouncing bomb (otherwise known as an 'Upkeep') and the story of the Dambusters.

The main draw at East Kirkby though is the beautifully restored *Just Jane* Avro Lancaster bomber, which greets our arrival. Though not certificated airworthy, the magnificent – even *more* magnificent for the proximity you get to this 'gentle' beast – aircraft is licensed to taxi along the runways, and on certain days carries passengers to experience the cramped conditions endured by the crew. We deliberately arrive on such a day and as each of the four Rolls-Royce Merlin engines fires up within feet of our trembling bodies, the thumping reverberates through our bellies. Emotionally charged, I am not the only one to be seen wiping away a tear.

Returning to Coningsby after lunch in the wartime NAAFI at East Kirkby, we join a guided tour of the hangars at the Battle of Britain Memorial Flight Visitor Centre. The Avro Lancaster in formation with its Hurricane and Spitfire companions is perhaps one of the most iconic sights in the skies on big commemorative and celebratory occasions.

The squadron is based at RAF Coningsby and tours of the hangar are a must. Our tour guide, Clive Rowley MBE RAF (Retired), overawes Dominic. A fighter pilot flying fast jets with the RAF for more than 36 years, Clive culminated his career flying Spitfires for the Battle of Britain Memorial Flight as the Commanding Officer. We could not ask for a more experienced guide! His talk on each of the aircraft – six Spitfires, two Hurricanes, one of only two Lancasters left flying in the world, two Chipmunks and a Dakota – provides insight into some of the personal lives of their aircrew that flew them; their stories are inspiring.

Returning to our pitch at Woodhall Spa that night, feeling humbler than we had when we left that morning, a walk through the woods of Moor Farm Nature Reserve surrounding the campsite gives us an opportunity for quiet reflection on the heritage that we've seen and the stories we've heard. With stealth-like clusters of clouds replacing the roar of the practising Typhoons as the evening draws in over the woods, silence is given new meaning.

Next morning, we drive past the entrance to the former **RAF Scampton**, the airbase with most significance to the Dambusters. It closed in 2022, but it's still possible to see the listed 1936 buildings used during World War II, which housed the office of Wing Commander Guy Gibson, commanding officer of 617 Squadron. Also here is the grave of his legendary black labrador – a mascot for 617 Squadron, tragically killed the night before the Dams Raid and then buried as it was being carried out. Sorting fact from fiction, it was from RAF Scampton that 617 Squadron departed for the raid, and to which sadly not all returned. The base was also used as one of the locations for the iconic film.

A check of the road atlas will see that there's a bulge in the road beside RAF Scampton. The Roman-straight A15 (Ermine Street) had to be redirected to

↑ *Just Jane* Avro Lancaster Bomber at Lincolnshire Aviation Heritage Centre (Kev Gregory/Shutterstock)
→ Battle of Britain Memorial Flight Visitor Centre (CM)

extend the runway for Vulcan bombers, which were also one-time residents of the base during the Cold War.

With the airfield sitting on top of the Lincoln Cliff, at the foot of the escarpment is the tiny village of **Scampton**, which we visit to see the memorabilia in the Dambusters Inn and the tiny churchyard, where the graves of Commonwealth and German aircrew rest side by side. There is a heritage board at the church outlining the importance of RAF Scampton to aviation history.

It's only appropriate that our tour of Lincolnshire's aviation sites should culminate in a visit to **Lincoln**. A city of two halves, with a very steep hill to climb in between, it is where Bomber Command would let off steam at the Saracen's Head pub near Stonebow (a small plaque marks the spot).

On a hill overlooking the city is the International Bomber Command Centre. The memorial site and exhibition provide recognition of, and highlight, the global co-operation of personnel from more than 60 nations that came to join the RAF as volunteers in Bomber Command during World War II. It's free to wander around the memorial site, with guided tours available, though a visit to the exhibition offers insight into Bomber Command's role plus the contrasting opinions of war.

High on the hill opposite stands Lincoln Cathedral. It became a spiritual guiding beacon for airmen returning after long night raids, with many talking of the shimmering stained glass windows welcoming them home.

ESSENTIALS

GETTING THERE & AROUND Cranwell Aviation Heritage Museum is just off the A17, west of Sleaford. North on Rauceby Ln, B1429 west then A17/A607 north/ B1178 east/A15 north to RAF Waddington Aircraft Viewing Enclosure (WAVE). A15 south/B1202 to Metheringham/B1189 south/A153 to Tattershall. B1192 to Woodhall Spa. Rural road to Kirkby-on-Bain/A153 south/A155 east to Lincolnshire Aviation Heritage Centre at East Kirkby. A155 west/A153 south to Coningsby for Battle of Britain Memorial Flight Visitor Centre. A153 east/Wharfe Ln north/Kirkby Ln west/Wellsyke Ln north to Woodhall Spa CCC Site. Rural lanes north to Bucknall/B1190 to Bardney/B1202 north then rural lanes northwest to RAF Scampton via Langworth, Scothern & Welton. A15 south/A1500 west/B1398 north to Scampton. A15 south/B1188 to International Bomber Command Centre. B1188 north/A4134 southwest/B1378 northwest to Hartsholme Country Park.

Parking without height barriers: all the airfields & other sites that we visited have easy parking. The entrance to the car park at Tattershall Castle is narrow with a tight bend; visitors with coachbuilt motorhomes may prefer to park in the village. If not staying overnight in Lincoln, there's the Lawn Car Park on Union Rd; otherwise see opposite.

We visit the Airmen's Chapel within the cathedral, and to pay our respects to the Bomber Command memorial there. In our ears is the sound of the cathedral's organ being retuned. As we leave the chapel, a deep, gong-like note tolls.

ACCOMMODATION We stayed at: Woodhall Spa CCC Site, Woodhall Spa; Hartsholme Country Park Campsite, Lincoln (buses run from the park entrance to the city centre).

FIND OUT MORE

Aviation Heritage Lincolnshire
⬦ aviationheritagelincolnshire.com
**International Bomber Command
Centre** ⬦ internationalbcc.co.uk

**Lincolnshire Aviation Heritage
Centre** East Kirkby Airfield
⬦ lincsaviation.co.uk
Visit Lincolnshire ⬦ visitlincolnshire.com
Visit Lincoln ⬦ visitlincoln.com

TOP TIP: RAF SCAMPTON Such is the historical importance of RAF Scampton that, while it closed from operational use in 2022, the heritage of the site is being put front and centre of any redevelopment. At the time of writing there is no museum or visitor centre on-site, but various proposals are under consideration – so do check the tourist board websites before you come to the area to add this to your itinerary if possible.

↑ Lincoln Cathedral from Steep Hill (Frank Fell/Robert Harding Picture Library/SuperStock)

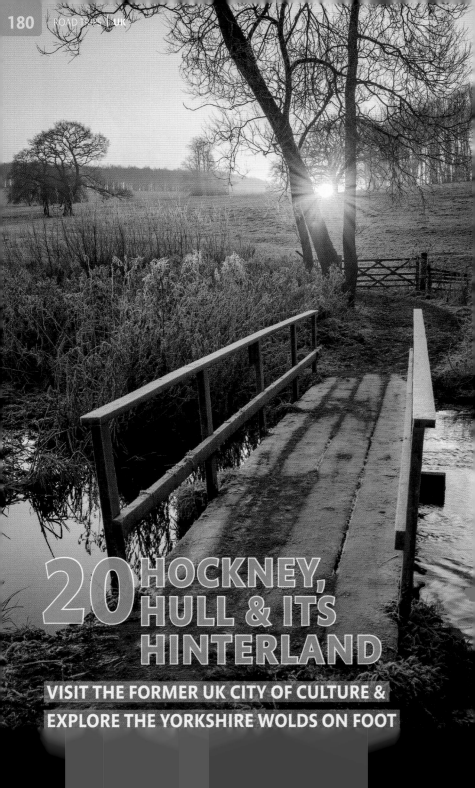

20 HOCKNEY, HULL & ITS HINTERLAND

VISIT THE FORMER UK CITY OF CULTURE & EXPLORE THE YORKSHIRE WOLDS ON FOOT

WHERE	East Yorkshire
DISTANCE/TIME	110 miles/4 days
START/FINISH	Wintringham/Kingston-upon-Hull

Climbing away from the deserted medieval village of Wharram Percy along a track trodden over centuries, I have to watch my step. Swallows rest on the dusty ground around my feet and every few yards a plume of marbled white butterflies lifts into the air. An anomalous patch of poppies stains the ripening barley field beside me, and the piecemeal collage of corn yellow and lime green fields beyond seems all the more animated against a purple sky. Turning around at the top of the rise, into view come the North York Moors, the vales of York and Pickering, the Howardian Hills and, in the distance, a thin line of dales. It's as if the whole of Yorkshire appears before me.

The Yorkshire Wolds are not so high profile as their county cousins, the North York Moors and the Yorkshire Dales, which attract the greater number of visitors. It makes the Wolds even more special; a hidden, forgotten corner of Yorkshire tucked between the bright coastal lights of Scarborough and Bridlington to the east, and the city of York to the west. As a gentle, undulating landscape, the Wolds are also perfect for easy-going walks.

One of 15 National Trails within England, the 79-mile Yorkshire Wolds Way helps to show off the very best of the Wolds' incredible chalk landscape, from the hilltops with huge skies and big vistas to the minutiae of the remarkable glacial valleys. Long-distance linear walking routes, though, are often difficult to accomplish with a motorhome. Fortunately, a series of short, mainly circular walking trails has been created utilising the Yorkshire Wolds Way.

Before I pull on my walking boots, my visit to the area begins with a stroll through the perfumed fields of Woldie's Lavender & Nature Farm at **Wintringham**. More than 60 types of lavender are grown at this small farm, the essential oils from which are extracted in the country's only wood-fired distillery on site.

Visually striking, the lavender fields and accompanying wildflower meadows are a haven for wildlife and, with a giant naturally planted Games Maze, are perfect for young families to enjoy.

Woldie's is conveniently situated within half a mile of Wolds Way Caravan & Camping, the location for the start of my first walk on Knapton Wold. In an area renowned for distant vistas, the walk, a little over two miles in length, provides some of the most extensive views in the Wolds, with a 180° panorama over the Vale of York, the North York Moors and across to the Yorkshire coast.

En route, I come across *Enclosure Rites*, one of several art installations along the Yorkshire Wolds Way. The unnerving, carved faceless figures of the artwork refer to mysterious chalk figures found discarded in Iron Age settlements in the area.

← Londesborough Park (lortek/Shutterstock)

The minor roads throughout the Wolds are quiet and relaxing to drive; from Settrington Brow, another viewpoint with a short walk, I make my way south to Duggleby and Wharram-le-Street, for a wander to view an age-old village. **Wharram Percy** is the most famous and intensively studied example of a deserted medieval village in England. Between 1950 and 1990, large parts of the former settlement were excavated to reveal, alongside documentary evidence, a bustling village that flourished between the 12th and 14th centuries.

The ruins of the medieval church of St Martin along with an 18th-century farm cottage are all that remain standing, tucked away in a secluded valley, though you can see evidence of the traditional medieval longhouses and recognisable streets with the aid of information panels. Regardless, located along the Yorkshire Wolds Way, the valley is a haven of peace.

Continuing south, I drive the first of several valleys to **Thixendale**, a very attractive village of tender pink brick, tucked deep along a former glacier. Travelling along the bed of these steep-sided valleys, one can easily see the glacial formation, created in the last Ice Age. Today the chalk grassland slopes and valley floors are suntraps, brimming with a botanist's collection of wildflowers, stunted hawthorn bushes, butterflies and birds. It's an incomparable landscape, with one dry valley after another interlocking like knuckles.

On Sundays, the community of Thixendale serves Village Hall Teas (with the proceeds going to the upkeep of the building). The meeting place is a popular stop-off for walkers and cyclists, and my tea quenches a thirst after my morning walks. I continue northwest along the elongated valley, where hundreds of butterflies suck the nectar from field scabious and musk thistles, before reaching the hilltop road that runs from Malton to Pocklington. Heading south on a signposted Scenic Drive to **Huggate**, the vistas over the red rooftops of Uncleby and the crumpled hillside of Garrowby Hill, the highest point on the Wolds (and the summit of Bishop Wilton Wold), appear gin-clear and vast.

It's little wonder that the Yorkshire-born artist David Hockney needed giant canvases to create his *Bigger Picture* series of paintings, painted from memory and in the open air around the Yorkshire Wolds during the 1990s. Huggate, my next stop, was where Hockney worked as a schoolboy and it's in the surrounding fields that he created his largest ever painting, *Bigger Trees near Warter*, put together from 50 canvases.

Everything seems big in the Yorkshire Wolds and my lunch at The Wolds Inn in Huggate is no different! A Sunday roast is most definitely a feast to suit a longer walk – though it takes me by surprise when asked by the waitress if I want one, two or three Yorkshire puddings with my beef!

I need just the one to keep me going on my afternoon walk, an easy-going five-mile trek that begins beside the pub and joins the Yorkshire Wolds Way for

↑ Church at the abandoned village of Wharram Percy (Roger Driscoll/Shutterstock) → One of the many glacial valleys in the Wolds (AlmacUK/Shutterstock)

views in all directions. Heat haze rises over the barley fields but beyond the wispy golden ears, I can make out the Humber Bridge 25 miles hence.

The shortest walk on my visit to the Yorkshire Wolds is, arguably, the prettiest: a there-and back saunter through **Londesborough Park**. Dragonflies and damselflies accompany my sun-drenched footsteps through the open parkland to the estate lakes where a family of swans keep watch.

On my return, I notice four urns at the entrance to the abandoned walled garden within the park. Twelve other identical urns, which once stood here, now form part of the decoration in The Slopes, a Georgian landscaped pleasure garden created by the 6th Duke and Duchess of Devonshire in Buxton, Derbyshire. The family, owners of the celebrated Chatsworth House, also in Derbyshire, once owned Londesborough Park. They demolished the little-used Hall at Londesborough in 1818 and took works of art and furnishings to decorate Chatsworth.

At **Market Weighton**, I follow the three-mile Hudson Way Rail Trail, which uses the former track between Market Weighton and Beverley. It's named after York-born George Hudson, 'The Railway King', who created the line (and once owned Londesborough Park). But, of all the walks, it's the least appealing and I continue to Beverley by road.

By contrast, **Beverley** appeals as one of the loveliest towns in England. The approach along Westwood, where cows graze the common beside the renowned Beverley Racecourse, provides magnificent views of both Beverley Minster and the medieval St Mary's Church. It's a wonderful introduction to the town.

The focal point of Beverley is the Minster, an architectural masterpiece. Aside from the magnificent interior, one of the best places from which to view it is Beverley's Beck, a historic industrial waterway that leads to the River Hull.

And it's from Beverley that I make my way to **Kingston-upon-Hull**. As the UK City of Culture in 2017, Hull has seen significant investment in recent years and the cultural festival highlighted the city as a major visitor attraction. Hull is chock full of cultural museums and attractions, and most are free of charge to enter.

I begin with a walk through the Land of Green Ginger, an ancient narrow lane within the heart of Hull's Old Town area and which, allegedly, is home to the world's smallest window, placed within the door of The George Hotel. I explore Hull's seafaring history at the Maritime Museum, housed in the grand former headquarters of the Hull Dock Company.

I view the remarkable and colourful ceiling in Hull Minster, admire the numerous architectural elements on Trinity House, City Hall and the immense Guildhall – and eye up the impressive collection of artworks in the Ferens Art

Gallery, home to numerous masterpieces by European Old Masters in addition to contemporary British artists.

I stroll around the marina and vibrant old Fruit Market that's taking a new lease of life with quirky cafés and restaurants in disused warehouses, and take a turn on the deck of the Spurn Lightship, which once helped ships navigate the notorious River Humber.

But by far the most thought-provoking of Hull's cultural attractions is the Wilberforce Museum. Housed in the birthplace of William Wilberforce, the 18th-century campaigner for the abolition of the slave trade, there are exhibitions about his life, the history of slavery and his abolition campaign, and a contemporary look at modern slavery and human rights.

Crossing the Humber Bridge – one of the longest single-span suspension bridges in the world – at the end of my visit to Hull and East Yorkshire, I leave behind an extraordinary landscape with remnants from a prehistoric past and a city regenerating itself for the future. I take with me a desire to return and visit both town and country again.

ESSENTIALS

GETTING THERE & AROUND
Woldie's Lavender (Wintringham) is 1 mile south of the A64 between York & Scarborough. Rural lane to Wolds Way Caravan & Camping. A64 west/rural lane south to Settrington. Rural lane south & east to Duggleby/Wharram-le-Street. Rural lanes south to Thixendale. Rural lane southwest then Roman Rd south (south of Uncleby)/A166 east/rural lane southeast to Huggate. Rural lanes south to Londesborough. Rural lane southwest/A1079 northwest then rural lane to Everingham (for campsite). A1079 to Market Weighton/Beverley. A164 south/A63 east to Hull (Priory Park & Ride). Note: Humber Bridge (A15) has a toll.

Parking without height barriers: each of the Easy Access Walks utilising the Yorkshire Wolds Way (see below) provides details of parking, with no problems for motorhomes. There's a small free car park for Wharram Percy Medieval Village, though coachbuilt motorhomes may have difficulty at weekends when walks from here are popular. The Wolds Inn at Huggate has a large car park with space for motorhomes. To visit Hull, I used the Priory Park & Ride near Hessle.

ACCOMMODATION
I stayed at: Wolds Way Caravan & Camping, West Knapton; Common Farm CL, Everingham (CAMC members only; page xiv); Willow Lane Caravan Site, Beverley (CCC members only; page xiv).

FIND OUT MORE
Visit Hull and East Yorkshire
⌖ visithullandeastyorkshire.com

Yorkshire Wolds National Trail
⌖ nationaltrail.co.uk/yorkshire-wolds-way

21 ESCAPADES IN ESKDALE

A SEARCH FOR PEACE & QUIET IN A MICROCOSM OF THE NORTH YORK MOORS NATIONAL PARK

WHERE	North Yorkshire
DISTANCE/TIME	51 miles/3 days
START/FINISH	Whitby/Westerdale

I could be escaping. For that's really what I'm doing, running away from the rigours of daily life for a few brief moments of quiet and solitude in a dead-end valley, picking up memories of panoramas, silent lanes and unassuming villages along the way. I like being alone, sometimes.

Eskdale is an anomaly in the North York Moors National Park. While most of the rivers and dales within the park run north to south, the River Esk, in the north of the park, winds its way west to east. Sprouting from the Cleveland Hills the river, initially flowing northwards, runs along the hemmed-in Westerdale, then turns a corner at the mouth of the valley to flow east through – naturally – Eskdale. Its journey ends amid the affably clustered houses of Whitby, where the

↑ Whitby, where the River Esk enters the North Sea (allouphoto/Shutterstock)

river seeps steadily into the North Sea, taking with it boats of fishermen eager to put a fish supper on the plates of Whitby's innumerable restaurants.

And that's where I begin my tour. In a fish and chip restaurant. **Whitby** can be alluded to as the king of fish and chips, with more than 20 such restaurants in the coastal town, including The Quayside, once crowned Fish and Chip Shop of the Year at the National Fish and Chip Awards. Very tasty they are too, wrapped in paper zinging with vinegar and eaten along the quayside of the Esk. Here I watch the sunlight dance over Whitby's red rooftops as the white lacy latticework of the Swing Bridge lets little boats come and go along the river. It's the last bridge across the Esk before it flows out to sea. I cross many more on my tour upriver.

By morning I'm back in Whitby, at the train station for a trip on a North York Moors Railway heritage train. The railway, which runs from Whitby to Pickering on the southern edge of the North York Moors National Park, is considered one of the most pleasurable steam train routes in Britain. For the first part of

its journey, it utilises the Esk Valley Line – a useful way to get about in Eskdale without the campervan.

Leaving Whitby on my well-sprung seat feels special. People throng the platform to wave goodbye to the string of wooden carriages with regal blue-and-red plush furnishings. Silver luggage racks – the kind you pay a fortune for in retro interior design shops – hang from the carriage walls and there's a vintage smell associated with 'real' travel.

Immediately we begin to shuffle alongside the tidal Esk, the river slightly sludgy without much water. Through pretty Ruswarp, where rowing boats ply the river, plumes of steam shroud the countryside; before long, the Esk has lost its girth.

The train journey crosses the Esk nine times between Whitby and Grosmont, a good introduction to the river. At one moment, the train stops directly above it – an opportunity to enjoy the horizon vista through the steamy wisps rather than stare directly at the watery ribbon a considerable depth below!

At each station, long lenses appear on the platform eager to snap that perfect picture of the slender machine passing by. Through the long tunnel at Grosmont, perfect darkness descends. I realise it's important to sit back, embrace Slow and not expect slick Japanese Bullet scheduling. There's time enough to soak up the vintage atmosphere of the flower-festooned railway stations advertising ancient boxes of Colman's mustard.

Just as heather begins to show its vibrant side on the moors above, my destination comes into view. **Newtondale Halt** is a request stop, seemingly in the middle of nowhere, except for the edge of the North Riding Forest Park. The nearest road is more than a mile away so it's only the occasional walker that steps on and off the train here.

With the steam plumes disappearing around the corner, I have what feels like the whole of the national park to myself. Complete silence envelops the dale except for the soft chatter of water and the resonance of breeze through quivering foliage. Birdsong keeps me company on my short walk in the woodland glades among foxgloves before I return to the platform. Anxious initially not to miss my return train, now I hope for it to be long overdue so I can spend more time here.

The pleasant introductions to the Esk over, I pick up the 'van to start my tour of the dale by road, with tea and cake at Beacon Farm in the tiny village of Sneaton. From the tearoom decking there are far-reaching views of Whitby's rooftops and the gothic ruins of St Mary's Abbey. These become more apparent as I wind my way along the road through Ugglebarnby and Eskdaleside. Hotchpotch fields in hues of green give fodder to patchwork cows here in what appears, during summer at least, to be a pastoral idyll of tranquillity.

At **Grosmont**, little more than the railway station and a post office, I join the merry throng of long lenses to click away at a steaming train before taking the

↑ North York Moors Railway at Goathland Station (Milosz Maslanka/Shutterstock) ← Newtondale Halt (Daniel J Rao/Shutterstock)

short walk to the engine sheds. Here railway enthusiasts tinker, turning rusty bits of metal into gleaming, fully functioning works of art to ply the train tracks. The journey continues to **Beck Hole**, in my humble opinion the prettiest village in the national park. In a bracken-entrenched den, a half-dozen rose-covered cottages sit around a tiny village green and a knobbly beck where West Beck and Eiler Beck meet to become the Murk Esk. Wooded and very steep, contorted hills lie either side.

My stay in Beck Hole is prolonged with a visit to the Birch Hall Inn, standing on the edge of the bubbling beck. Extreme quirkiness best describes this hostelry, often accoladed as one of the top pubs in Britain. There are two tiny bar rooms, with a sweet shop in between. Atmospherically dingy, the peeling retro wallpapers are held in place by aging prints and sepia photos; it is a place to be charmed. Beckswatter is the village brew but, as I'm driving, I sip my lemonade in the pub garden, accompanied by the tantalising song of Eiler Beck.

From Beck Hole it's possible to walk the Rail Ale Trail, a four-mile route along a disused part of the railway, through verdant countryside back to Grosmont. Slightly off-track from Eskdale, I continue my way to Goathland, the one-time residence of *Heartbeat* and film location for *Harry Potter and the Philosopher's Stone*.

Everyone who comes to the Moors, it seems, comes to Goathland. It's busy – by the coachload – and I join a queue of young and old descending the narrow path to reach Mallyan Spout, a waterfall on West Beck. There's a 142yd rock scramble to approach the waterfall and with ever-present people; I've seen more dramatic water features for considerably less effort earlier in my tour, at Falling Foss, near Little Beck (a short walk from the North York Moors Caravan and Motorhome Club Site at Sneaton). My recommendation is to visit Mallyan Spout in early morning, mid-week, to avoid crowds.

Returning to Eskdale, I cross the river again at **Egton Bridge**. A village to rival Beck Hole in geniality, there's a pleasing pub at either end and, in between, a set of stepping stones to cross the river. Here, again, is the possibility to see the area on foot, along the Esk Valley Walk that follows the river for its full length and beyond. I follow alongside to Carr End and Glaisdale (by road, in my case) and find arguably the prettiest stretch of the Esk as it passes beneath the historic Beggar's Bridge.

Overshadowed now by a towering viaduct, this 17th-century packhorse bridge is an endearing token of a man's love: Thomas Ferris, a poor farmer's son fell in love with the squire's daughter, who lived on the other side of the river. Refused her hand in marriage unless he made his fortune, he did just that, and built the bridge as a reminder of the countless times he'd had to wade through the Esk during their courtship. He got his girl!

↑ The moors above Egton Bridge (Anne Coatesy/Shutterstock) → Road leading to Goathland (Daniel J Rao/Alamy)

From the hilltop village of Glaisdale, I turn away from Eskdale to take a circular tour of the like-named Glaisdale, a dead-end valley that runs as an angled spur to its neighbour. With a flat, farmed floor and wincingly sharp sides, the dale is where I hear what silence sounds like. Sat at the dale's head for a mug of tea, no-one passes by and, once again, I relish the quiet moment. These roads are not suitable for large coachbuilts; indeed, for any size of campervan I recommend parking (responsibly) in the village and heading out on two wheels for a gentle cycle ride around the dale. As a circular ride, and with relatively flat roads, it's a great route for families.

At my **Lealholm** campsite that evening, the drooping sun drenches wild roses with pink sateen. The moors beckon. I set out on foot to climb Glaisdale Moor where I can view what appears to be the whole of Eskdale. The sun's light bathes the valley, illuminating its drainpipe shape and the striped fields of cut hay within.

By morning I'm on the trail of the river again as I wander around Lealholm. The village, a harmonious collection of blackened millstone houses, straddles the Esk, with a pretty pub and tearooms beside the bridge. I spend my time playfully jumping the stones of the second staddle-stone crossing I've come across in as many days, this one the more attractive of the pair.

Like the day before, I depart from Eskdale at a skew to explore conjoined twins, Great Fryup Dale and Little Fryup Dale. The two valleys, which meet at a shudderingly craggy, scarred head, are divided by a long, wooded hill simply named Heads. Both have becks that flow into the Esk. Little Fryup Dale is the more accessible of the two – again the pair are great for cycling – though the duo are at their most striking at the head.

I rejoin Eskdale at the crumbling ruins of Danby Castle. With motivating views along the eastern length of the valley, the river is crossed once more alongside the ancient Duck Bridge, a second moss-covered packhorse bridge, built in the 1300s. The route takes me to **Danby** where I visit Danby Lodge National Park Centre. In an old Georgian house, the visitor centre is a thoughtful place on the wildflower-strewn banks of the Esk. The centre also houses the 'Inspired by...' gallery, an oak post-and-beamed exhibition space for art and craft inspired by the national park.

My inspiration comes from climbing high above Danby to sit atop Beacon Hill. The views above the purple brilliance of the heathered moors and along Eskdale are remarkable. But look northeast, and the view is out across the North Sea into which the Esk flows. I'm nearing my journey's end, though. Not far from the source of the river and close to the head of Westerdale, I pull up into the tree-lined Meadowcroft CL. With little beyond except the foothills of Westerdale Moor and the trickle of Tower Beck, a tributary of the Esk, by my side, I find seclusion. I'm very glad of my momentary solitary confinement.

↑ Fryupdale (Andrew Fletcher/Shutterstock) ← Duck Bridge near Danby (Mark Bulmer/Shutterstock)

ESSENTIALS

GETTING THERE & AROUND I approached the area on the A171 Scarborough to Whitby. B1416 to Sneaton (for CAMC campsite & Beacon Farm). Rural lanes west to Ugglebarnby/Sleights; Eskdaleside to Grosmont. Fair Head Ln east to Sleights Moor. A169 south & rural lane west then south to Beck Hole. Rural lane southeast to Goathland. Cross West Beck then north to Egton Bridge. Rural lanes west to village of Glaisdale. Circular tour of Glaisdale via Glaisdale Side to Yew Grange & return via New House Farm to village (cycling recommended). Rural lane west to Lealholm (for campsite) & Houlsyke; south then east then turn south again at Wheat Bank Farm. Along Great Fryup Dale to Street; Street Ln & Nuns Green Ln to Little Fryup Dale; north along Little Fryup Dale to Danby Castle & Danby Lodge National Park Centre. Detour northeast to Beacon Hill. Danby to Westerdale (campsite).

Small campervans will have no problems with any of the roads within Eskdale, but large coachbuilts may struggle around Glaisdale (page 193) & Beck Hole (see opposite).

↑ Glaisdale (Daniel J Rao/Shutterstock)

Parking without height barriers: in Whitby, motorhomes should use the park & ride (junction of A171/B1460; open Apr–Oct) or the long-stay Marina Back Car Park (max 3.5t & fitting within 1 car parking space). Grosmont & Danby Lodge National Park Centre have good-sized car parks (motorhomes may use coach bays) with pay & display parking. The village of Beck Hole is not suitable for large coachbuilt motorhomes; park at the top of the steep hill to the east & descend on foot into the village. Goathland has a national park car park & on-street parking.

ACCOMMODATION
I stayed at: North Yorkshire Moors CAMC Site, Sneaton; Wild Slack Farm CL, Lealholm & Meadowcroft CL (CAMC members only; page xiv). Beacon Farm, Sneaton, also offers camping.

FIND OUT MORE
North York Moors National Park
⌖ northyorkmoors.org.uk

North Yorkshire Moors Railway
⌖ nymr.co.uk

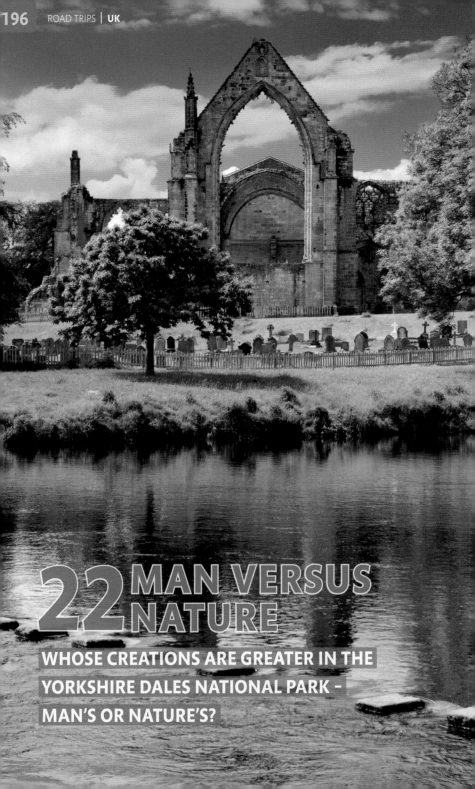

22 MAN VERSUS NATURE

WHOSE CREATIONS ARE GREATER IN THE YORKSHIRE DALES NATIONAL PARK – MAN'S OR NATURE'S?

WHERE	Yorkshire Dales National Park
DISTANCE/TIME	98 miles/6 days
START/FINISH	Bolton Abbey/Malham

Boundaries are almost always man's creation. And nearly seventy years ago man drew a boundary around an area of Yorkshire and deemed it a national park – the Yorkshire Dales National Park. It was created, in part, by two Yorkshire Quakers, Arthur Raistrick (voted 'Dalesman of the Millennium' when he died, aged 95, in 1991) and John Dower, who was Secretary for the Standing Committee on National Parks. Dower wrote a report in 1944 that set the scene for national parks in England and Wales.

Both men were passionate about the area in which they lived and were aware of the great contribution farming and local culture made to the special landscape qualities there. So, I thought I'd pitch battle: which 'attractions' within the Dales will win me over – those created by man or by nature?

With 680 square miles of national park covering twenty main dales, I know that my task must be narrowed. I begin my search at the entrance to the Dales, north of Ilkley – **Bolton Priory**. Man certainly knows a picturesque spot when he sees one. For the ruined remains (and never-finished sections) of the 12th-century Augustinian priory sit close to the River Wharfe. While the priory may have looked grandiose once, the ruins look more atmospheric against their backdrop, with the sun playing games through the open arches.

Venturing further into the national park, I reach nearby Barden Tower. The roofless ruin was built purely as a lavish 15th-century residence for a local lord. Despite the tower's imposing nature, seated between the steep wooded nursery slopes of Barden Moor and Barden Fell, it's the dale itself that grabs my attention as the rain-pitted river sidles past.

Beyond my initial brushes with the priory and tower, I begin to see man's great contribution to the Dales further north, first at **Grassington** then at Kettlewell. These two charming villages ooze community spirit. The clusters of buildings, their very being, appear to grow from the ground as if a part of nature. And everywhere, silvery walls desperately try to contain the glossy spread of child's-yellow buttercups strewn across the surrounding meadows.

Grassington sits just above the Wharfe, with the attractive Linton Falls a ten-minute walk from the national park car park. The village collection of shops, tearooms and country pubs sited around the main square makes a charming introduction to **Wharfedale**.

Kettlewell, further upstream, sits right beside the river, with a magnificent backdrop of craggy slopes either side. I climb the slopes to the north of Kettlewell, very much deemed a walker's village, for magnificent views along Wharfedale.

← Bolton Priory beside the River Wharfe (Reimar/Shutterstock)

Beyond Buckden, the road to Newbiggin is impressive enough, carving its way through Bishopdale. But I opt to continue my exploration of Upper Wharfedale and the lesser-known **Langstrothdale**. I choose well. Even within the context of a national park, the landscape of these two dales is considered extra-special. Home to many rare species of plant, the countryside is astounding. Passing through Hubberholme, little more than a quirky pub, farm and church, the Wharfe runs along the side of the churchyard. It's worth a stop. While the sacred ground is the final resting place of playwright and broadcaster J B Priestley (who considered Hubberholme to be 'the smallest, pleasantest place in the world'), the oak pews of the church are home to scuttling mice – of the wooden variety, carved by the famous Mouseman of Kilburn.

Beyond, I witness a serene and secluded wilderness – sublime beauty. Both the road and the Dales Way footpath run alongside the shallow and bubbling River Wharfe as it trips and falls over itself. Climbing up and over the fells into Sleddale, I realise I have barely drawn breath for miles before arriving in Hawes, the gateway to Wensleydale.

I skip Hawes for now, to stride along the more open 'plains' of **Wensleydale**. With a bigger and bolder character than Wharfedale, this valley seems to do everything greater than its southern neighbour – a considerably greater number of stone walls criss-cross the countryside, a bigger river (the Ure, of which the River Wharfe is a tributary), bigger villages and bigger waterfalls. Much bigger.

Making the water features of the Wharfe look like immature youngsters, the **Aysgarth Falls** show their might. I use the plural advisedly, for it's a triple flight: Upper, Middle and Lower Falls. One of the best vantage points to see the Upper Falls is the bridge above (taking care of traffic on the road), a favoured spot of painter J M W Turner. Arguably, Middle and Lower Falls are more spectacular.

Accessed by a delightful woodland walk, there's a viewing point above Middle Falls, which are made even more picturesque by the backdrop of Aysgarth Church. Turner seemed to think so anyway, for he used it as the subject for one of his paintings. My favourite, however, is Lower Falls. Via a set of stone steps fit for a giant, you can scramble down to the river's edge and cast a glance upwards at these falls as they, quite literally, fall to your feet with the volume of water appearing to float above the giant slabs of limestone. For viewing, they're at their best after a hefty rainfall; during my visit the river appears as if someone has emptied a giant jar of Marmite into the water.

Now I have a set of waterfalls to compare, I make for another. In the pretty village of **Hardraw**, well worth a visit if you wish to escape the crowds in Hawes, or if you're hiking along the Pennine Way, is The Green Dragon Inn. It's about as attractively spit and sawdust as you can get, with a centuries-old smell, aging pews, and delightfully mismatching tables beneath low-beamed ceilings and mood-

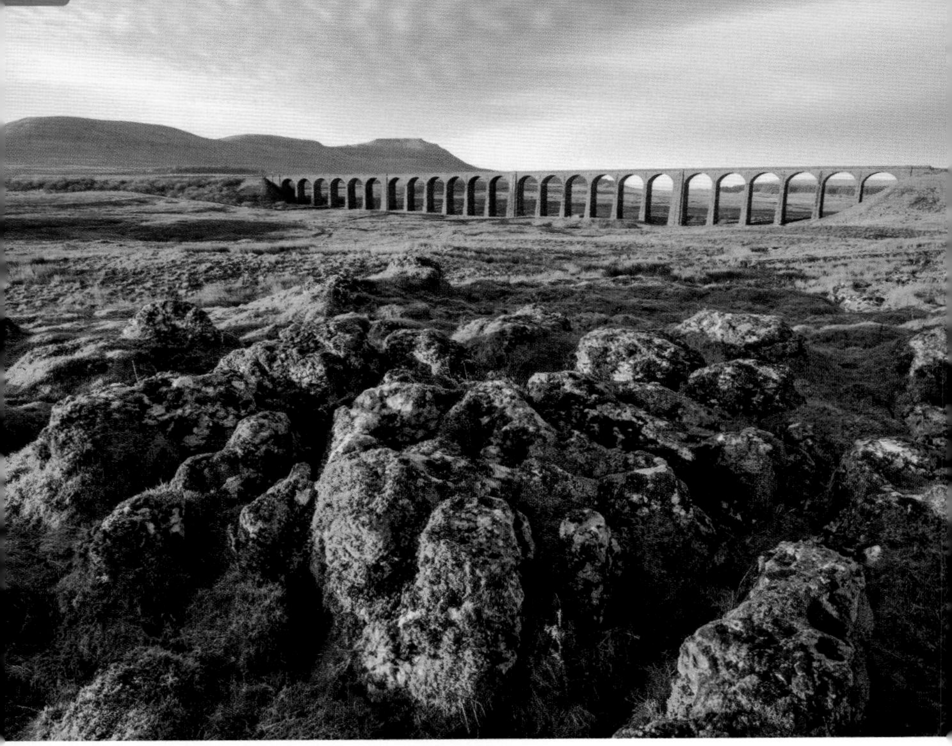

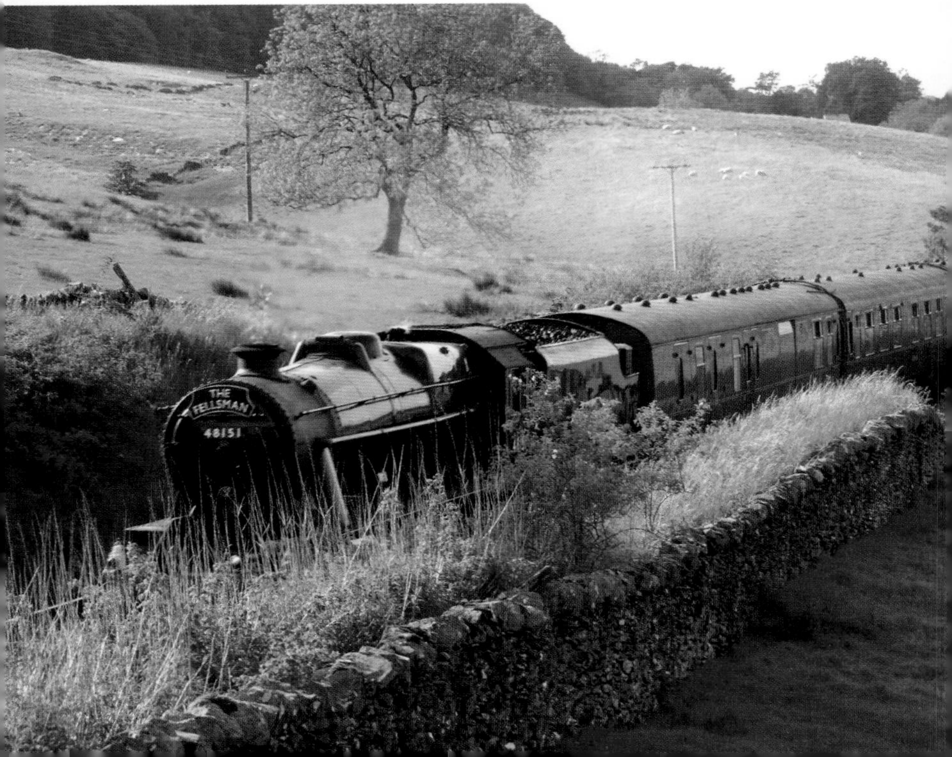
THE
FELLSMAN
48151

enhancing light that's so dim you have to adjust to the day again when you step outdoors. To reach Hardraw Force, the highest unbroken waterfall in England, it's necessary to walk through the Green Dragon (paying a nominal fee). Once out in daylight, the waterfall is like a power shower pounding into the depths of Hardraw Beck. The noise brings with it a sense of calm.

I have no time to visit the more northerly Swaledale on this occasion, but I do feel it necessary to drive along what is potentially man's finest contribution to road-building within the Dales – Buttertubs Pass. A serpentine route, it's the kind of road that was built for touring, with the vistas along the way astonishing and endearing in equal measure. It makes one respect every fold and furrow of the landscape.

Returning to Hawes, however, I am under no doubt of man's best contribution to the Dales thus far – cheese. My visit to Wensleydale Creamery, perfectly timed to coincide with lunch, involves lots of it – first watching its production in vast vats of liquid, then tasting it on toast in Calvert's Restaurant, before sampling other variations in the shop. Wensleydale and cranberries is meant to be!

On this day, man's involvement is winning the battle and it continues to do so when I approach the **Ribblehead Viaduct** southwest of Hawes. This exquisite piece of industrial beauty, carrying the Settle–Carlisle railway, gracefully curves and bends its way between the Dales' Three Peaks – Whernside, Ingleborough and Pen-y-Ghent. And here, man's winning streak ends, for now. For suddenly I have a trio of landmarks so striking as to divert the gaze from stone-built to glacial melt. Beyond the viaduct, on the road to Ingleton and under the watchful eye of Ingleborough, Twistleton Scars and Raven Scar provide the rocky liner for a U-shaped glacial valley. It's clear to see and matches in perfect symmetry the viaduct arches.

Also clear to see are the long lenses beginning to gather, pointing at the winding railway. *The Fellsman* is due to come through – in one hour. Time enough for me to reach my campsite, Cragg Hill Farm, and gain a personal grandstand view as the railway runs alongside. While the sun sinks over the western edge of Pen-y-Ghent and lonely lambs are bottle-fed by the campsite farmer, I watch as the steam train whistles past my pitch. My brain is in torment – man or nature?

With a return to the foot of Blea Moor for an early morning walk beside the viaduct and patches of limestone scar, I venture to ask another walker for some guidance on further notable landmarks. By chance he's a local man, soon off to work – at Ingleborough Caves. Perfect. Unsure whether to opt for the White Scar Caves or his place of work, I ask which are the best to see. Naturally, the defence comes for Ingleborough. Asked why, the reply is, 'You can get dropped off by coach at the entrance to one while you have to work to get to the other.'

↑ Ribblehead Viaduct (Daniel_Kay/Shutterstock) ← *The Fellsman*, seen from Cragg Hill Farm Campsite (CM)

Sure enough, as I pass the entrance to White Scar Caves, two coachloads of tourists arrive. On my arrival in the idyllic village of **Clapham**, my 1.3-mile walk to the entrance of Ingleborough Caves takes me along the Ingleborough Estate Nature Trail. Following Clapham Beck, which flows from the cave, passing through glorious woodland out into the scar-ridden valley, it doesn't exactly feel as if I have to 'work' to reach the entrance.

With hard hat supplied, it's my fellow walker John who introduces our small party of intrepid cavemen to the stalagmites and stalactites of Ingleborough Cave. The dripping underworld is surreal, one of immense architectural splendour that makes one appreciate and respect what you don't always realise is beneath your stumbling feet.

My feet, after the walk beneath the world, are on top of it as I haul myself up through the mammoth gorge of Trow Gill to reach Gaping Gill. Here, amid the bowl-shaped open fell and with the east face of Ingleborough before me, the trickling Fell Beck drops 322ft into the giant cavern of Gaping Gill. Would that I had more time to join the hardy souls that are descending beneath the earth's crust. Instead, I'm in need of rest for my final day to determine the victor.

Staying at Hurries Farm that evening where the owner David Wellock can show, from the hill above his farmhouse, the very fields that he grew up in and

↑ Malhamdale from the limestone pavement above Malham Cove (Dave Head/Shutterstock)

the very house in which he was born, I gain once again that sense of community upon which the Dales is built. Man is shaping up well in the contest.

As the dawn breaks on my final day of deliberation, I opt for a walk in **Malhamdale**. A circular trek from Malham – the embodiment of the Dales – takes you past the enchanting, fairylike Janet's Foss waterfall and up through the unforgiving jaws of Gordale Scar.

Beyond, crossing a vibrant bottle-green open landscape blemished by rocky outcrops, I reach the still, blue world of Malham Tarn. It's a glacial lake that serenely and unpretentiously lays claim to being the highest natural lake in England. Lying in a natural bowl, with a summer blue reflected in the water and the stillness of limited human life around, the tarn is a place of reflection in every sense.

My return journey on foot takes me from the edge of the tarn along the Pennine Way to the very edge of Malham Cove. There, above the undeniable artwork of Malham's limestone pavement and with a bird's-eye view of the Dales, I realise my final decision as to which is greater, man or nature, is an easy one.

ESSENTIALS

GETTING THERE & AROUND
I approached the area via A65 Ilkley to Skipton. B6160 Bolton Abbey to Kettlewell then Buckden. Rural roads along Langstrothdale to Hawes via Hubberholme. Rural roads to Hardraw, Simonstone & Buttertubs Pass. Reverse route back to Hawes; B6255 to Ribblehead Viaduct, then B6479 to Horton-in-Ribblesdale; B6255 to Ingleton then A65 to Clapham & Hellifield, then rural road to Otterburn & Malham.

I had no problems with any of the roads within the Dales; the only section that I would not recommend for coachbuilts of any size is beyond Malham village up to Malham Tarn (Malham Rakes & Cove Rd).

Parking without height barriers: The national park owns car parks at Grassington, Buckden, Hawes, Aysgarth Falls, Malham & Clapham, all accessible to motorhomes. Parking is per day. Motorhomes will have little problem parking up roadside nr the Ribblehead Viaduct. Parking at Bolton Abbey Estate is included in the entrance fee.

ACCOMMODATION
I stayed at: Wharfe Camp, Kettlewell (adults only); Hurries Farm CL, Otterburn (CAMC members only; see page xiv); Cragg Hill Farm, Horton-in-Ribblesdale; Shaw Ghyll Caravan & Camping Site, Simonstone.

FIND OUT MORE
Yorkshire Dales National Park
⊘ yorkshiredales.org.uk

23 NORTHERN HIGHLIGHTS

EXPLORE THE POWER OF THE PENNINES
ON THIS TRANS-PENNINE ROUTE

WHERE	Lancashire/West Yorkshire/South Yorkshire
DISTANCE/TIME	185 miles/6 days
START/FINISH	Clitheroe/Wentworth Castle Gardens

It's massive. Pendle Hill. A colossus of Lancashire. Wherever I travel for miles around, it follows. It's there. A titan that looms. It rises, like a sleeping giant, laid shoulder to toe, north to south, from a verdant valley of tiny pastures flecked with handsome oaks, bonsai-like against the naked hulk. I become so attached to its presence in a very short space of time that when it disappears from view I long to see it again.

And so it is that I begin a tour across the Pennines, in sight of Pendle Hill. **Clitheroe** is my starting point, a small provincial market town in the Ribble Valley, at the western foot of its dominating landmark. A climb to Clitheroe's Norman castle keep affords views of the long length of the hill, and of the town's high street, lined with a healthy number of cafés and bistros.

I spy a road that slices through Pendle Hill, the Nick of Pendle, and, after my wander of Clitheroe's streets, choose to follow it. The road, which leads to

↑ Pendle Hill (Kevin Eaves/Shutterstock)

Sabden – a small village that was once known for its calico printing mills – draws a curving ascent of Pendle's western face. At the 994ft-high brow, it's not only the 180° views to the west, south and east that inspire, but the immense bulk of Pendle Hill that rises infinitely to the north.

A blustery wind blows. Sheep straddle the stony crags of the Nick and shelter beneath knolls. Beyond, my route passes along the eastern face of Pendle Hill to Barley, a handsome village, and a traditional starting point for an ascent. The weather is benign – neither fearsomely hot nor dangerously murky, and I decide that the time is right to climb Pendle Hill on foot.

The hill's eastern face is punishingly sheer. I see a couple of hardened fell runners attempt the stony-stepped climb, grimacing; I opt for a circular route that's longer but eases walkers in gently, rising past Lower and Upper Ogden Reservoirs into the V-shaped wilds of Ogden Clough. Then a steep ascent beside craggy Boar Clough, pitted and scarred by watery incisions but ornamented with sateen purple bells on foxglove spikes.

On ankle-busting rocky paths, I climb past the prettiest lime-green sponges of sphagnum moss and quivering buds of cotton grass – detailing the importance

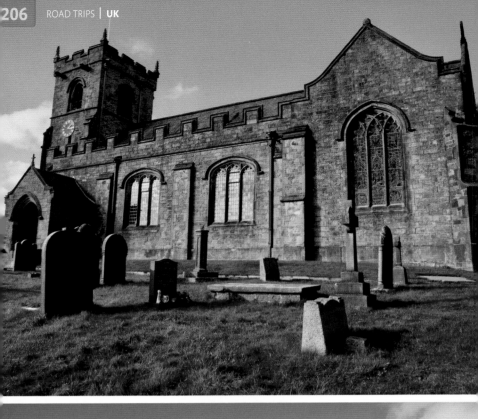

of Pendle's peaty carbon dioxide storage system – towards the hill's summit. The bleak moorland extends interminably in every direction, but as I climb ever higher, I find distant views towards England's west coast and, to the east, more Pennine expanse.

As I reach the trig point, close to the eastern edge, the sun bursts from overcast skies, like some triumphal fanfare that casts a glorious glow over the Forest of Bowland. It shows the luscious green landscape of grazed fields and fells in its best light. I can't wait to explore further.

Returning to Barley via the stone-stepped descent of the eastern escarpment is slow, to soak up the views as 'ground-level' draws closer. Reunited with the campervan, I drive along the base of Pendle Hill's northern face to the village of **Downham**.

The Forest of Bowland is designated as an Area of Outstanding Natural Beauty that covers 312 square miles. Downham, close to the eastern boundary of the AONB, is considered one of its finest villages, with a cluster of rose-clad stone cottages around a 15th-century church, a village green and a shallow brook. With no overhead wires, TV aerials or satellite dishes in sight, there's little to distract from the flawless quality of the village. From my remote campsite nearby, where every crease in Pendle Hill's western slope appears under a magnifying glass, I watch the sinking sun soften the hill's sharp edge as its beige cloak of summer seedheads takes on a healthy pink blush.

I wake to find much of the hulk's body has vanished behind morning mist and appreciate the timing of my walk. An ascent would be futile now, and hazardous, highlighting the necessity to prepare for any walk on bleak Pennine moors.

I set off in the campervan on the first of two circular routes exploring the Forest of Bowland and a string of villages as the sky clears to leave the Ribble Valley resplendent in summer tones. Passing through Chatburn, I take the road to Grindleton, crossing the Ribble as rows of ripened hay are gathered in the river meadows. An elderly flat-capped farmer, hands resting on his shepherd's crook, looks on to survey that all is well with the crop. So, too, does omnipresent Pendle Hill.

Views of Pendle Hill extend along the road from Grindleton to **Sawley**, where the Ribble bumbles past stone cottages and makes a U-turn towards the hill. The village is known for its Cistercian abbey that sits under the watchful eye of the hill. While the outline of a vast 13th-century religious complex lies in the grass, little remains of the uneven abbey walls, crowned by a thin layer of fluttering sward and with the ancient mortar a nursery for miniature ferns.

I continue first to the tiny hamlet of **Holden**, where I discover one of the finest plantsman's nurseries in Britain worthy of a road trip (and with a fine selection of eats at the Shepherd's Hut café), then to **Bolton-by-Bowland** where black-and-

↑ St Leonard's church, Downham (Keith Heaton/Shutterstock) ← Cycling is a great way to see the Forest of Bowland (Pete Stuart/Shutterstock)

white painted cottages adorned by bunting intermingle with elegant stone houses around a village green.

My tour continues north to Wigglesworth, then turns south to Tosside, where I cross from Lancashire to North Yorkshire and back. The county border runs through the centre of the red and white rose village. Beyond, en route to Slaidburn, I detour to Gisburn Forest and Stocks Reservoir.

The forest appears as a giant slab of dense pine trees from afar but, having penetrated its dark façade, quiet roads lead through an open forest of oak, silver birch and hazel. There's bike hire to explore off-road forest tracks from the Gisburn Forest Hub and an appealing eight-mile walk that circumnavigates Stocks Reservoir.

Between the two, accessed by road or a link walk, is Dalehead Church, a tiny chapel removed from its original village site to make way for the reservoir in the 1930s and rebuilt stone by stone in its present, remote location in the woods. Its meadow churchyard is designated as a Biological Heritage Site for its species-rich list of 130 wildflowers, including orchids and scented fluffy clouds of meadowsweet.

The wildflowers continue when I walk from the village of **Slaidburn** – on a par with Downham for rich beauty and location – alongside the River Hodder. A group of lovably downy fledgling long-tailed tits, still learning to balance plump body against oversized tail, work the riverside hedgerow as I make my way to Bell Sykes Meadows. The traditionally farmed fields, rammed with wildflowers, are collectively designated as a Coronation Meadow showcasing the best in Lancashire and used as a donor seed site to populate other meadows in the county with localised species. The short, circular walk provides admirable views of Slaidburn and the rolling hills around, completed with tea in the village Riverside Tearooms.

With the skies brooding, I return to Clitheroe, passing through Newton-in-Bowland. Within the core of the AONB, the scenery around the village is wilder, the ring of fells enclosing and untamed. Views of Pendle Hill appear again on the approach to Waddington, a sprawling but alluring village on the outskirts of Clitheroe. The imposing hulk today is dark and menacing.

Flat-bottomed clouds prick the sky when I depart for my second circular tour of the AONB the following morning. Through Bashall Eaves, I take a winding road beside gnarled oak trees before a steep wooded descent to Whitewell. Beyond the village, the views open over the River Hodder valley, where undulating pillow mounds are more hospitable than bleak moors.

At **Dunsop Bridge**, an aesthetic match for Downham and Slaidburn, I take a short walk to follow the River Dunsop upstream. The serenity of the riverside amble – ideal for pushchairs and wheelchairs as the entire circuit is on paved tracks – is disturbed only by an unruly family of ducklings who dabble in the

↑ Clitheroe (CM) → River Dunsop (CM)

shallows. The moors around Dunsop Bridge, on view from the footpath, have been calculated by Ordnance Survey to host the geographical centre of Great Britain. A footpath leads to the earmarked point, but there's a relentless climb onto bleak and open moorland to reach it.

Returning to the village, I continue by camper to Langden Brook where members of the Ribble River Trust are paddling in the stream to amass fish stocks prior to the deposit of hundreds of tons of gravel at the intake. 'The gravel, when it gets washed downstream in the next high water, is a fantastic habitat for the fish to spawn,' says a member of the environmental charity, 'allowing the fish stocks a chance to prosper when released back into the river.' It's evidence on my tour of the kind of environmental management taking place to maintain a sustainable ecosystem within the Forest of Bowland.

Beyond becomes my 'new favourite' touring route as the fells close in ever tighter and higher above. The landscape becomes, again, wild and remote, the road curving through waves of bracken approaching the Trough of Bowland. I'm not sure what to expect over the brow of the trough. I find silence among the pines and oaks, like ancient Caledonian forest, bilberries – and a young grouse sat in the road!

The route travels west towards Lancaster – this is the road that the famous 17th-century Lancashire witches were led along from their homes around Pendle Hill to face trial and death for reputedly heinous crimes. It's a chilling thought while crossing the bleak moors, but one that fades when, approaching the Jubilee Tower viewpoint, I spy the Lake District fells, the expanse of Morecambe Bay and Blackpool Tower.

In the village of **Quernmore**, where the AONB swallows up the Lune Valley, I turn off for Oakenclough with a drive that provides a constant view of the sea and, in the foreground, gentle pastures filled with sheep that I've now become accustomed to seeing throughout the Forest of Bowland. The bulk of Bleasdale Moor comes into view, then Beacon Fell Country Park, a landmark tree-lined mound. At its foot is Eccles Moss Farm, home to Goosnargh Gin, run by Richard and Rachel Trenchard. Every one of the seven gins they make at the distillery is related to the Forest of Bowland in some way, including a seasonal summer gin that includes botanicals from the Bell Sykes Coronation Meadows.

Two miles south is Beesley Farm, home to Mrs Kirkham's, renowned for making award-winning Lancashire cheese. There's a pungent aroma entering the small farm shop. I taste Mild and Tasty varieties next to the ripening room where large truckles of cheese sit in various stages of maturation.

My route returns to Clitheroe through Longridge and Hurst Green, re-entering the AONB for a pleasant drive.

Leaving the Forest of Bowland, Clitheroe and Pendle Hill behind, my tour continues to cross the Pennines, to begin an exploration of the Industrial

Revolution in Yorkshire. Like Bowland, the Forest of Trawden, through which I pass crossing the county border into West Yorkshire, is not forested but merely refers to ancient hunting ground. There seems little to hunt for as I cross the desolate fells east of Colne towards Oxenhope and the Worth Valley. The isolation is less welcome, with nowhere beyond Wycoller Country Park to stop or pull across. As I begin to approach Oxenhope, up and down a series of steep slopes that create three surrounding valleys, I begin to understand the reality of crossing the Pennines and am grateful for a change from driving for a while, with a ride on the Keighley and Worth Valley Railway.

The five-mile railway, which was created to assist various textile mills in the three conjoined valleys, has long been associated with *The Railway Children*, much of the filming of the 1970 movie (and its 2022 sequel *The Railway Children Return)* taking place on and around the station at Oakworth.

I hop on a steam train at **Oxenhope**, the most southerly of the six stations along the line, for the round-trip to Keighley. While the trains and the stations, in vintage design, are kept looking florally beautiful by the 500-strong band of wonderful volunteers, it is not an entirely idyllic pastoral journey. The stretch between Haworth and Damens, passing through Oakworth, is the prettiest section – but these beanpod valleys are choked with modern development and the view from the railway carriage is not one of rolling hills but that of unkempt builders' yards and long-forgotten dumping grounds. Nonetheless, the 25-minute journey, listening to the muffled toot of the train echoing up the valley, and appreciating the dedication of the volunteers in maintaining the railway and exhibitions, is a worthwhile experience.

On the return journey, I alight at **Haworth** station for the notable climb from the valley floor to the cobbled streets of the village. Haworth attracts sizeable numbers of visitors – far more than anywhere I saw in the Forest of Bowland – though a step away from the main street lined with tourist shops and cafés finds quieter lanes to reflect on the view over the surrounding hills. This is Brontë Country, signs repeatedly remind visitors, and every opportunity is utilised by businesses, from take-away restaurants to tyre fitters, to cash in on the Brontë name.

I have no time on this occasion to step out onto Haworth Moor in search of locations associated with *Wuthering Heights* but do step into the Brontë Parsonage Museum to learn more about the humble Brontë family and view what is reputed to be the room in which *Jane Eyre*, *The Tenant of Wildfell Hall* and other classics were written.

Having returned to Oxenhope on the next steam train, I drive to East Riddlesden Hall, on the outskirts of Keighley. Saved from falling into ruin by a pair of brothers who donated the 17th-century manor house to the National Trust, it offers a glimpse into the wealth of James Murgatroyd, who bought the

↑ Oxenhope, Keighley and Worth Valley Railway (Emily Marie Wilson/Shutterstock) ➜ Haworth, once home to the Brontë sisters (Natalia Sidorova/Shutterstock)

house and accompanying 2,000-acre estate having made his fortune in the Halifax woollen cloth industry. Keighley is a busy town and the hall, together with its intimate gardens, offer a tranquil retreat.

It's to Halifax that I head after an overnight stay in **Oakworth** but, rather than travel direct, I take the road from Keighley to Hebden Bridge, which rises out of the valley at Oxenhope to venture over Oxenhope Moor. The roads across the valleys around Keighley, Haworth and Oxenhope do not make especially relaxing driving, so to park up on the hilltop is welcome. The view back is of the interlinking valleys towards Keighley in the distance and, to the west, Wadsworth Moor, Boulsworth Hill and, on a bright day, the Forest of Bowland.

As the road descends towards Peckett Well and Hebden Bridge, I see the extraordinarily steep wooded slopes of Hardcastle Crags, of Heptonstall on the hillside and, across the valley, Stoodley Pike monument asserting itself like a sentry guard surveying the Calder Valley. Tightly knit terraced houses appear on the steep hillsides.

Hebden Bridge is exceedingly busy when I arrive. The streets are alive, the cafés, bars, pubs and street-food vendors feverishly active. Hebden Bridge is known as Trouser Town, its mills once renowned for making corduroy. The Rochdale Canal, together with the River Calder and Hebden Water, flow through the town; slender mill chimneys dot the skyline alongside the canal and close to the ancient packhorse bridge that gives the town its name.

The town is a delight but so, too, is **Heptonstall**, a historic village that's situated high above Hebden Bridge, and which provides excellent views of the town below and the surrounding hills. It's an intense ascent to reach by road, with some unremarkable modern development on the outskirts. But the historic village centre, including the ruins of its former church with giant crazy-paving gravestones, old cloth hall, coaching inns and excellent Towngate Tearoom – plus access to the Pennine Way – charms any visitor.

The road to Halifax follows the Rochdale Canal. **Halifax** is not on everyone's tourist itinerary but at least one of its buildings certainly should be. The Grade I listed Piece Hall is unique. It is the sole surviving Georgian cloth hall in the world. Its architectural brilliance showcases Yorkshire's one-time dominance in hand-woven textiles. Its scale is astounding, its beauty something to rival that of Georgian Bath or Edinburgh's New Town.

The beautifully restored structure, a four-sided colonnade, is alive with little boutiques, bars and cafés while the open-air central atrium is used for concerts and events throughout the year. A 15-minute walk leads me to Dean Clough, an excellent example of Yorkshire's textile industry on the grandest scale. The former textile mill site, which made carpets that were exported across the world, dominates the skyline. The attractive buildings – all stone and glass – are on an

← Hebden Bridge (Mike Devereux/Shutterstock)

unprecedented scale. The site, which has won numerous awards for its restoration, is now occupied by restaurants, shops and businesses. Also within a five-minute walk of The Piece Hall is Halifax Minster, the final resting place of Anne Lister and it's to her former home, Shibden Hall, that I head next, on the edge of Halifax.

Anne Lister, and Shibden Hall, have come to prominence on television screens in recent years through the biographical drama *Gentleman Jack*. Anne, a formidable woman in an industrial age, was given the derogatory title for her appearance, the way in which she dressed, her mannerisms and her financial interests in canals, railways, quarries and coal mines. She inherited Shibden Hall and the agricultural estate, and lived there for much of her adult life. Like East Riddlesden Hall, Shibden Hall and its grounds offer an element of tranquillity on the edge of a bustling town; the parkland, which is free to wander in, is very popular while a self-guided tour of the house offers insight into wealth and life during the Industrial Revolution.

My trans-Pennine route from Halifax continues to follow the ups and downs of the hills – passing through unexpected delights such as **Slaithwaite**, whose main street runs alongside the Huddersfield Narrow Canal and River Colne, and **Holmfirth**, a charming market town with bucolic surroundings that were brought to life on television screens in the 1980s through *Last of the Summer Wine* but more recently has been prized for its vineyard.

I'm heading for Cannon Hall Park, west of Barnsley in South Yorkshire. The impressive hall, while dating back to the 13th century, was substantially expanded over three centuries from the 17th, through wealth generated by the local iron industry. The family home, now owned by Barnsley Council, houses high quality collections of art, ceramics and furniture; these, together with 70 acres of parkland and gardens, are open to the public free of charge.

Barnsley Council also owns my next stop, Elsecar Heritage Centre. Like Dean Clough, this large complex, together with the wider model industrial village of **Elsecar**, highlights an industrial heritage – here ironworks and coal mining – including The Earl's Great Engine, considered a masterpiece of engineering for the Industrial Revolution as it prevented coal mines from flooding. The heritage centre complex is free to enter; there's plenty to see and learn of the local trade and its importance across the world, with interpretation panels to guide visitors throughout the site. Like Dean Clough, this too has gained new life with retail shops and cafés.

Elsecar was created as a showstopper of industrial entrepreneurship by the Earls Fitzwilliam, whose vast country estate borders the village. Like Elsecar, the Fitzwilliams' former family home, Wentworth Woodhouse, is a showstopper – at 606ft long, the stone east front of the house is the longest of any country house in Europe.

↑ Piece Hall, Halifax (Alastair Wallace/Shutterstock) → Holmfirth (travellight/Shutterstock)

The house today is in the hands of a preservation trust who have in place a 25-year plan to restore and renovate the buildings and the park to their former glory. A self-guided tour of the cool interior highlights the opulent marble floors and gilt ceilings. The 70 acres of gardens are no less admirable, with a walk beneath the shady woodland gardens to appreciate the extended views across the South Yorkshire countryside, now in the lower foothills of the Pennines. In the garden meadows, deckchairs and lawn games are provided for families.

Wentworth Woodhouse – originally built in 1670 for Sir Gervase Cutler, a Royalist knight and loyal supporter of Charles I – was inherited by Earl Fitzwilliam in the late 18th century. Step back to the beginning of that century and the estate was the subject of a bitter family feud between two branches of the Wentworth family, the house being left to a nephew rather than a cousin. That cousin, Thomas Wentworth, believed he had birthright claim to the estate. It was not granted so, in resentment, he bought and enlarged the estate at Stainborough Castle, seven

ESSENTIALS

GETTING THERE & AROUND Clitheroe to Barley on rural lanes via Sabden & Fence; Barley to Downham/Worston (for campsite). Rural lanes Worston to Grindleton, Sawley, Holden, Bolton-by-Bowland to Wigglesworth. B6478 to Slaidburn, with a detour on rural lane to Gisburn Forest/Stocks Reservoir. B6478 to Clitheroe/B6243 to campsite. Rural lanes to Quernmore via Bashall Eaves & Dunsop Bridge, then to Oakenclough, Whitechapel & Longridge. B6243 to Clitheroe.

Rural roads from Clitheroe to Downham, Barley & Barrowford then A6068 to Laneshaw Bridge; rural roads across Keighley Moor to Oxenhope. A6033/A629/B6265 to East Riddlesden Hall. B6143 to Oakworth. Rural roads via Stanbury to Oxenhope & A6033 to Hebden Bridge then A646 to Halifax (& A58 for Shibden Hall). A629/A62 to Slaithwaite/B6107 to Holmfirth/A635 to Cawthorne. Rural lanes from Cawthorne to Stainborough via Silkstone/A628. Rural lane to A6195 (briefly)/A6135 & B6090 to Elsecar Heritage Centre. Rural lane & B6090 to Wentworth Woodhouse. Rural lane to A6135/A6195 then Rockley Ln to Wentworth Castle Gardens. Note: Wentworth Castle Gardens, Elsecar Heritage Centre & Wentworth Woodhouse are all well signposted; follow the brown tourist signs. Depending on the timing of your visit in relation to opening times, it may be preferable to visit Wentworth Castle Gardens first, then Elsecar, then Wentworth Woodhouse, in linear fashion. I made a circular tour on my final day, returning to Cinderhill CS for an extra night.

Parking without height barriers: there are pay & display car parks at Barley, Bolton-by-Bowland, Slaidburn & Dunsop Bridge. In Clitheroe, park at Mitchell St Car Park or Booth's (2hrs' free parking for customers). Oxenhope has a large free car park at KWVR station for railway users (park here & purchase a Rover rail ticket, allowing stop-offs at all stations).

miles west, renaming it Wentworth Castle! It's here that I finish my tour, with an exploration of the gardens and wider deer-park estate. The Palladian mansion is not open to the public, but the gardens are. Like Wentworth Woodhouse, they are work-in-progress with an ongoing restoration programme, including an impressive Victorian horticultural conservatory.

A walk to the top of the gardens, through the formal, symmetrical Union Jack Garden that was fashionable of its time (representing the recent union of England and Scotland), brings me to the Stainborough Castle itself. It is no medieval fortress: a mere folly that Thomas built as a sham ruin in pretense of inheriting a historic estate to impress and irritate his relation at Wentworth Woodhouse.

I climb to the top of the castle. The views across the estate over South Yorkshire and the rolling Pennines are clear and clean. There is little to demonstrate that three hundred years ago – or even as little as forty years ago – this area, or those I have travelled through crossing the Pennines over the past few days, were thick with the smoke and steam of heavy industry. It appears mere folly.

Hebden Bridge has discount parking by Innovation on Hangingroyd Ln, or you may find it easier to park at Bowling Green Car Park in Heptonstall (free all day) & take the bus to Hebden Bridge. At Halifax is Eureka! car park on Discovery Rd and a huge pay & display car parking area at Dean Clough. All other tourist attractions featured have large car parks.

ACCOMMODATION I stayed at: Angram Green CS, Worston; Clitheroe CCC Site; Newsholme Manor CS, Oakworth; Cinderhill CS, Cawthorne.

FIND OUT MORE
Visit Lancashire visitlancashire.com   **Visit Calderdale** visitcalderdale.com
Forest of Bowland AONB **Discover Halifax** discoverhalifax.co.uk
forestofbowland.com

TOP TIP: TODMORDEN AS AN ALTERNATIVE If Hebden
Bridge is too busy and you prefer a quieter town, take the 4.5-mile towpath west to Todmorden, made wealthy by the cotton trade during the Industrial Revolution. This lovely town of cobbled streets, right on the border with Lancashire, has some exceptional buildings, including the Town Hall, the façade of which represents cotton spinning (for Lancashire) and the wool trade (for Yorkshire) as it once straddled the county boundary. There are lovely places to eat, art galleries (try the Water Street Gallery beside the canal) and walks to Stoodley Pike, which has a viewing balcony 40ft above ground level – after a climb of 39 steps in darkness! Todmorden is also on the Calderdale Way long-distance trail.

24 THE BIG TEES: WILD ABOUT MEADOWS

WALK AMONG SOME OF ENGLAND'S LAST REMAINING HAY MEADOWS IN THE NORTH PENNINES AONB

WHERE	County Durham/Cumbria
DISTANCE/TIME	112 miles/4 days
START/FINISH	Cow Green Reservoir/Barnard Castle

Switching the campervan engine off far along Baldersdale, there is silence. The air is so hushed that as I open the driver's door quietly it creates a cacophonous din that appears to echo across the fells.

Aroused by our attempts at quiet, a bird rises into the air, its long, curved beak a giveaway sign of the curlew as it shrieks into life. Then another. And another.

I gaze into a small, square field of dazzling yellow, the glossy buttercups of the hay meadow hemmed in by walls built of clumpy stones. The intensity of floral colour shines brilliantly against the bottomless blue of Hury Reservoir beyond.

↑ Hannah's Meadow, Baldersdale (CM)

My 12-year-old daughter Lara whispers, 'Look over there,' and nods at a black bird that raises its head above the sward. 'It can't be,' I reply, but before I've so much as taken sight, a pair of rare black grouse lift off the ground and, in some cackling salute, appear to wiggle their white bottoms when they fly past as if to mock my measured reach for the camera.

'I think I might become a birdwatcher,' says Lara. 'I'm enjoying this,' she reveals as she attempts to take pictures of a disobliging quartet of stripy pheasant chicks. It's a far cry from the usual pre-teen ramblings and my guess is that, once home, ornithology might be at the back of her mind. But, for now, we're revelling in the magic of summertime amid Teesdale's hay meadows.

You don't have to be a fanatical twitcher or a botanist to appreciate the density of birds or wildflowers in Teesdale. Located in the heart of the North Pennines Area of Outstanding Natural Beauty, the dale is rich in natural beauty. Indeed, 40% of the UK's remaining 2,700 acres of upland hay meadows are in the North Pennines, where low-intensity traditional livestock farming encourages a preservation of internationally important species.

The hay meadows are at their best during spring and summer, when migrating birds visit to breed and when the most astonishing collection of wildflowers bursts into bloom, from March to the last few warm days of October.

↑ Black grouse (Sergey Uryadnikov/Shutterstock)

With the Camping and Caravanning Club Site at Barnard Castle as our base, Lara and I plan a series of short walks to explore and appreciate these upland hay meadows and the surrounding moors. There's beauty to be seen from the campervan windows, but there's no denying that the best sights and the finest views require stepping out.

We begin with a three-mile walk over **Widdybank Fell**. As rain begins to prickle our faces, and the wind whips across the silvery-grey Cow Green Reservoir, it sometimes feels like a hike. But the Widdybank Fell Nature Trail is actually a doddle, the entire route along a tarmac track that's easy for buggies and wheelchairs to access.

There's a picnic area at the Cow Green car park, the starting point for the walk, from where you can see the highest point on the Pennine ridge, Cross Fell. But it's the nature trail that provides the best scenery. Widdybank Fell is within the Moor House–Upper Teesdale National Nature Reserve, one of the largest reserves in England and Britain's leading site for research into the effects of a changing climate on the natural environment. Stretching across parts of County Durham and Cumbria, the reserve contains a wide range of North Pennine upland habitats, including the limestone grassland and blanket bog seen around Widdybank Fell.

Besides the fluttering cotton grass, a classic plant of peat bogs, we come across several of the limestone-loving arctic and alpine plants for which **Upper Teesdale** is renowned, including the mountain pansy and bird's-eye primrose. These delicate flowers, along with the electric blue spring gentian (for which our visit was just too late) form part of the Teesdale Assemblage, a group of 20 internationally important plants.

But the highlight of the walk is to see Cauldron Snout. This waterfall, crashing down over a precipice beyond the reservoir, is the first of three along the River Tees' 85-mile journey to the North Sea. Vociferous and brash, the thundering waterfall lures visitors down the rocky Pennine Way to admire its youthful energy from below.

Cauldron Snout is one of the first truly accessible locations to see the Tees after the river's birth at the foot of Cross Fell. Eager to see more of it, we drive east to begin the Upper Teesdale Wildflower Walk, a stroll just shy of four miles that follows the Pennine Way along the banks of the Tees before returning through a series of hay meadows. These magnificent meadows are bursting with colour right to the water's edge. It's where, as the views of the dale become all encompassing, we come across our first globe flowers, another of Teesdale's summer specialities.

We rise with the sun the following morning to drive along Lunedale, a westerly spur off Teesdale, and over Welbeck Fell towards the Cumbrian village of **Dufton**.

↑ High Cup Nick (Jonathan Sutcliffe/Shutterstock) ➔ Bird's-eye primrose (Kersti Lindstrom/Shutterstock)

The sightings of birds and wildflowers are plentiful, the views enormous but nothing to prepare us for the panorama that unfolds on our walk up Dufton Fell. Following the Pennine Way once again, our climb on foot takes us northeast out of Dufton. With every step, a glance back reveals ever more extravagant views over the Howgill Fells, the Yorkshire Dales and the Eden Valley to the south as we marvel at Dufton Pike and Murton Pike, two volcano-shaped peaks that, like sentry posts, guard the entrance to High Cup Gill, one of Britain's finest glacial valleys.

The six-mile walk is beyond superlatives. Our lunchtime stop at High Cup Nick, the head of the valley, is remarkable and provides a view that, I believe, everyone should see at least once in their lifetime. The walk requires a little effort though the climb isn't as steep as I'd anticipated. An alternative, easier option (but a longer route) is to follow the Pennine Way across Dufton Fell from Cow Green Reservoir. Neither route, however, should be attempted in bad weather.

The North Pennines AONB is also a Global Geopark, a place recognised by UNESCO as having outstanding geology and landscape. Lured back by Teesdale's magnetic beauty, we return to visit the dale's most well-known pair of geological features, High Force and Low Force.

High Force, the larger of the two waterfalls downstream of Cauldron Snout, plunges 68ft over the Whin Sill, a geological feature of the North Pennines, before the River Tees carves its way through an Ice Age gorge to Low Force. Both waterfalls can be seen with a five-minute walk from picnic areas at **Bowlees** (for Low Force) and High Force. We choose to walk the High Force Bowlees Geotrail, a four-mile route that takes in both waterfalls and the surrounding landscape, geology and wildlife.

The riverbank footpath (also The Pennine Way) between Low Force and High Force is mesmeric in beauty. It's regarded as another fine location to see the Teesdale Assemblage along with one of Teesdale's unique features, the remains of an ancient Ice Age juniper wood, the largest in England. Juniper is famous for flavouring gin, but the scent erupting from the prickly evergreen shrubs is quite a tonic in the sunshine.

If High Force is the most grandiose display we see along the River Tees, our penultimate walk involves one of the humblest. Like Lunedale, Baldersdale is a small westerly spur. It was known, for those who remember the 1980s, as the home of Hannah Hauxwell, a spinster who lived alone on her small farm overlooking the Blackton Reservoir, without electrics or running water and who eked out a measly existence with limited livestock. She shot to 'fame' with several television documentaries.

Hannah's Meadow is now a nature reserve and designated as a Coronation Meadow, regarded as an 'outstanding example of our remaining meadows', a lost

← High Force waterfall (Veronique Stone/Shutterstock)

landscape. With understated, rustic elegance, it has an appeal that makes one want to sit and enjoy the serenity of the countryside. We leave our longest walk, along the Teesdale Railway Path, until last. Teesdale Railway was built in the 19th century between Barnard Castle and the delightful village of Middleton-in-Teesdale. The last train ran on the track in 1965 and the railway line is now a picturesque footpath. Ten miles in length, the walking route (also open to cyclists and horseriders) can be broken into sections with opportunities to 'alight' at the original stations in Cotherstone, Mickleton and Romaldkirk, three appealing villages along the way (the latter being the final resting place of Hannah Hauxwell, in the church graveyard). There are pubs and cafés in each village for refreshment stops. The walk can also be accessed, with a slight deviation, directly from the Barnard Castle Club Site and the adjacent village of Lartington.

The views along the railway path are gentle, the wildflowers astounding. Our steps, as we approach the end of our walk, are slow. It's not through tiredness or lethargy, simply a reluctance to allow our time in Teesdale to end. There are some places you don't want to leave. Teesdale and the North Pennines is one of them.

ESSENTIALS

GETTING THERE & AROUND
Cow Green Reservoir (signposted at Langdon Beck) is accessed off the B6277 between Barnard Castle & Alston. B6277 to Barnard Castle then B6277/B6276 to Brough/A66 to Appleby-in-Westmorland, rural road to Dufton, then Long Marton (for Clickham Farm CS). Back along A66 to Brough then B6276 to Middleton-in-Teesdale & B6277 northwest to Bowlees Visitor Centre; southeast to Barnard Castle. B6277 northwest, then rural roads around Baldersdale, to Hury & Balderhead Reservoirs. Reverse route to campsite.

The roads around Baldersdale are not suitable for large coachbuilt motorhomes, but they're perfect for walking & cycling. This includes the quiet country lane along Baldersdale that is a 2-min walk from Hannah's Meadow (roadside parking).

The B6277 between Alston & Barnard Castle is one of the prettiest drives in England. For an extension to the beginning of this route, I'd recommend starting in Alston (at 1,000ft, sharing the title of highest market town in England) or making a loop via Alston to return to Teesdale via Weardale on the A689 & B6278.

Parking without height barriers: for Widdybank Fell Nature Trail there's a car park at Cow Green Reservoir. For Upper Teesdale Wildflower Walk, park at Hanging Shaw car park. The Dufton Pike Open Access Walk can begin from the car park in the village of Dufton. Park at Bowlees Visitor Centre for the High Force & Bowlees Geotrail. Fiddler House & Hury House have car parks well located for Baldersdale Hay Time Walk 3.

I recommend beginning the Teesdale Railway Path/Taste Trail (same route) from the Barnard Castle CCC Site. It's a linear walk so use bus 95 or 96 for the return journey to the bus stop at the end of the lane to the campsite.

ACCOMMODATION
We stayed at: Clickham Farm CS, Appleby-in-Westmorland (CCC members only; page xiv); Barnard Castle CCC Site (open to all; includes Ready Camp glamping units for those without own camping facilities).

FIND OUT MORE
North Pennines AONB Walking routes ⌂ explorenorthpennines.org.uk/recreation-opportunity/walking

TOP TIP: WALKING IN TEESDALE AND THE NORTH PENNINES
The seven walks that we followed are only a few of the many opportunities for walking in the North Pennines AONB. Details and directions for all the walks we did can be downloaded from the website above.

The reception area at Barnard Castle Camping & Caravanning Club Site also has a large folder of walks, including a pretty walk direct from the site to the town centre of Barnard Castle.

↑ Romaldkirk (CM)

25 MAGICAL MOURNE

TOUR THE ANCIENT KINGDOM OF MOURNE

WHERE	County Down, Northern Ireland
DISTANCE/TIME	127 miles/4 days
START/FINISH	Kilkeel/Rostrevor

I t's early morning and a pale sky lights up the shimmering blue waters of Carlingford Lough as it calmly encircles the steadfast Haulbowline Lighthouse. The relenting, soft sand of Cranfield's blue-flag beach is naturally rippled by the ebbing tide; the compressed grains yield to our every footstep.

Beyond the small flotilla of fishing boats bobbing at the entrance to Greencastle, with its cluster of half-dozen coastal dwellings, rise the magical Mourne Mountains. So busy are we gazing at the serene panorama to our walk, that we almost tread on a seal pup enjoying an early morning sunbathe on the beach. Our campsite host, Richard Chestnutt, had assured such a sighting.

The family and I, on a rare occasion when Daddy can travel too, had arrived the previous evening eagerly anticipating three days of walking in this beautiful part of Northern Ireland. The Mourne Mountains, covering an area approximately fifteen miles by eight in the district of Newry and Mourne, lie at the southernmost

↑ Carlingford Lough overlooking the Mourne Mountains (Pavel_Voitukovic/Shutterstock)

point of County Down. To the south, beyond Carlingford Lough, lie the Cooley Mountains and the Republic of Ireland. The skyline views of both sets of mountains from our campsite, Chestnutt Holiday Parks, are astounding.

Of the sixty plus mountains in Mourne, twelve rise above 2,000ft. We have no intention of climbing all twelve – indeed one would suffice in three days! Instead, we choose a selection of walks from short, easy-going coastal strolls to more demanding mountain climbs.

Our first, described above, takes us direct from the campsite in West Cranfield on a circular five-mile walk, along the beach to **Greencastle** and back using quiet lanes between gentle pastures. With the Mourne Mountains not too distant, the walk provides an impeccable introduction to the area.

We take a short driving tour through **Kilkeel**, Mourne's principal town and the seafood capital of County Down, to Annalong. The little harbour of this tiny fishing village is overlooked by a corn mill, restored to full working order and open to visitors, where our second walk begins. This one-mile amble along the coastal path gives a brief opportunity to enjoy both the views across the Irish Sea and the mountains to the west.

Continuing north, driving along the coast on the signposted *Mourne Coastal Route,* we gain further views of the mountains, including Slieve Donard, the highest in the area at 2,788ft, which plummets to the sea. We approach the picturesque and popular coastal town of Newcastle before our drive takes us inland for the first time, past Tollymore Forest Park. A must for a return visit, the landscaped park is filled with appealing 18th-century follies. It provided oak wood for the interiors of White Star Liners, including the *Titanic,* which was built in Belfast.

As we turn each corner, there's a realisation of how dramatic and incredibly beautiful the region is. We uncover another valley, with the ground rising sharply on occasions here, craggy outcrops there, and smooth undulations elsewhere.

We finish our driving tour with one last walk for the day – a visit to Silent Valley, four miles north of Kilkeel. Within this north-south crease between the mountains of Slievenaglogh and Slieve Binnian lie two reservoirs. Ben Crom Reservoir, further north, can be reached on an extended seven-mile walk; we opt for a 1½-mile circular walk to the dam of the Silent Valley Reservoir. As a landscaped park, there are several other waymarked walks each presenting a different type of scene from a short nature trail in the woods to more demanding approaches to the peaks.

Inspired by our gentle low-level introduction to the mountains, the following day breeds a yearning to be among them. Parking at Carrick Little, just to the west of **Annalong**, we take a five-mile return walk to Blue Lough.

↑ Tollymore Forest Park in autumn (Dawid K Photography/Shutterstock)

Along stony tracks and crossing mountain streams, the trek provides a sense of being in the mountains, with superb panoramic views all around, while retaining gentle gradients. On a blisteringly hot day, the highlight is our approach to the

TOP TIP: WALKS IN THE MOURNE MOUNTAINS

My walking tour of the Mourne Mountains and Ring of Gullion is based upon a series of walking routes by Visit Mourne Mountains, available to download from ◊ visitmournemountains.co.uk/dbimgs/Mourne-Walking-Route-Cards.pdf

There are more than 20 walks detailed. While these include directions and maps, I recommend taking the Ordnance Survey map from the 1:50,000 *Discoverer Series: Sheet 29 The Mournes* for the longer-distance walks and when selecting your own routes. Walks we covered include:

Annalong Coastal Path: A one mile-walk along a gravel footpath with sea views. Rated as an easy family walk, it takes approximately 30 minutes. Accessible for pushchairs. Parking is by the Corn Mill.

Silent Valley: An easy family walk of 1.5 miles, with tarmac and gravel paths, suitable for both pushchairs and wheelchairs. Longer and more challenging waymarked trails are possible. Refreshments are available. There is an entrance fee for vehicles and pedestrians.

The Fairy Glen: An easy 15-minute riverside walk of one mile, accessible either from Rostrevor village or Kilbroney Park (campsite); suitable for both pushchairs and wheelchairs. A more challenging mountain hike to the summit of nearby Slieve Martin is also available direct from the campsite.

Cranfield to Greencastle and Mill Bay: A five-mile walk, taking approximately 2¼ hours on both beach and quiet minor lanes providing scenic coastal and mountain views. Accessible direct from Chestnutt Holiday Park.

Slieve Gullion: A spectacular eight-mile walk initially along quiet lanes, then to the summit of Slieve Gullion over rugged moorland and tracks between forest plantations. Steep and lengthy climbs involved with careful footwork required in places. No shade at any point and nowhere to obtain refreshments except the start/finish (Slieve Gullion Forest Park), so take all necessary provisions. Not suitable for very young children and all walkers should be relatively fit and agile. Parking at the Forest Park. Anticipate a minimum of four hours.

The Blue Lough: A linear route of 2.5 miles (each way) to the Blue Lough using distinct footpaths with gentle gradients, though assured footing required. Limited shade. Spectacular scenery and an extra climb over rough terrain takes you to a further viewpoint overlooking Ben Crom Reservoir. Park in designated car park at Carrick Little Walkers Car Park, two miles from Annalong. Details of this walk can be downloaded from: ◊ walkni.com/mourne-mountains/blue-lough.

Blue Lough. What a place to swim! Tempted by the cooling, crystal water and the idyllic 360° backdrop, it takes no time for the children to wade in as we, in more refined manner, plunge our toes in.

Staying at a wooded campsite in the Victorian resort of Rostrevor that evening, we take a short stroll across Kilbroney Park into town, where we catch up with the bubbling Kilbroney River. A very easy stroll under the shade of the *Fairy Glen*, an understandable name for this tree-lined river walk popular with locals, is what's needed after a day in the sun.

Accustomed to our mountain climate, we're now after giant views, and we select a giant mountain upon which to get them. To the west of **Newry**, the largest town in the area, is the Ring of Gullion. Like the Mourne Mountains it is designated as an Area of Outstanding Natural Beauty and is a geological phenomenon.

A long, central mountain – Slieve Gullion – is central to a ring of smaller, volcano-like hills with a scooped valley between the two. The Ring is most prominent from above, so we feel it necessary to climb the matriarchal mountain. At 1,889ft, and with another day of heat, it's far from a race to the top; rather a gentle climb, stopping to admire the view of the Ring and beyond on repeated occasions. And the view is enormous.

Our trekker's picnic spot is at the top where, like an oasis on a mountain with no shade, Callagh Barras Lough greets us. Another dip is necessary in this infinity-like natural pool as we question if we can ever find another as high to match its beauty.

ESSENTIALS

GETTING THERE & AROUND Irish Ferries Holyhead to Dublin or Stena Line Liverpool to Belfast. Road travel is quick and easy on to the M1 direct from the ferry port at Dublin with a comfortable journey time of 1½hrs to Newry. Use the toll tunnel from the ferry on to the M1, rather than navigating Dublin's suburbs; it's worth every. Alternatively, Newry is an hour from Belfast Harbour via M1/A1.

From Kilkeel (Chestnutt Holiday Parks) A2 to Annalong/Newcastle; B180/B27 to Silent Valley Reservoir via Tollymore Forest Park & Attical. Return to campsite via Kilkeel. To Carrick Little Walkers Car Park (for Blue Lough walk) via Kilkeel. Then, Head Rd west, B27 north/west to Hilltown then south on Rostrevor Rd to Rostrevor for Kilbroney Caravan Park. A2 to Newry/B113 to Slieve Gullion Forest Park. Return to Newry then B8 to Spelga Dam. B27/rural track to Deers Meadow Car Park (for Spelga Dam). Then back to Rostrevor via Hilltown as before.

Parking: No height barriers were encountered at any of the car park facilities for the walks listed on page 231.

That evening – our last – we sit beside the Spelga Dam, 19 miles northeast in the centre of the Mournes, and watch the sun setting over the water as we reflect on our visit. 'Daddy,' enquires our nine-year-old, 'is Ireland your favourite?'

With eyes fixed on the mountains, his reply is with little hesitation. 'Yes, I think it is.'

ACCOMMODATION We stayed at: Chestnutt Holiday Parks, Kilkeel; Kilbroney Caravan Park, Rostrevor.

FIND OUT MORE

Irish Ferries ⌖ irishferries.com
Stena Line ⌖ stenaline.co.uk
Visit Mourne Mountains
⌖ visitmournemountains.co.uk

Ring of Gullion AONB
⌖ ringofgullion.org
Discover Northern Ireland
⌖ discovernorthernireland.com
Camping Ireland ⌖ campingireland.ie

TOP TIP: SWIM SAFELY Open water swimming can be dangerous. Please take into consideration your swimming capabilities and experience before taking a dip. We found the two pools mentioned in this chapter to be safe to swim, based upon our known levels of competence and the weather conditions on a good summer's day.

↑ Ben Crom Reservoir from Slieve Binnian (Shutterstock/James Kennedy NI)

26 TREASURE IRELAND

VISIT NATIONAL TRUST PROPERTIES & LANDMARKS IN NORTHERN IRELAND

WHERE	Northern Ireland
DISTANCE/TIME	475 miles/5 days
START/FINISH	Belfast (circular route)

Samson and Goliath shimmer golden yellow beneath a setting sun as I stand at the summit of Black Mountain. These giant gantry cranes, the symbol of *Titanic*-maker Harland and Wolff's domination in shipbuilding, cradle Belfast as I turn my head to the south for the smooth lines of the Mourne Mountains. The sun's weakening warmth glows upon my back, but it glistens more over the seemingly limitless surface of Lough Neagh. To the north, rays dance across Island Magee and the Causeway Coast, intermittently sprinkling the green fields with slivers of light.

My waltz up Black Mountain is the very last in a series of visits to National Trust land within a short week and it provides an opportunity to survey and reminisce about the many parts of Northern Ireland that I have visited on my circular tour of the province, which had begun days earlier with a scenic drive along Belfast Lough to Island Magee.

↑ Mussenden Temple and Downhill Demesne (Ballygally View Images/Shutterstock)

Island Magee is a small peninsula on which the National Trust owns several notable landmarks, including The Gobbins, a long stretch of sheer cliff face. It can't be reached by road, but rather a momentous coastal walk, leaving the campervan in the car park.

My preference is for agreeable walks around the tiny hamlet of Portmuck, on the northeast coast of Island Magee. With little more than a handful of quaint dwellings and a minuscule, sheltered bay, it's a good destination for a quiet picnic on an empty beach and walks along the shoreline. There's a small car park but the village is accessed along a narrow lane that I wouldn't recommend for vehicles more than 23ft (7m) long.

More easily accessible to all is Skernaghan Point and Brown's Bay at the northern tip of the peninsula. With an award-winning silky-sand beach and a headland to view the length of Antrim's east coast, it's an atmospheric place worth lingering a while.

Leaving Island Magee behind, I follow the coast north, with commendable views of the Antrim Glens, to **Cushendun**. The Trust owns the village, one of black-and-white houses beneath slate roofs that sit comfortably against a backdrop of hills, and with an outlook over a gorgeously soft bay. Commissioned by the first and last Lord Cushendun for his wife, several of the village buildings were designed by the renowned architect Clough Williams-Ellis, of Portmeirion fame (page 149). It is impossible not to spend some time in Cushendun, such is the allure of the village.

Practically speaking, it's necessary for coachbuilts and A-class motorhomes to follow the A2 north from Cushendun, a route that takes in the best of the Glens of Antrim, including the NT-owned Cushleake Mountain. Smaller campervans however have the privilege of accessing the narrower and more twisty coastal route past Torr Head to Murlough Bay. Here, the land lies contorted by crags that plummet to an azure sea with folds in the earth lined by a billiard-green sward. Both Murlough Bay and neighbouring Fair Head, a bank of 650-foot cliffs, offer outstanding walking territory with views of the retreat-like Rathlin Island and, on a clear day, the Scottish islands of Islay and Jura.

Ireland is repeatedly referred to as The Emerald Isle owing to its vivid green rural appearance. But head to the north coast of Antrim and you'll find emerald *seas*, too. Beyond the attractive seaside town of Ballycastle, popular with families, is one of Northern Ireland's most frequented attractions, the **Carrick-a-Rede** Rope Bridge. It's not for the faint-hearted and I witness several people walk the two-thirds of a mile necessary to reach the bridge, only to opt out of the crossing. Their nerves are understandable, for the oscillating bridge, originally erected by salmon fishermen, dangles 100 feet above a 65-foot chasm.

Crossing the bridge is one of those must-do attractions that I consider is something of nothing as one joins the throng of coach-led tourists; cross to the small island to watch the movements of the island birdlife – and raise a nostril to the pungent, nay acrid, ammonia-scented poo they leave behind – and you're 'done'. The walk to the bridge is nonetheless stimulating and offers opportunities to scrutinise the jewelled coastline.

My preference to the rope bridge is for the quieter coast around Ballintoy and the sweeping National Trust Whitepark Bay. With a sea colour to rival the most precious gemstones, the coast leads past the precarious ruins of Dunseverick Castle to Ireland's ultimate attraction – the **Giant's Causeway**.

If crossing the rope bridge is underwhelming, stepping over the land of giants is not. Nothing can prepare for the natural beauty of the Giant's Causeway, be it the sheer expanse of the area, the mountainous backdrop and cavernous cliffs, the crystal-clear rock pools illuminating a hexagonal underworld or the bizarre effect of polygonal rock plunging towards the sea. If ever there's beauty in natural pattern, the Giant's Causeway is an expressive example.

Scotland is lost by daybreak. While the previous evening's sun had turned each jigsaw piece of the Causeway to molten rock smouldering beneath the

→ Giant's Causeway (CM)

incoming tide and the Mull of Kintyre had looked within touching distance, now the Antrim coastline lurks amid a fine mist of sea spray and fog, the harebells on top of Magheracross adding a hint of colour to the otherwise ghostly world. The National Trust's Portstewart Strand appears to stretch infinitely into the distance (it stretches for four miles, anyway) as the beachside flags whistle to hardened dog walkers braving an inclement wind.

Not a beach to laze upon on such a day, I move further west to **Downhill Demesne**. For even on such a day, there are strained views of the coastline while walking on the headland, both to Portstewart Strand and, west, towards Derry and Benone Strand.

Within the grounds are the ruins of Downhill House, built by an eccentric Earl-Bishop. Older than its windowless frontage portrays, from the roofless interior there's a sense of the incredible location the bishop found for his palatial parties – revelries that involved the investigative owner placing flour on the floorboards to divulge bedroom liaisons during the night!

Mussenden Temple, a rotunda that all but hangs over the edge of the cliff at the rear of the ruins, expresses the bishop's own love for a woman. Built in honour of his beloved cousin, it provides picture frame windows through which to view the neighbouring beaches.

Inland, within a mile of the Temple, is Hezlett House. The traditional rustic, thatched cottage with a peaceful orchard and floral front garden, is one of the oldest thatched properties left in Northern Ireland. Its tiny rooms tell the story of 17th-century rural life.

Within an hour, I'm wandering the grounds of another 17th-century home on a grander scale. Springhill House is a family home of English plantation settlers. With white walls touching the green canvas of the surrounding estate, Springhill is arguably one of the prettiest homes in Northern Ireland.

Crossing from Cookstown to Omagh, the countryside opens out and I become mesmerised by the Sperrin Mountains as I pass through. They're home to the Wellbrook Beetling Mill, a relic of the 19th-century linen industry. Unfortunately closed on my trip, I move on to **County Fermanagh** and its lakeland area; first the vast, sealike Lower Lough Erne followed by its more southerly counterpart.

Of the two, Upper Lough Erne, south of the island town of Enniskillen, is undoubtedly the more scenic. It's here that The National Trust owns the **Crom Estate**, more than 2,000 acres of tranquil countryside. I explore watery nooks and crannies by canoe, trek through woodlands, take pretty walks along the shore and across footbridges to flawless, uninhabited islands. This is a special place.

Close by are two National Trust properties, Castle Coole and Florence Court. Both offer a glimpse into 18th-century life and picturesque walks around the respective estates. Florence Court has the more dramatic backdrop of the pair,

↑ Portstewart Strand Beach (Ballygally View Images/Shutterstock) ← Northern Ireland has some stunning coastal roads (Nahlik/Shutterstock)

with the rugged limestone Cuilcagh Mountains in view. There's more opportunity for a ramble here, too – or a cycle ride – with 8,649 acres to explore. Of appeal to me is the huge walled kitchen garden that's been part of a mammoth restoration project in recent years. Gradually filled with vegetables and the sweetest of sweet peas and roses, it provides a pleasant, orderly contrast to the wilderness of the neighbouring mountains.

In County Armagh, two National Trust houses are within five miles of one another, making a good visiting pair. Following brief stops at both The Argory, where visitors can launch a canoe on the River Blackwater, and Ardress House, in fruit-growing territory and surrounded by apple orchards, I move east.

Whether from a distance – at first the faint outline – or close by, the full glory of the Mourne Mountains is a wondrous sight. Slieve Donard, magnificently bold as its eastern edge slides towards the sea, is the highest of the Mournes at 2,790ft. The mountains are worthy of more than the passing glance that I have time for on this occasion and I begrudgingly resist the temptation to become entranced by their alluring beauty and turn towards Strangford Lough.

Filled with saltwater courtesy of the tiny Narrows – the entrance to the lough from the Irish Sea – much of its foreshore and islands are owned by or leased to the Trust. With its shoreside position at the southern edge of the lough, some of the finest views are from **Castle Ward**, whose estate provides miles of walking and cycling trails suitable for all. There are canoes to hire from the on-site activity organisers, though I find solace enough in a walk along the Shore Trail, past castle ruins and with views of the colourful painted houses in the pretty town of **Portaferry**.

↑ Cuilcagh Mountains (Adam.Bialek/Shutterstock)

There is more colour to see at **Mount Stewart,** one of the National Trust's most popular destinations. Adjacent to the lough, a tour of the former home of socialite Lady Londonderry displays the brilliance of Mount Stewart's interior decoration, alongside numerous exhibits. Would I could pull a book from its library shelves and settle down for an evening in front of the fire.

It's the grounds however that are greatly celebrated – a frequent contender for the world's top gardens – with the front of the house showing off rare plants sited alongside common favourites. Electric blue delphiniums sit close to near-electric hydrangeas while, elsewhere, restful wildflower meadows hum to the sound of nature beneath gargantuan *Wellingtonia* and western red cedar.

Following a tour of the province, it feels fitting to finish with a celebratory drink. And so, I enter **Belfast** and The Crown Bar. If Fermanagh's Crom Estate is special for one reason, The Crown Bar is unique in another way, as the finest example of a Victorian gin palace. Ceramic tiles, woodwork and glass abound in this masterful show of interior decoration, where period gas lamps and cosy snugs fire the imagination of secret chatter amid the partitions.

I'm reliably informed that the evening music is worthy of an overnight stop, and I wish I could stay. But I have one more place that's calling. For upon my arrival in port five days earlier, the first sight that stimulated the senses was the ridge of mountains that lines the 'back' of Belfast. These I must climb.

With limited time before the ferry departure, I all but run up the National-Trust-owned **Divis and Black Mountain.** From the summit, there are views over the whole of Belfast and more: Strangford Lough, the Ards Peninsula, the Mourne Mountains – and my ferry waiting in the harbour. I'm sure I can see the ship's captain waving at me to hurry up, too. Reluctantly, I oblige.

↑ The Crown bar, Belfast (CM)

ESSENTIALS

GETTING THERE & AROUND | I travelled from Liverpool (Birkenhead) to Belfast with Stena Line. The crossing takes 8hrs & I'd recommend the overnight ferry, arriving refreshed & ready to begin touring immediately. However, it's worth booking a private cabin on day crossings. Stena Line also operate a Cairnryan–Belfast service.

M2 Belfast port to Six Mile Water Caravan Park. M2/A57/B58/B90 to The Gobbins & Portmuck (Island Magee). Rural roads to Brown's Bay. A2 to Cushendun. Torr Rd to Murlough Bay (coachbuilts/A-class motorhomes use A2). B15 to Carrick-a-Rede. A2/Causeway Rd to Giant's Causeway & Ballyness Caravan Park. B17/A2 to Downhill Desmesne. A2 southeast to Hezlett House then A2/A29/B18 to Springhill. A29/Orritor Rd to Wellbrook Beetling Mill. A505/B83/B122/B80 to Enniskillen. A46 north to Blaney Caravan Park. A46 south to Castle Coole. A4/A32 to Florence Court. Marble Arch Rd west to Rushin House Caravan Park. A509/rural roads to Crom Estate. A4 to The Argory then rural roads to Ardress House. B28/A27 to Clare Glen. A51/A50/A25 to Castle Ward. A25 to Portaferry ferry crossing then A20 to Mount Stewart. A20 to Dundonald Touring Caravan Park. A55/A2 to Belfast (The Odyssey). A12/B38 to Divis & Black Mountain. Reverse route to Belfast port.

Vehicles on the ferry from Strangford to Portaferry are charged according to length – a 19–26ft (6–8m) motorhome currently costs £10 for a one-way crossing or £5.80 under 19ft (6m). There is no charge for bicycles, though cyclists pay a £1 'passenger' fare.

Parking without height barriers: I had no problems parking at any of the National Trust properties or landmarks. I also found numerous roadside parking and picnic places with no height restrictions, particularly along the Causeway Coastal Route, allowing plenty of opportunities to stop and enjoy the view. In

↑ Belfast from Divis and Black Mountain (stephen barnes/Northern Ireland/Alamy)

Belfast, The Odyssey is an extensive car park, with on-site security, just 5mins' walk from both the Titanic Quarter and the city centre. At Murlough Bay, coachbuilts and A-Class motorhomes should access via Ballycastle. The road to Murlough Bay has a steep slope not suitable for motorhomes. However, the roadsides beyond are wide enough to pull off and there is a hardstanding car park halfway along the road before the descent to the Bay, with room for 'vans to park and manoeuvre.

ACCOMMODATION
I stayed at: Six Mile Water Caravan Park, Co Antrim; Ballyness Caravan Park, Co Antrim; Blaney Caravan Park, Co Fermanagh; Rushin House Caravan & Camping Park, Co Fermanagh; Clare Glen Caravan & Camping Park, Co Armagh; Dundonald Touring Caravan Park, Co Antrim.

FIND OUT MORE

Stena Line
stenaline.co.uk/routes/liverpool-belfast

Tourism Ireland ireland.com

Discover Northern Ireland
discovernorthernireland.com

National Trust
nationaltrust.org.uk

Irish Camping & Caravanning Council campingireland.ie

TOP TIP: NATIONAL TRUST MEMBERSHIP
Those who plan to visit several National Trust properties during their time in Northern Ireland should consider joining as members to get free access to all NT-owned properties and car parks. If you have an existing membership in England and Wales, it is also valid throughout Northern Ireland – but be aware that the National Trusts for Scotland and the Republic of Ireland are entirely separate organisations.

27 WILD WITH NATURE, WILD WITH CONSENT

VISIT NORTHUMBERLAND FOR SOME 'WILD NIGHTS'

WHERE	Northumberland
DISTANCE/TIME	71 miles/2½ days
START/FINISH	Berwick-upon-Tweed/Elwick

It's one of those mornings where the water of Ross Bay, on the Northumbrian coast, is so glossy only the shards of light from the softening sun shatter the stillness. Where even the take-off from an anomalous flying gull, creating pools of ringlets, seems offensive when all its feathered companions choose to contemplate their shadows, motionless on the water.

Moments earlier, I'd watched a late summer sunrise beside **Lindisfarne**. No one will reach the island just now; the famous causeway refuge box stands alone on the horizon.

Autumn begins to hang on the downy thistle heads and make the straw-yellow grass seeds and knapweeds droop. An egret stands guard over the marshy pools and rivulets that glint in the early morning light. Only a wren, hidden among a hedgerow rich with hawthorn berries and rosehips, breaks the silence.

As the warmth rises, a small pearl-bordered fritillary braves the early morning and spreads itself wide on the lichened timber of Elwick bird hide. This is Lindisfarne National Nature Reserve, and there is much wildlife here to be thankful for.

I've pitched my campervan a mere 200yds away, mindful of the privilege of staying so close to areas of environmental importance; I'm staying overnight on a Wild With Consent site, and I have exclusive use – as you will too, should you choose to visit. It overlooks Holy Island (Lindisfarne's alternative name) with an all-but-private view of Lindisfarne Castle.

My short Northumberland break had begun two days earlier, in **Berwick-upon-Tweed**. As a coastal town, close to the border with Scotland, it has a military landscape of historic fortifications and a dominating barracks, now managed by English Heritage. There's a pleasant walk around the fortifications.

Many visitors to Northumberland remain along the coast but I'm keen to explore inland to find quiet, wild locations. I find them soon enough, travelling along the B6353 to the village of **Ford**. Turning off for Ford Moss Nature Reserve, I have wide-open views of the Cheviot Hills, which lie in the northernmost part of Northumberland National Park, and a wilderness to call my own for a short walk.

The nature reserve is a lowland peat bog. In part there's an element of the manmade about it; a lone brick chimney stack is a reminder of a one-time mining landscape. Today, it's gorse, heather, rock-roses and bracken that surround the rich lowland habitat, on this occasion feeding countless large white butterflies enjoying the sunshine.

← Lindisfarne Castle on Holy Island (eye35.pix/Alamy)

↑ Cheviot Hills/Dave Head/Shutterstock

Ford Moss is a part of the vast Ford and Etal Estate, where the two namesake villages are central. There's a restful quality to both villages, each very different in style. Ford is made up of a series of stone villas, with a village green, a medieval castle and attractive church with views. The highlight is Lady Waterford Hall, its interior walls painted with Pre-Raphaelite murals.

Etal, meanwhile, contrasts with a ribbon of white cottages that lead towards the stone ruins of Etal Castle, and the only thatched pub (The Black Bull) in Northumberland. The River Till affords the opportunity for a peaceful riverside walk between the two villages; both offer an attractive tearoom apiece.

It's another river that draws me to the border village of **Norham**. The agreeable village centres around one wide street, lined with a higgledy-roofed row of terraced houses, each different in style. On the hillside above is Norham Castle. These gigantic pink ruins (free to visit) were beloved by the artist J M W Turner, who painted them with an obsessive frequency.

I glimpse the tantalising River Tweed between the trees below. Suddenly I'm castled out and eager for nature once more. Access to the river on foot is over the Norham and Ladykirk Bridge. The river marks the border between England and Scotland; my restful riverbank walk among the meadowsweet and sickly scented Himalayan balsam takes me along the Scottish side, where herons stand one-legged, fishing.

Norham is a handful of miles from my first Wild With Consent site in West Learmouth. My exclusive pitch is beside the Willow Burn, a tiny stream that ultimately flows into the Tweed. The site is remote, away from the farm-and-a-barn hamlet, tucked into a field along a single-track road.

I have the land to myself, and a walk up the hill of the newly tree-planted field gives way to striking views, and an unexpected up-close encounter with a bemused hare. My stay is a peaceful one.

There are plenty of opportunities for walking and cycling along quiet lanes from the site. This border country is also battle country. The site of the Battle of Flodden, where the English defeated the Scots in a one-day bloody onslaught in 1513, is within a three-mile cycle ride of the West Learmouth site. There's a circular walking route to get the lie of the land and a feel for the devastation of the battle.

I continue by road to the coast and time the journey right to cross the causeway to Holy Island. It's a busy day on the island, with most visitors whiling away a morning in the village or trailing to Lindisfarne Castle.

I peel off onto a footpath for a solitary circumnavigation of the island and Lindisfarne National Nature Reserve, to discover a wildly beautiful sea-level landscape of sand dunes, silent bays and enough flora and fauna to satisfy my craving for nature – roe deer, a spectacular array of wildflowers that includes orchids and delicate grass-of-Parnassus, and a selection of seabirds.

↑ River Tweed near Norham (CM) ← Brown hare (Czesznak Zsolt/Shutterstock)

ESSENTIALS

GETTING THERE & AROUND From Berwick-upon-Tweed A1/B6525/B6353 to Ford (detour to nature reserve) & Etal; B6354/A698/B6470 Etal to Norham; A698 Cornhill-on-Tweed, then rural roads to West Learmouth. Rural roads to Branxton (for Battle of Flodden site) then A697/B6353/A1 to Beal & Holy Island via the causeway. Rural roads Beal to Holburn (for St Cuthbert's Cave). Rural road south towards Chatton then B6349 to Belford/rural road to Elwick.

Check causeway crossing times to Holy Island (⚓ lindisfarne.org.uk) & be sure to leave plenty of time for the return journey to the mainland, anticipating heavy traffic in peak season. Crossing times are also posted on a noticeboard at Beal.

Parking without height barriers: Berwick-upon-Tweed has easy parking for motorhomes by the Parade square in front of the barracks. Parking is free for 3hrs, displaying a parking disk – parking attendants check vigilantly! – which can be obtained from the car park machine or from Berwick Visitor Centre & museum on Walkergate. Holy Island has a huge pay & display car park; it's possible to pay online, by phone or with coins. Ford & Etal have free parking, with easy access for motorhomes. At Norham, there's free parking at Norham Castle, & a small parking area beside River Tweed on the Scottish side.

↑ St Cuthbert's Cave (Dave Head/Shutterstock)

I venture back onto the mainland in the campervan to find more wildly remote beauty all but a stone's throw from the coast. While visitors in number continue to flock to Holy Island – where the patron saint of Northumbria, Cuthbert, was initially buried – I take a short walk in the Kyloe Hills to visit **St Cuthbert's Cave**. It's reputedly where monks rested while carrying his remains to Durham. The walk, initially up a sunken lane tunnelled by tall rosebay willowherb and then through woods of heavily scented Scots pine, is sublime. The views west become ever bigger as, with each inclining step, fields of wheat, pasture and rolling hills break out to vast panoramas of the Cheviots.

Above the cave, a climb to the rocky outcrops at the top of Greensheen Hill frames the panorama with a sea of purple heather to the west and, to the east, a wild landscape of lakes among bog and moorland with grazing cattle and sheep. Beyond, the coast and Lindisfarne.

It sets me up nicely for a stay at my final Wild With Consent site in **Elwick**, a farmer's field along a stone track. The field is carefully mown, and there's plenty of space for large coachbuilt motorhomes.

In the evening, sitting in the dark looking out from my personal pitch, it's an enigmatic sight to see car lights crossing to Holy Island, as if gliding silently over the water, when low tide gives up its sub-aqua causeway once more. I'll happily consent to sit here a while longer.

ACCOMMODATION
I stayed at: Wild With Consent sites at West Learmouth (small campervans only) & Elwick (any size of motorhome).

Wild With Consent connects motorcaravanners and campervanners with private landowners in Northumberland (and elsewhere in the UK). The scheme offers exclusive off-the-beaten track locations, where 'vans may pitch up in natural and often wild surroundings. With only 1 pitch available per location, you will always have exclusive use. Stays are limited to 1 night . Check their website for the suitability of each site to your vehicle size. Visitors book online & receive directions prior to arrival. There are currently a dozen or so sites from which to choose within Northumberland, each one costs £20–75. As sites are in wild locations, visitors must follow a *Leave Only Footprints Code of Conduct* and adhere to the Countryside Code to avoid any undue harm to the surroundings.

Wild With Consent sites are only for self-contained campervans and motorhomes. Alternatives for tent camping, or to stay at a full-facility campsite: Coldstream Holiday Park, Coldstream; Barn at Beal Campsite, Beal.

FIND OUT MORE
Wild With Consent
⚲ wildwithconsent.com

Northumberland Tourist Board
⚲ visitnorthumberland.com

28 GOING WILD FOR LAKES & LOCHS

ENJOY THE PERMITTED OPTION TO WILD CAMP IN A MOTORHOME OR TENT

WHERE	Argyll & Bute
DISTANCE/TIME	250 miles/5 days
START/FINISH	Luss/Balmaha

There are some moments that you don't want to end – and wild camping beside Loch Achray in Loch Lomond and The Trossachs National Park is one of them.

I'm sitting outdoors in the darkness on one of those velvet nights, watching the western light fade, the shapes of the hills and point of Ben Venue backlit by a ribbon of fluorescent orange.

The rough shadows of trees and distant car lights flicker in the reflections of Loch Achray. I can hear only the sound of ducks making home for the night, the wingbeats from passing geese looking for somewhere, anywhere. Then silence in the calm and the dark. I am alone and I don't want to shut the campervan door on the moment.

Created in 2002, Loch Lomond and The Trossachs National Park, at 720 square miles, affords the largest body of lake/loch in the UK together with many other

↑ Loch Lomond (Dougie Milne Photography/Shutterstock)

large lochs, two forest parks (Queen Elizabeth and Argyll) and a host of mountains and rolling lowland.

Wild camping here is as much a part of the national park as Loch Lomond is. But to kerb antisocial habits, the national park authority introduced a management system in 2018, whereby parts of the national park around Loch Lomond and within Queen Elizabeth Forest Park are under a Camping Management Zone. It means you can only camp (in a motorhome/campervan or tent) in designated locations with a pre-booked permit. I thought I'd give it a try.

I begin my wild camping experience, with the aim to cram in as much walking as I can, on the southwestern shore of Loch Lomond and the scenic conservation village of **Luss**. A blanket of charcoal grey clouds drops its contents so solidly that I'm not aware that neighbouring Beinn Eich and its foothills even exist. It's not the greatest of starts but Luss is so charming and colourful that it fails to dampen the shabbiest of days.

My first walk – Luss Heritage Path – is a gentle introduction to the area, less than two miles by footpath into Luss Glen and returning to the village along the banks of Luss Water, a small bumbling burn that enters Loch Lomond. The

green-coloured slate makes the river glassy alongside meadows of grazing sheep while colourful pots of flowers in pretty lochside cottage gardens appear all the more vibrant with the monotone sky.

Luss was once known as 'the dark village' because it lies in the shadow of surrounding hills. Those non-existent hills finally come into being, making the village appear in miniature, as I enjoy a hearty bowl of soup in the village café.

With my first wild camping night at Inveruglas, beside Loch Lomond, soggy and uneventful, I drive west along Glen Croe to the popular beauty spot **Rest and Be Thankful**. The picnic site lives up to its name – one cannot fail to appreciate the first-class views along the length of the glen and the surrounding hills. But the rest is only temporary as I leave the main road to descend beside the River Goil, with eyes agog at the incomprehensible beauty, to **Lochgoilhead**.

As its name implies, this peaceful village sits at the head of Loch Goil, a fjord-like sea loch. A school party of kayakers appreciates its calm water, where seals are often seen, as I set off on a short circular walk along The Donich Trail, above the village. The walk utilises part of the Cowal Way, a long-distance path with its name taken from this area of the national park, the Cowal Peninsula.

Cowal is known as one of the best places to see red squirrels in the national park but it's not until I reach Benmore Botanic Gardens, having taken a circular coastal tour along the shores of Loch Long and Holy Loch, that I spot one.

Benmore Botanic Gardens is a showcase mountainside garden. It is famous for its magnificent collection of trees and shrubs, with its assemblage of rhododendrons considered one of the finest in the world – there are more than 300 species represented.

There's an easy-walking tarmac route that remains on the flat and takes in the remarkable 150-year-old Redwood Avenue. But take the time to explore the 120-acre garden to its extremities and climb to the various hilltop viewpoints and you're rewarded with glorious views of surrounding hills and nearby Holy Loch. The descent, through the rhododendron bushes, is no less majestic and after my visit I tag on a less-demanding flat walk – the three-mile River Eachaig and Massan Circuit, which follows these two enticing rivers as they come together.

My return journey to Inveruglas takes me back via mysterious and skinny Loch Eck and the northern reaches of the vast and wider Long Fyne. I could have continued along the main road, but I'm longing to see more of the Argyll Forest Park that I had come through on my way to Lochgoilhead.

A climb up Hell's Glen is unremarkable, but for the rear-view mirror vistas of Loch Fyne. As I descend into the forest, though, that same feeling of astonishment I'd felt earlier in the day returns. Once again, I have remote roads to myself and the canopy of trees – not conifers as I expected, but oaks and birch – is uplifting.

↑ Luss village (RowanArtCreation/Shutterstock) ← Glen Croe seen from Rest and Be Thankful (dnaveh/Shutterstock)

Greenery has not quite arrived and the dappled sunlight seems brushed on to the road by the bristles of the leafless branches.

When I leave my camping spot at Inveruglas in early morning, the mist that hangs over the ever-narrowing northern tip of Loch Lomond makes it appear mystical. My first stop is at the Falls of Falloch, four miles north of Loch Lomond, for a short walk. The waterfall is notable but nothing by comparison to my ultimate destination for the day, the Falls of Dochart at **Killin**.

I punctuate the journey with walks beside the River Dochart and the string of lochs that the river feeds – Loch Dochart and Loch Lubhair – making the acquaintance of Highland cattle and sheep, and the chance to see a golden eagle that frequents the crags above.

In Killin, a popular tourist haunt owing to the falls, I follow the village heritage trail, via interpretation panels. It takes in the Scandinavian-looking St Fillan's Church, an old tweed mill and the ancient island burial ground of Clan McNab. I also enjoy the easy two-mile Auchmore Circuit from the village, which crosses through the Auchmore Estate and provides lovely views of Loch Tay.

But it's the photogenic Falls of Dochart, in the centre of Killin, that draw the crowds. With low water, the vast stretch of rocky outcrops lend themselves as picnic tables while the refreshing water tumbles around though, when the river is in spate, picnics are best eaten elsewhere!

Turning south along Glen Ogle, it's Loch Earn that I come across first. The loch is popular and busy with anglers, though the road along the southern shore is more peaceful and scenic; there are plenty of places to pull off and value the views across the loch to **St Fillans**, a very handsome village at the far-eastern end of the loch, with places to eat and drink.

My preference is for the quieter Balquhidder Glen where, once again, the most astounding scenery unfolds. Balquhidder village is popular with visitors to the grave of Scottish folk hero Rob Roy MacGregor, who lived and died here.

But I drive the twelve miles alongside first Loch Voil and latterly Loch Doine to the end-of-the-road car park.

The twelve miles are to be savoured slowly, and while the car park may be at the end of the road, it's not strictly a dead end. For the views extend for miles east and west; they are superlative, and the walking provides an opportunity to explore some of the most tranquil wilderness that Loch Lomond and The Trossachs National Park supplies.

Callander, beyond Loch Lubnaig, is my next stop. This busy and attractive town is at the heart of the Trossachs. It's obvious that many people simply pass through, but it really is worth spending time here and a stop at any of the numerous eateries in Callander is a worthy reward after a variety of walks in the town and the surrounding hills.

↑ Killin's historical stone bridge (Mino Surkala/Shutterstock) → Callander and the River Teith (TreasureGalore/Shutterstock)

There's a town heritage trail, useful to gather your bearings, and signposted routes north into the wooded hills to Callander Crags and the Bracklin Falls. But my favourite is a walk around Callander Meadows, only a mile long, which follows the River Teith. The river is shallow and slow moving – there are pools for swimming – and the meadow bursts with wildflowers. It's a lovely walk for families as the circular route is hard surfaced and there are plenty of places to picnic.

My tour takes me west to Loch Venachar, where the ripples of water lapping at the shoreline is all that I can hear. I park up nearby at Little Druim Wood. Owned by The Woodland Trust Scotland, this small ancient deciduous woodland, with a play and sculpture trail, is part of the vast Glen Finglas Estate, which itself is part of the Great Trossachs Forest National Nature Reserve.

There's a visitor centre to learn more about the estate and the importance of the forest. I begin a walk here that climbs Lendrick Hill. The circular route picks up a small section of the Great Trossachs Path, a 30-mile trail from the eastern shore of Loch Lomond to Callander. The views across the valley, of Loch Achray and Loch Venachar and towards the Queen Elizabeth Forest Park, are astounding even on a grey day. The clouds won't break and Ben Venue, which towers above Loch Katrine and the other lochs, appears hazy in the distance. Nonetheless, the flora and fauna at my feet – dark green fritillary butterflies, harebells, sneezewort and foxgloves – divert my gaze from the distant mountains.

Between Loch Venachar and Loch Achray sits the tiny village of **Brig o'Turk**, where I pick up a late lunchtime snack in the quaint, pine-clad tearoom. From here, it's a 20-minute scenic walk to Ruskin Viewpoint. John Ruskin, the poet, author, artist and social critic, was a frequent visitor to the Trossachs during the 19th century. He was influenced by Sir Walter Scott's *The Lady of the Lake* and the Romantic notion of nature. He loved Glen Finglas, and the artist John Everett Millais painted what is regarded as one of the most important pictures of Ruskin here, with a backdrop of the rocky gorge and waterfall.

It's late afternoon by the time I reach **Queen Elizabeth Forest Park**, created in 1953 to honour Her Majesty's coronation. It's big – some 50,000 acres – stretching from the eastern shores of Loch Lomond in the west to Callander in the east.

The view from my walk on Lendrick Hill had been pleasing enough, but it's nothing by comparison to the scenery along the Duke's Pass, arguably one of the best short touring routes in Scotland. It's surpassed, though, by a tour of Three Lochs Forest Drive, a seven-mile one-way route within the forest park. With panoramic views high up in one moment, lochside the next, the drive is outstanding. The road is unmetalled and I recommend spending at least a day here to account for the numerous walks accessible from the route (car parks and stopping points are endless) and to take time on the road.

↑ Loch Achray (Dale Kelly/Shutterstock)   ← Duke's Pass, Queen Elizabeth Forest Park (jwramsay/Shutterstock)

However, the entrance barrier shuts at 4pm, and the exit at 5pm, so most day visitors have gone by early evening – which means, if you have a permit to camp overnight, as I do, you'll find the entire, vast area is populated with a handful of campers only.

The camping spots are limited and stretched out along the seven miles. Tent campers are not mixed with motorhomes, and the motorhome spots allow for just two or three 'vans. At my location, overlooking beautiful Loch Achray close to the end of the trail, I have the whole of the eastern end of the loch shore exclusively.

I could walk and walk from my wild camping pitch: into the pine woods; along the now-silent forest drive; up into the hills or down to the pub at Brig o'Turk; there's plenty of choice. But, at this moment in time, abandoning Loch Achray and its magical charms is out of the question. I must sit, to watch the sun slide behind Ben Venue and illuminate the sky like a fireball.

I wish I'd booked to stay longer beside Loch Achray. But, much as I want to linger, my wanderlust is ready to fit in another string of lakes, on the road heading northwest from **Aberfoyle**. There are three lochs to pass along the way and, beyond the black and mysterious Loch Ard, the road becomes single track with passing places.

On this occasion, I have first Loch Chon and latterly Loch Arklet, the most remote of all the lochs I encounter, to myself.

↑ Fishing on Lake of Menteith (Ulmus Media/Shutterstock)

Its beauty takes me by surprise. Turn a corner and it's suddenly there, sunken in a vast bowl. The early morning light is such that the bronzed hillsides reflect in Arklet's peaceful water like tiger stripes, and it's impossible to see where the water ends and the hills begin. I could not have selected a more inspiring location for breakfast and a short walk. Thirty minutes later and the tiger stripes are gone.

Reversing my route (the road halts at Loch Lomond's eastern shore) to Aberfoyle, I venture to the Lake of Menteith (the national park's only loch that's named as a lake) and board the tiny ferry for a ten-minute crossing to Inchmahome.

Both Robert the Bruce and Mary Queen of Scots found solace on this minuscule, wooded island, with its 13th-century priory ruins. It remains a sanctuary today, a place to escape Loch Lomond's busy shores – just 260 people had visited Inchmahome the day before my visit.

As the hum of the boat disappears into the distance, it's only birdsong that 'disturbs' the air while I stroll around the edge of the island; it takes all of ten minutes to complete at a pace, but lingering to appreciate the swathes of bluebells, the gently lapping shoreline and the restfulness of the location is what Inchmahome is all about.

Running out of time, there is one last place I'm keen to walk before I leave the area. It's a bank holiday weekend and Balmaha, on the eastern shore of Loch Lomond, appears overwhelmed by visitors, all eager to enjoy the warm weather beside the water. A trail of walkers are tramping up iconic Conic Hill, and the attractive Oak Tree Inn and ice-cream parlour are doing a roaring trade.

While all the world sunbathes at Balmaha, I hop on-board *Lady Jane*, a fine glossy-lacquered boat, for a five-minute on-demand boat trip to Inchcailloch, an island that I arrive to find deserted.

Inchcailloch is smothered by the most beautiful gentle, shady deciduous woodland and, in spring, the island changes hue beneath a blanket of bluebells. There are footpaths around, across and up the cone-shaped island and I choose to head towards the summit. There, at the same height as the island's treetops, Loch Lomond and The Trossachs National Park appears spread out like a giant map.

I can see the vastness of Loch Lomond and how many islands it embraces. I can see how varied the landscape is, from baked brown and vivid green slopes to flat meadows and seas of oak. And there, rising above them all, I catch a hazy glimpse of Ben Lomond, the national park's highest peak. My little summit of Inchcailloch is diminutive by comparison but, were *Lady Jane* not returning to collect me, I'd gladly stay sitting on it.

ESSENTIALS

GETTING THERE & AROUND
A82 Luss to Inveruglas then reverse route to Tarbet; A83 to Rest & Be Thankful/B828 to Lochgoilhead. B839 north then A815 south. Rural road from Whistlefield Inn to Blairmore via Ardentinny/A880 to Benmore. A815 north/B839/B828 to Rest & Be Thankful. A83/A82 to Inveruglas. A82 north to Crianlarich/A85 east/A827 to Killin. Reverse route to A85 then continue south to Glen Ogle & circular tour of Loch Earn. A84 south then rural road west to Loch Doine (car park beyond). Reverse route then A84 south to Callander. A84/A821 to Three Lochs Forest Drive entrance. A821 south to Aberfoyle, then B829 to Loch Arklet & Inversnaid Hotel. Reverse route to Aberfoyle then A81 to Lake of Menteith. Return to Aberfoyle then A81/A811/B837 to Balmaha.

All the roads that I ventured along are acceptable for coachbuilt motorhomes, except for the section from Callander to The Crags & Bracklin Falls, which is steep & narrow with deep gutters; there is limited turning space if the Falls car park is full. To access the Bracklin Falls walk, it is better to park at Callander Meadows and enjoy the walk from town via the very pretty Callander Crags.

Parking without height barriers: there is suitable parking at Luss South Car Park in Luss and The Meadows Car Park in Callander. In Balmaha is the Visitor Centre Car Park. Parking a large motorhome here on a busy summer weekend could be problematic unless you arrive early, but Balmaha is within walking distance (along the West Highland Way) of Milarrochy Bay CCC Site & Cashel. Camping in the Forest site (see opposite) for recommended extended stays in the locale. Lochgoilhead has a central village car park.

ACCOMMODATION

ACCOMMODATION I stayed at: Maragowan CAMC Site, Killin (open to non-members); Cashel Camping in the Forest; Three Lochs Forest Drive Camping Management Zone; Inveruglas Camping Management Zone.

Permits are required for Mar–Sep stays at designated sites in the Camping Management Zone, available online; see below. They may be booked up to 4wks in advance (they do get booked up at times) and cost £4/night per motorhome/tent (max 3 consecutive nights). You will receive your permit via email (to print & display in your 'van) along with detailed directions. The camping permit locations have no facilities; there is a chemical waste disposal point at the National Park Visitor Centre car park on Loch Lubnaig.

At Three Lochs Forest Drive, there is also a £2 drive-through access charge.

FIND OUT MORE

Loch Lomond & the Trossachs National Park ⏴ lochlomond-trossachs.org

Camping Management Zone permits ⏴ lochlomond-trossachs.org/things-to-do/camping/get-a-permit/

TOP TIP: LOCAL WALKS

TOP TIP: LOCAL WALKS There are many signposted walking trails with detailed descriptions and directions available for download from the website above. All the walks I did were taken from here.

Recommended Ordnance Survey maps for walking in the area: *OL38 Loch Lomond South, OL39 Loch Lomond North* and *OL46 The Trossachs*. I recommend taking good old-fashioned paper maps; I had to assist a walker who had no signal for his digital version!

↑ Highland cattle at home in northern Scotland (BenWatts/Shutterstock)

29 GREAT SCOT: A LAND OF STORIES

A COMBINATION OF HISTORIC SITES WITH ICONIC SIGHTS ON A TOUR OF CENTRAL SCOTLAND

WHERE	Stirlingshire/Falkirk/West, Mid & East Lothian/ Scottish Borders (Berwickshire)
DISTANCE/TIME	131miles/4 days
START/FINISH	Stirling/St Abbs

'We are mere transients, who sing,' it reads, chiselled hard into a solid timber ring at the Battle of Bannockburn memorial site. To a background of atmospheric reverberations, the poetic words echo softly across the gentle, rolling landscape, in sight of imposing Stirling Castle which sits aloft a solitary rocky crag.

This is where Robert the Bruce, now straddled across his horse in bronze, battle-axe at the ready, defeated the English King Edward II in 1314 during the Wars of Scottish Independence. The Battle of Bannockburn is regarded as the most significant battle in Scottish history – and Stirling Castle, one of the most important castles in Scotland.

The historic city of Stirling seems a fine place for my daughter Lara and me to begin a short tour of Scotland, taking in some of the country's history, its stories and iconic sights, modern and old.

↑ Stirling Castle (cornfield/Shutterstock)

Stirling was a prominent focal point in royal Scottish history for centuries, seeing births, deaths, wars and coronations. The restored castle is open to the public and its grounds provide prominent views over the attractive Old Town, the Forth Valley, the Ochil Hills to the northeast and the National Wallace Monument. This, too, is situated on top of a wooded crag, the monument dedicated to William Wallace who, some 17 years earlier than the Battle of Bannockburn, defeated Edward I, the father of Edward II, at the Battle of Stirling Bridge. It's possible to climb the landmark via its spiral staircase – be warned, there are 246 steps to its crown!

Within seven miles of Stirling is The Pineapple, one of the world's most unusual follies. This extraordinary piece of architecture, built in 1761, sits adjacent to a six-acre walled garden, part of Dunmore Park, where exotic fruits were once grown. The unusual stone cupola is intricately carved like a pineapple, though no exact reason for its fruit-like design is known.

The Pineapple is rented as a holiday let, but visitors may enter the walled garden free of charge to view the external architecture. The garden, filled with an orchard of fruit trees, is a lovely place to sit with a picnic.

Our tour continues south to visit first the Falkirk Wheel and latterly The Kelpies. Opened in 2002, the Falkirk Wheel is a masterful modern work of art – and a piece of engineering that connects the Forth and Clyde Canal with the Union Canal. It's impossible not to be mesmerised watching the giant wheel as it turns

↑ The Falkirk Wheel (Alan Bilsborough/Shutterstock)

to raise – and lower – boats from one level to another. Boat trips may be booked to experience the lift with a short journey along the canal.

Less than five miles from the Falkirk Wheel sit The Kelpies, on the banks of the Forth and Clyde Canal. These giant steel equine sculptures dominate Helix Park and provide a popular family day out as there are places to eat and play, and trails to walk (including the towpath from the Falkirk Wheel). It's possible to book a tour to view inside the structures, too.

As its name suggests, the Forth and Clyde Canal links two of Scotland's most notable rivers, those that flow through, respectively, Edinburgh and Glasgow. We follow the former to the capital for an overnight stay at the CAMC site that would overlook the Firth of Forth were it not for the impeding trees.

On our way we stop in the photogenic town of **South Queensferry**. This town is filled with delectable places to eat – everything from upmarket seafood restaurants to fabulous stone-baked take-away pizzas.

It's also one of the best places from which to view the famous trio of bridges: the Forth Road Bridge, the Forth Rail Bridge (a UNESCO World Heritage Site) and the more recently opened Queensferry Crossing, which carries the M90 motorway across the Firth of Forth. Foot passengers may cross the Forth Road Bridge for outstanding views of the iconic rusty-red railway crossing. Alternatively, passengers may board the *Maid of the Forth* for a sightseeing tour on the water.

Our stay in **Edinburgh**, on this occasion, is brief, with just time for an evening stroll along the banks of the Forth. Access to the beach from the campsite is via a steep footpath through woodland opposite the site entrance; or turn left out of the entrance and walk along the quiet road for 200yds to descend on a gentler slope. The beach promenade also acts as a tarmacked cycleway all the way to Leith, where the visitor attraction, the Royal Yacht *Britannia* is docked.

We continue our tour by skirting Edinburgh on the ring road and exiting the A1 at Wallyford to join the East Lothian Coastal Trail. The 31-mile touring route follows the coast through pretty villages such as Cockenzie and Port Seton, with its tiny fishing harbour and coastal cottages showcasing castellated roofs, and **Gullane**, the centre of 'Scotland's Golf Coast' with golf courses one after another.

Here, we stop for incredible homemade ice cream at Imma's, opposite the red-rock ruins of the village's 12th-century church, although we spot plenty of other good-looking eateries along the main street. The wild headlands and beaches offer fabulous coastal walks, though we enjoy a walk around the charming village of **Dirleton**, with the Castle Inn pub overlooking the village green and the ruins of Dirleton Castle. Open to the public, the walled gardens that surround the medieval fortress (which was badly damaged when it came under siege by Oliver Cromwell's troops in 1650) include, at 705ft, the world's longest herbaceous

↑ The Kelpies (Gavin Ritchie/Shutterstock) ← The Three Bridges: Forth Rail Bridge, Forth Road Bridge and Queensferry Crossing (Iain Masterton/Alamy)

border – allegedly! Regardless of length, it is an impressive sight and a beautiful place to visit.

So, too, is neighbouring **North Berwick**, a popular town with lots of independent shops to browse, a family golf course beside the town's two beaches (West Bay and Milsey Bay), a shallow saltwater lido, and an anomalous conical-shaped hill, North Berwick Law, to climb for coastal views. The town also gives us our first glimpse of Bass Rock.

This famous volcanic rock erupts more than 350ft from the sea, rather like Uluru does from the desert in Australia. It's home to a vast colony of gannets – indeed, there are so many birds that the rock's surface appears silvery white from the resulting mass.

We have a better sighting of Bass Rock from Gun Head; it's a scenic spot to sit while enjoying a tasty snack from Drift, a trendy shipping-container café that sits on the edge of the promontory. The steep cliffs provide contrast to our later visit to John Muir Country Park, on the edge of **Dunbar**.

Here, named after the naturalist John Muir, who was born in the town, the country park offers acres of space for walking, together with access to a vast sandy

SOUVENIR
EIGHT FABULOUS THINGS TO DO ON THIS ROAD TRIP

1. Visit Stirling Castle to view the beautifully restored Great Hall, the largest banqueting hall in Scotland, built for royal feasts and pageants.
2. Climb the National Wallace Monument for extraordinary views over the Forth valley and Ochil Hills.
3. Become immersed in medieval warfare as events unfold before your eyes through the audio-visual experience at the Battle of Bannockburn Visitor Centre.
4. Travel by water between Glasgow and Edinburgh on the Forth–Clyde Canoe Trail. If you don't want to take the trip alone, there are paddle activity providers to help you on your way.
5. Walk the ¾-mile causeway to Cramond Island, a tidal island in the Firth of Forth, within walking distance of the Edinburgh Caravan & Motorhome Club Site. Time your walk well, to get back before the tide comes in!
6. Discover the life and legacy of John Muir at his Birthplace Museum in Dunbar – and step out at the start of the John Muir Way coast-to-coast walk.
7. Explore the beauty of St Abbs Head, a National Nature Reserve with rugged coastal scenery; if you walk the Smuggler's Trail, you'll pass through the reserve.
8. Find out more about the history of smuggling along the Berwickshire coast at Gunsgreen House in Eyemouth. The imposing house was built by a smuggler!

beach and views of Belhaven, an appealing village west of Dunbar. The landscape is that of wild-grass meadows and salt marsh, where little streams interconnect as they run to the sea. Wildflowers are in abundance, with clusters of sea asters, sea buckthorn and dog roses smothering the ground. With a beachside surf school, it's also a popular place for learning to ride the waves.

In the evening, following a stroll around Dunbar Harbour and the pretty town, we sit overlooking Bass Rock from our campsite pitch. It appears gargantuan from the ultramarine sea in the evening sunshine. By morning, both sea and rock merge as a steely grey.

We leave the East Lothian Coastal Trail driving route behind and, moments later, pick up the Berwickshire Coastal Trail, diverting off the main A1 to visit the tiny village of **Cove**. As its name implies, the village – no more than a dozen or so cottages – hugs the cliff top of a sheltered cove.

The plan had been to walk, in sections, the Smuggler's Trail, which begins (or ends) in Cove and runs along to Burnmouth, close to the border with England. But the dense fog that swirls over the coast doesn't provide the finest conditions for walking a clifftop path. The inclement weather does, however, allow the occasional

↑ Lobster pots by the harbour at Dunbar (Phil Silverman/Shutterstock)

ESSENTIALS

GETTING THERE & AROUND Stirling is accessed off the M9, Junction 9 (south) & Junction 10 (north). A91 to Bannockburn, then A905 towards Falkirk for The Pineapple & The Kelpies. A9/B816 for Falkirk Wheel. A904 to South Queensferry; A90 for Edinburgh CAMC Site. A902 then A720/A1 (Edinburgh ring road anticlockwise); off at Wallyford then B1348/A198 (following East Lothian Coastal Trail) & A1087 to Dunbar. A1 to Cove; rural roads then A1107 to Coldingham & Eyemouth. Return to Coldingham for B6438 to St Abbs.

All the roads that I ventured along are acceptable for coachbuilt motorhomes.

Parking without height barriers: in Stirling, there's Castleview or Springkerse Park & Ride (free bus); but note that campervans & motorhomes may not park at Stirling Castle. The Pineapple has a small car park accessible by campervans, but no space to manoeuvre coachbuilts; overhanging trees on the access road effectively limit height to 6ft 6in (2m). Falkirk Wheel & The Kelpies (Helix Country Park) have dedicated (paid) motorhome parking. At South Queensferry, there's parking at Newhalls Rd or Scotmid (customers only). For Edinburgh, use St Leonard's Car Park or the 5 park & rides. North Berwick has on-street parking options. For Dunbar, there's parking at John Muir Country Park (turn right at 6ft 9in/2.1m height barrier for over-height vehicle parking) or at Dunbar Harbour. Park at Victoria Rd Car Park in Eyemouth. Note, the car park in St Abbs has a steep single-track

↑ The harbour at St Abbs (Phil Silverman/Shutterstock)

break to see just how jagged and steep the cliffs are. The surrounding countryside is, in places, a collage of agricultural fields and hedgerows; in others, wild and remote moorland bog, layered with tough grasses, tufted cotton buds, bracken and the rich pinks and purples of heather.

It's so misty and wet that, instead of the planned walk, we choose a sea-based exploration of the cliffs in a RIB, with a fast splash-and-dash trip from Eyemouth to Pettico Wick, stopping at the beautiful harbour of **St Abbs**. Perhaps more so than had we walked, tracing along the foot of the cliffs, we can see why smugglers in days of old relished this area of coastline so much for hiding booty in the numerous caverns, holes, crevices and creases. The speedy trip provides a very different perspective of the suede green folds and sharp, blackened craggy lumps of rock mellowed by seawater and time.

For our final night we choose to stop harbourside in the little village of St Abbs. The day's rain ceases and the light changes over the rocks as we watch the tide come in and fishing boats disappear over the horizon. It's a strange light, pink and pale, creating mirror pools and ripples that slosh and plop beside the harbour wall as one rock after another vanishes from view.

We are mere transients, passing through. We leave St Abbs and the rhythm of the tide with muted morning colours. The seagulls sing.

approach with a sharp bend (with clear view) at the bottom. Approach with caution. Parking is pay & display.

The recommended Ordnance Survey Explorer **map** for walking the Berwickshire Smuggler's trail is OL346 *Berwick-upon-Tweed*.

ACCOMMODATION
During my visit, I stayed at: The Woods Caravan Park, Alva (Clackmananshire); Edinburgh CAMC Site; Dunbar CCC Site; St Abbs Harbour (overnight motorhome stopover allowed; put the money through harbourmaster's letterbox). Overnight motorhome stopovers are also available at the Falkirk Wheel & Dunbar Harbour for a small fee.

FIND OUT MORE
Visit Scotland visitscotland.com
Stirling stirling.gov.uk/tourism-visitors/
Falkirk Wheel
scottishcanals.co.uk/falkirk-wheel/
Berwickshire Coast
visitberwickshirecoast.co.uk

Berwickshire Smugglers Trail
gunsgreenhouse.org/smugglers-trail.html
Eyemouth RIB Trips
eyemouthribtrips.co.uk

30 HIGHLAND RING

WHERE	Highlands
DISTANCE/TIME	697 miles/7 days
START/FINISH	Inverness (circular route)

Climbing up from a sea of lakes as the timid sun appears to blow grisly clouds from the sky, we turn a corner at Rispond to find a jewel-decked sea and silver-sand beach set against the most brilliant purple banks of wild thyme. We are close to the most northwesterly point of our Scottish road trip and the sun has just come out to play. We sense the best is yet to come.

The Scottish Highlands are brimming with superlatives: the northernmost point and town on mainland Britain; the best waterfalls to see leaping salmon; the deepest gorge in Britain; the oldest National Nature Reserve in the UK; Europe's largest herring port; the shortest street in the world; the biggest dolphins in the world... the list goes on.

Added to that catalogue of superlatives is 'one of the best driving routes in the world', the North Coast 500. The 500-mile (officially 516) road trip starts and ends in the Highlands' capital, Inverness, and takes in the north Highlands' most dramatic coastal scenery. My son Dominic and I were revelling in its beauty, with or without the sun.

After an explorative walk around Inverness, taking in the historic castle from where the best views of the city and the River Ness can be seen, our trip begins with a mooch around the **Moray Firth** by boat. *Dolphin Spirit* operates wildlife-watching tours, with sightings of the 200 bottlenose dolphins that live in the Moray Firth a regular occurrence. We're unlucky not to see any of these largest and most northerly dolphins in the world during our Dolphin Space Programme-approved trip, though we do spot harbour seals basking on the rocks and a couple of otters dipping through the inky-black water.

We are more fortunate when we park up at our campsite in pretty **Rosemarkie**, overlooking the firth. A gentle walk along the beach brings us to Chanonry Point, famous as one of the best places in the world to see these graceful creatures. And sure enough, as the tide comes in, so too does a dolphin and her calf. There are no circus acrobatics, just a playful flirtation with the water – and their salmon supper. Courtesy of the feeding dolphins, some salmon will never make it to their spawning grounds upstream.

Rosemarkie and nearby **Cromarty**, where we make a brief stop, both lie on an area known as the Black Isle. Neither island nor black, this picturesque peninsula divides the Moray Firth and Cromarty Firth – and would get missed without a detour from the '500'.

We find the Black Isle soothingly beautiful, a rolling landscape of potato fields and swaying barley, woodland, and coastal wildlife. Even in the rain the little

← Invernerss and the River Ness (Karol Kozlowski/Shutterstock)

fishing village of Cromarty proves idyllic, with its narrow lanes and alleyways, whitewashed cottages ornamented by stepped gables and the intoxicating wet scent of a rose – and a comforting coffee and cake from Sutor Creek.

By the time we've gone off-route to discover the Mermaid of the North sculpture in the Seaboard Village of **Balintore** and, later, the famous Falls of Shin, it becomes apparent that we are using the NC500 as a skeleton from which to explore further afield. The latter a 25-mile detour inland, is regarded as among the best places to see leaping salmon on their migratory route back to the spawning beds upstream.

There's an exhibition centre close to the waterfall that explains the life cycle of wild salmon and the importance of salmon rivers in Scotland, but it doesn't match viewing a salmon's struggle to return 'home'. Of the dozen or so we see attempt the falls, only one manages the desperate fight to swim against the flow, the others simply battered by the force of the falls. It's a humbling experience to watch.

So mesmerised by the salmon and a wander by the sparkling waters of the Shin, we arrive too late to enter Dunrobin Castle, the most northerly of Scotland's grand houses. The home of the Dukes of Sutherland, Dunrobin's spires and turrets would look more in keeping beside the River Loire in France than perched above the North Sea. We take a long drive north, the scenery progressively more remote, wild bog mingling with buttercup meadows. As we climb up on to extreme moorland, the weather turns, sea fog hovers and, approaching Wick, we decide it's beneficial to stop driving for the day.

Wick is the largest town in Caithness, which is the most northerly of Scotland's ancient counties, the pair 'established' by Viking invaders. In Victorian times, Wick was also the largest and most important herring port in Europe. With a ten-minute walk beside the River Wick from our campsite into town, we can see that heritage laid out before us. Numerous handsome buildings remain in what is the only complete example of town planning by the 19th-century engineer Thomas Telford. But despite Wick's heritage and its Guinness World Record credentials as home to the shortest street in the world, the town today is in desperate need of investment to maintain its appeal with visitors. Hopefully those touring the NC500 will be able to add to the local economy.

Wick's loss of tourist trade is partly due to its location just south of John O'Groats, where every road tripper makes a beeline. We delay our visit to the tourist hotspot by visiting deserted Noss Head, just north of Wick. With views of the Orkney Islands, our walk along the headland takes us to Castle Sinclair Girnigoe.

In our judgement, **Noss Head** is a must-see location on the NC500. The ruined castle perches precariously on a rocky promontory, with the vast crescent of Sinclair's Bay stretching beyond. In summer, the headland is abundant with

← Noss Head and Castle Sinclair Girnigoe (RIEGER Bertrand/hem/Hemis/SuperStock)

birdlife and a magnificent collection of wildflowers, including rare northern marsh orchids.

John O'Groats is named after Jan de Groot, a Dutchman who settled in the area some 500 years ago and started the first regular ferry service to Orkney. A passenger ferry continues to sail daily today during the summer months, but we weren't awestruck by the dispersed village.

Regarded by many as the northeastern tip of mainland Britain, it's nearby **Duncansby Head** that actually claims this honour. Bird colonies of shags, kittiwakes, gulls and puffins reside on any shelf available – and there are plenty, with sharp cliff faces and broken slices of rock. These include the sandstone Stacks of Duncansby, two pyramidal lumps around which the sea swirls menacingly. Drifts of pastel pink sea thrift and tufts of cotton grass tremble on the clifftops as the light shifts and dances over a mauve sea and whisper-blue sky. But the lighting effects over this particular stage are nothing by comparison to the sallow all-night light that was to come.

A storm is approaching. The scattered, roofless structures of the derelict crofters' cottages among the fields of buttercups and spiky bog appear to soak up every raindrop like a sponge and I'm grateful to step out of the torrent and inside The Queen Mother's Castle of Mey.

Purchased in 1952 soon after the death of her husband, King George VI, The Queen Mother stayed in Mey every year for holidays until her death in 2002. It was the only house she owned personally; a guided tour shows much of the family side to The Queen Mother, including where she would feed her corgis!

The walled gardens are outstanding. But the castle overlooks the Pentland Firth and, had it not been for the wet lashings of rain, we'd have admired them much longer. Instead, we make our way to **Dunnet Head**, the most northerly point on mainland Britain, where the tempestuous waves crash about the cliffs with alarming spectacle – and deem the lighthouse even more essential.

By evening the storm has tamed and, throughout the night, a wonderful soft and pallid pink light ensues. There is no midnight sun, but the light never really wavers.

Despite its Viking history we bypass Thurso, the most northerly town on the mainland, to continue west. The landscape between Thurso and Bettyhill is perhaps the least interesting of the 500-odd miles but, beyond the decommissioned power station at Dounreay, the route becomes increasingly scenic.

From Torrisdale Bay and our lunchtime diversion to the diminutive Skerray Harbour, the views become ever greater, and more dramatic with each bend in the road. As we cross the Kyle of Tongue and skirt Loch Eriboll, all thoughts and evidence of the previous day's storm have evaporated, leaving jewel-like shimmering bays. By Rispond, we arrive at the first of many empty, silvery white

↑ Puffins may be seen at Duncansby Head (AndreAnita/Shutterstock) → The picturesque landscape around Loch Eriboll (KobusSmit/Shutterstock)

SOUVENIR

Discovering places like The Jammery at Culkein (see opposite) is an aspect we loved along the North Coast 500. In the most seemingly remote places, we would come across an award-winning shop or café, spinning studio, wool dyer or art gallery. The route was created to improve the economy of remote parts of the Highlands and high-quality artisan craftspeople have set up in the most unlikely of places. Many on the west coast are part of the Assynt Crofters' Association, keeping the ancient tradition of remote living alive.

beaches, each one more inviting than the last – though **Balnakeil**, to come, stands out as the most beautiful of them all, overlooked by its ruined church and baronial manor house.

With a glowing sun culminating in an intense orange sunset, our evening is spent walking along clifftops and scrambling on rocks around Sango Sands Campsite before settling down to drift off to the swish of the flowing tide. By morning, we're watching seals take an early bathe in the bay.

It's here at Durness and Balnakeil Beach that we reach our most northwesterly point and the drive southwest is, initially, a rain-infested crossing of spectacular moorland. Desolate, treeless, boggy and mountainous in equal measure, this is seemingly the most remote part of the NC500 but by no means the most dramatic. That, we find, is still to come – as we cross into the Northwest Highland Geopark, the views approaching the rugged landscape of the Assynt leave us dumbstruck.

↑ The Jammery at Culkein (CM)

Crossing the Kylesku Bridge, we peel off towards Drumbeg, a narrow route that, despite being only nine miles in length, takes approximately an hour to travel. The views of outlying islands, lakes and stunted trees make this an inspiring section of the route but it's not suitable for all vehicles (see box, page 282).

A detour takes us to the Point of Stoer. Orcas had been spotted earlier that day around the headland. They'd disappeared by the time we arrive but, with clearing skies, distant mountains on the Outer Hebrides appear as faint blue hummocks. The detour is worthwhile, including a visit to the The Jammery at Culkein, where a young couple have set up making homemade jams and chutneys in a scenic, remote edge-of-nowhere village.

Descending towards Clachtoll and Rhicarn, the Assynt landscape becomes ever more astounding. Its combination of knobbly but smooth ancient rocks, imposing peaks and brooding lakes create a striking sight. And, while we clamber over rocks amid the sheep around our beachside campsite at Achmelvich that evening, my gaze is never far from the remarkable Suilven 'sugarloaf' mountain that dominates the skyline.

It's hard to comprehend, staring out across mystical Loch Assynt the following morning, that the mountainous rocks in front of us are more than 3,000 million years old. The air is still, the silence magical as we look at the age-old pine trees that grow from these tiny prehistoric islands in the jet-black water. We stop again to admire the ancient rocky panorama once more in Knockan Crag National Nature Reserve, an area created where two continents came crashing together,

↑ Kylesku Bridge (Cain images/Shutterstock)

now renowned for its geology. But nothing prepares us for the descent on foot to the death-defying Corrieshalloch Gorge, the deepest in Britain.

The narrow gorge is sheer-sided, channelling the River Droma down a series of waterfalls. There's a wobbly suspension bridge that crosses the gorge at its deepest point, with a cantilevered viewing platform hanging above the rock face further downstream. We take the longer of two walks to reach the gorge, where a microclimate provides a humid hike amid youthful pines, heather and rosebay willowherb, and views over Loch Broom, into which the Droma flows.

By the end of our day, we're appreciating a walk around the celebrated Inverewe Gardens. Created by Osgood Mackenzie in the 19th century from a windswept headland beside Loch Ewe, the gardens, now owned by the National Trust for Scotland, are filled with plants from around the world. But it's the lochside walled garden that is the most vibrant, with colourful stripes of fruit, cutting flowers and vegetables mingling with swags of scented roses. It's quite a transformation from the rugged and remote landscapes we have become accustomed to.

Our final day begins on foot, on the signposted Woodland Walk in Benn Eighe National Nature Reserve, the oldest reserve in the UK, which protects the largest remnant of ancient Scots pinewood in the western Highlands. There's the option of the four-mile Mountain Trail too, which climbs high enough to reach Arctic conditions, but our modest mile-long, 100yd climb provides magnificent views of Loch Maree and Slioch mountain through the splendour of the pine canopy.

Back on the road, turning west at Kinlochewe, the jagged quartzite slopes of Benn Eighe become ever-present, shimmering snow white in the sunshine. The bulky mass looms large along much of the glen before we reach the appealing coastal village of **Torridon**, where the village shop doubles up as a fine café and lunch stop overlooking Upper Loch Torridon.

We soon realise we have saved the best until last, though, and our drive from Shieldaig to Tornapress around the coastline of the Applecross Peninsula provides sensational views. This is not a road for bad weather, but we have timed it just right. Cloudless skies with limitless visibility mean that every corner we turn creates another vista, with endless peaks across the Highlands, the Isle of Skye and the Outer Hebrides.

At Applecross, leaving empty pink sandstone beaches behind, we begin the final steep climb to Bealach na Bà Viewpoint and the ensuing remarkable hairpin descent to Lochcarron.

Like a gentle cool down after intensive exercise, we're grateful for the road thereon to Dingwall and Inverness. The route drifts into open countryside, providing a gradual return to normality following the dramatic views of the previous days. In soft sunshine, we arrive back where we began, alongside the Moray Firth, just in time to see the dolphins come out to play.

↑ Views of Raasay and Skye from the North Coast 500 (CM) ← Bottlenose dolphins at Chanonry Point (grafxart/Shutterstock)

ESSENTIALS

GETTING THERE & AROUND
Inverness, the start and finish of the route, is easily accessed from the A9. Maps can be downloaded from the North Coast 500 website (see opposite) which detail the route in a clockwise direction. However, the reverse direction was recommended to us (by Yvette, owner of the *Dolphin Spirit*) to make the most of the west coast views; I would agree.

The NC500 touring route (not consistently signposted) is popular with motorhomes, and those that drive with care will have no problems, even on the single-track roads, where there are passing places every 50–100yds. We came across no height restrictions. However, there are two sections regarded as inappropriate for coachbuilt motorhomes, with alternative routes provided: the B869 Unapool to Stoer (large motorhomes should continue along A894 to Inchnadamph then A837 to Lochinver & B869 to Stoer); and from south of Shieldaig to Tornapress via Applecross and the Bealach Na Ba viewpoint, 41 miles of spectacular single-track driving (bypassed via A896). Both are generally quiet and remote (and, arguably, the most scenic along the route) but they are single-track roads with passing places and have low-hanging trees, blind bends and summits. We did come across several coachbuilt 'vans along the two unsuitable sections For safety, drivers must be confident at reversing their 'van long distances on these narrow roads.

We had no problems **parking** anywhere. The best place for large 'vans in Inverness is at the vast free car park beside the marina, from where Dolphin Spirit departs, a 15-min walk from the town centre. At Torridon, there's limited parking in the village; large 'vans should use the Countryside Centre car park and walk the mile-long Shore Path to the village.

When to go: May to September is best, as some of the roads may be closed due to snow or hazardous conditions during winter months. Most campsites are only open between the end of March and October.

↑ Knockan Crag National Nature Reserve (Micuzzzu/Shutterstock)

ACCOMMODATION
There are many campsites along the route, but we found the following particularly good: Rosemarkie CCC Site (on the shore of Moray Firth overlooking a mile-long sandy beach with Chanonry Point & the pretty village of Rosemarkie both within walking distance); Wick River Campsite (an attractive riverside site, 5mins' walk from town); Dunnet Bay CAMC Site (direct access to the sweeping bay, with some pitches overlooking the beach & Dunnet Head); Sango Sands Oasis (outstanding location with all pitches overlooking Pentland Firth & direct access to 2 virtually private beaches); Shore Caravan Site, Achmelvich (2 miles off NC500, on a headland with superb beach & places to go walking, but care should be taken on narrow approach road); Inverewe Gardens Poolewe CCC Site (fabulous location overlooking Loch Ewe & Inverewe Gardens); Dingwall CCC Site (at the head of Cromarty Firth, 10mins' walk to town).

FIND OUT MORE

North Coast 500
⌀ northcoast500.com

Dolphin Spirit
⌀ dolphinspirit.co.uk

Castle & Gardens of Mey
⌀ castleofmey.org.uk

Inverewe Gardens
⌀ nts.org.uk/inverewe

TOP TIP: FOOD & DRINK
St Andrew's Cathedral Café (Inverness): hot drinks & snacks & the opportunity to purchase a 'Suspended Coffee' – a hot drink for someone who wouldn't be able to afford it.
Sutor Creek (Cromarty): coffee & cake, take-away pizza, meals & desserts.
Cocoa Mountain (Balnakeil Craft Centre, Durness): hot chocolate & chocolates handmade on the premises.
The Jammery (Culkein): hot drinks, jams & chutneys, cakes & snacks.
Torridon Stores & Café (Torridon): daily lunchtime specials, soup, sandwiches & homemade cakes. Excellent coffee.

INDEX

Entries in **bold** refer to major entries

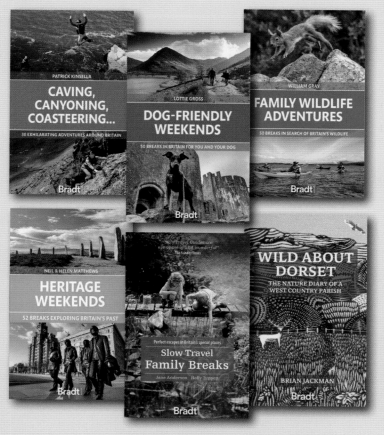

Bradt on
BRITAIN

Bradt GUIDES

TRAVEL TAKEN SERIOUSLY

bradtguides.com/shop

 BradtGuides   @BradtGuides @bradtguides

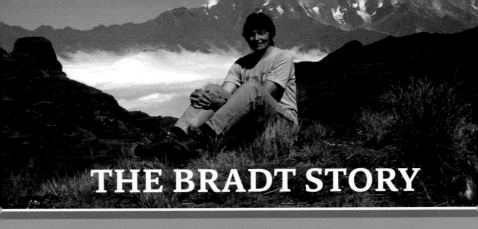

THE BRADT STORY

In the beginning

It all began in 1974 on an Amazon river barge. During an 18-month trip through South America, two adventurous young backpackers – Hilary Bradt and her then husband, George – decided to write about the hiking trails they had discovered through the Andes. *Backpacking Along Ancient Ways in Peru and Bolivia* included the very first descriptions of the Inca Trail. It was the start of a colourful journey to becoming one of the best-loved travel publishers in the world; you can read the full story on our website (bradtguides. com/ourstory).

Getting there first

Hilary quickly gained a reputation for being a true travel pioneer, and in the 1980s she started to focus on guides to places overlooked by other publishers. The Bradt Guides list became a roll call of guidebook 'firsts'. We published the first guide to Madagascar, followed by Mauritius, Czechoslovakia and Vietnam. The 1990s saw the beginning of our extensive coverage of Africa: Tanzania, Uganda, South Africa, and Eritrea. Later, post-conflict guides became a feature: Rwanda, Mozambique, Angola, and Sierra Leone, as well as the first standalone guides to the Baltic States following the fall of the Iron Curtain, and the first post-war guides to Bosnia, Kosovo and Albania.

Comprehensive – and with a conscience

Today, we are the world's largest independently owned travel publisher, with more than 200 titles. However, our ethos remains unchanged. Hilary is still keenly involved, and **we still get there first**: two-thirds of Bradt guides have no direct competition.

But we don't just get there first. Our guides are also known for being **more comprehensive** than any other series. We avoid templates and tick-lists. Each guide is a one-of-a-kind expression of an expert author's interests, knowledge and enthusiasm for telling it how it really is.

And a commitment to wildlife, conservation and respect for local communities has always been at the heart of our books. Bradt Guides was **championing sustainable travel** before any other guidebook publisher. We even have a series dedicated to Slow Travel in the UK, award-winning books that explore the country with a passion and depth you'll find nowhere else.

Thank you!

We can only do what we do because of the support of readers like you – people who value less-obvious experiences, less-visited places and a more thoughtful approach to travel. Those who, like us, take travel seriously.

TRAVEL TAKEN SERIOUSLY